Evil and Suffering
in the Bible

Wisdom Editions

Minneapolis

FIRST EDITION MAY 2020

Evil and Suffering in the Bible
Copyright © 2020 by Stephen J. Vicchio.
All rights reserved.

Printed in the United States of America.
10 9 8 7 6 5 4 3 2 1

Cover and interior design: Gary Lindberg

ISBN: 978-1-950743-26-1

This book is dedicated to my mentor, friend, and cousin, Peter Celli.

Contents

Evil and Suffering in the Bible

Stephen J. Vicchio, Ph.D.

Wisdom
Editions
Minneapolis, Minnesota

Preface

In 1946, French novelist Albert Camus wrote a novel he called *La Peste*, or "The Plague," that was published in Paris in 1947. It tells the story of a plague that settles in the North African city of Oran. In 1849, the same city experienced an epidemic of plague, though Camus' novel is set in the 1940s.

Camus' novel records the attitudes and views of several major characters about the appearance of the disease. This includes a physician, a journalist, a number of criminals, a clerk who works in public records and a Jesuit priest. The novel explores what these major characters believe the cause of the plague's appearance has been. The priest, early on, says the plague is the product of sin. Others, like the doctor, Dr. Rieux, believes it is a natural event. Many believe that the setting of the novel in the 1940s is an indication that the novel is an allegory about the Nazi occupation of France in the first half of the 1940s.

The plague spread wide and rapidly in the city. Clear records were kept of how many cases and deaths occurred. By the end of the novel, the plague dissipates, and the city goes back to normal. During the process, the economics of the city and its economy collapses.

The British publisher of Camus' novel, Penguin Classics, sold 226 copies of the book. In March of 2020, that figure had reached 38,000. We don't have to pause very long to wonder why so many copies of *The Plague* have been sold. The outbreak of the Corona Virus across the world has occasioned many readers to return to the novel.

We have begun this study of attitudes in the Bible toward the phenomena of evil and suffering at the beginning of the Corona Virus outbreak. We believed it might be a good idea to offer a book on what the Bible says about evil and suffering. To that end, this study consists of ten chapters, five about the Old Testament, one about the intertestamental period, and four chapters about materials in the New Testament.

Before my retirement in 2016, I had been trained as both a philosopher and a Biblical scholar. Thus, this study brings these skills together. All the classical Hebrew and Koine Greek translations are my own. In fact, I have provided two appendices that catalogs the many Hebrew and Greek words and expressions used herein.

This brings us to chapter one, an examination and introduction to what has been labeled by philosophers and Bible scholars, the issues of "Theodicy" and the "Problem of Evil."

Chapter One:
Introduction to Theodicy and the Problem of Evil

What man really fears is not so much extinction, but
extinction with insignificance.

—Ernest Becker, *Escape from Evil*

Apparently with no surprise
To any happy glower
He frost beheads it at its play—
In accidental power—
The blonde assassin passes on—
The sun proceeds unmoved
To measure off another day
For an approving God.

—Emily Dickinson, "Apparently With No Surprise"

I have been young, and now am not too old
And I have seen the righteous forsaken.
His health his honours and his quality taken.
This is not what we have formerly been told.

—Edmund Blunden, *Collected Poems*

Introduction

The purpose of this first chapter is to make some general remarks about
what has come to be known in the Judeo-Christian tradition as the

problem of theodicy or the problem of evil. The word "theodicy," from the Greek words *theos*, or God, and *dike*, or justice, was coined by the German philosopher G. W. Leibniz in his 1710 book entitled *Theodicy*.[1] Since that time a "theodicy" in the Judeo-Christian tradition was any answer or theological response to a question posed by Leibniz, "If God is all-good, all-knowing and all-powerful, then why is there so much evil and suffering in the world?" The name of the problem of theodicy also is sometimes simply called "The Problem of evil."

When we use the word "evil" in this study, we are referring to three separate forms of evil—moral, natural and metaphysical. Moral evils are those acts that bring suffering to others, like murder or rape. Natural evil refers to those examples of human suffering caused by natural events, like floods, earthquakes or plagues. Metaphysical evils are mental events that go beyond the physical like dread, anxiety or worry. When we speak of the problem of theodicy or the problem of evil, we mean examples of moral, natural and metaphysical evils.

The main tasks of this first chapter are the following. First, to introduce the problem. Second to place the Judeo-Christian tradition in the context of the religions of the world. Connected to this second task, we will make a fundamental distinction between what we will call the general problem of evil, as opposed to the specific problem of evil. These two goals will be followed by a third task, where we will enumerate and discuss the major theological and philosophical responses to the issues of theodicy and the problem of evil in the Judeo-Christian tradition, as well as in the Bible.

Theodicy and the Problem of Evil

As we have indicated, the problem of theodicy and the problem of evil can be summarized in this observation of Epicurus:

- Is God willing to prevent evil but not able, then he is not omnipotent.

- If he is able but not willing, then he is not malevolent.

- If he is both able and willing, then whence comes evil?

- If he is neither willing nor able, then why call him God?[2]

This formulation of the problem by Epicurus may be put another way. To wit:

> If God is all-good, all-knowing and all-powerful, then why is there so much evil and suffering in the world?[3]

Martin Amis, in his 2008 novel *The Second Plane*, also formulates the problem of evil in the same way. He observes:

> It is straight-forward—and never mind for now, about plagues and famines—If God existed, and is all-good, then why is there so much suffering in the world?[4]

Similar formulations of the problems at hand have been devised by numerous thinkers in the Judeo-Christian tradition, beginning with Epicurus (341–270 BCE), and continuing all the way to contemporary times. For example, contemporary philosopher Louis Pojman, in his book *Philosophy of Religion*, gives us this for his formulation of the problem of evil:

1. God is all-powerful (his powers include omniscience)
2. God is perfectly good.
3. Evil exists.[5]

Professor Pojman goes on to say, "But if he is perfectly good, why does he allow evil to exist? Why didn't he create a better world, if not one without evil, at least one with substantially less evil than in this world."[6] Dr. Pojman completes his thought:

> Many have contended that this paradox, first articulated by Epicurus, is not just a paradox but an implicit contradiction, for it contains premises that are inconsistent with one another.[7]

Other formulations of the issues of theodicy and the problem of evil have been suggested by eighteenth-century Scottish philosopher David Hume in his *Dialogues Concerning Natural Religion*;[8] in Gottfried Leibniz's 1710 Theodicy;[9] in Alvin Plantinga's 1974 book, *God, Freedom, and Evil*;[10] in William Rowe's 1979 essay, "The Problem of Evil and Some Varieties of Atheism" in the *American Philosophical*

Quarterly;[11] and J. L. Mackie's "Evil and Omnipotence," published in the journal *Mind*.[12]

And in each of these thinkers mentioned above, they all agree that the issues of theodicy and the problem of evil is this:

> If God is all-good, all-knowing and all-powerful, then
> why is there so much evil and suffering in the world?[13]

This brings us to a distinction between what we shall call the "General Problem of evil" as opposed to the "Specific Problem of evil," a problem only for the monotheistic faiths of Judaism, Christianity and Islam.

The General and the Specific Problems of Evil

Since the middle of the nineteenth century with the work of German scholar Max Weber in his book *Das Problem der Bedeutung* or "The Problem of Theodicy," there have been many prominent Western scholars who have developed heuristic models for interpreting views on the problem of evil or the issue of theodicy.[14] Weber discusses the issue of theodicy by raising the question about why the good sometimes suffer, while the evil man prospers. We would expect, Weber says, for the good man to prosper and the evil man to suffer.[15]

Weber also relates that the problem of evil raised in the context of "reconciling the world's imperfections with the prevailing concept of God." For him, it does not matter whether that conception of the Divine is monotheistic, dualistic, polytheistic or even, pantheistic. Weber tells us that evil and suffering "erodes our confidence in the Divine in the face of evil and suffering."[16]

Max Weber suggests a model for understanding the religions of the world by suggesting that there are three "primary types of religions." He calls these "Predestination, Dualism, and the Karmic View."[17] But underneath each of these views lays what Weber calls "the inner need for meaning."[18] As we shall see later in this first chapter, these three views correspond to what we later will call, "the Free Will" Defense, the "Religions of Solution" or Dualism, and the Retributive Justice View.

For Weber, the question of theodicy was not simply a problem for monotheism. "Theodicy arises," Weber says, "in the context of the incongruity between destiny and merit."[19] He maintains that every religion must find a place for, as well as the meaning of the phenomena of evil and suffering.

In the twentieth century, other thinkers like Peter Berger and Clifford Geertz also ground the issue of theodicy as a "need for social meaning."[20] For Berger, the purpose of religion is to provide a social context for a world that "often defies rationality." Instead, Berger tells us in his book, *The Sacred Canopy*, that "Each person, or community of persons, organizes their beliefs and their meaning in terms of what he calls a *Nomos*, an ancient Greek word that means "worldview."[21]

Each nomos, Berger tells us, "protects us from Chaos."[22] Indeed, Berger relates:

> Every Nomos is an area of meaning carved out of a vast
> mass of meaninglessness, a small clearing of lucidity in
> a formless, dark, always ominous jungle.[23]

For Peter Berger, then, religion is nothing more than the process of orienting ourselves in a world where evil and suffering often occur. Indeed, Berger defines a "theodicy" as, "Theonomic forces endemic to the human condition. Theodicy consists in the preserving of meaning in the face of experiences of evil and suffering."[24]

American scholar Clifford Geertz, in his essay "Religion as a Cultural System," also recognizes the innate need for "constructing social meaning," especially during experiences of evil and suffering. For Geertz, a religion is:

> A system of symbols which act to establish powerful,
> pervasive and long-lasting moods and motivations in
> men by formulating conceptions of a general order of
> existence and clothing these conceptions with such an
> air of factuality that the mood and motivation seem
> uniquely realistic.[25]

What all these three scholars have in common is that they all see religion, and its meaning, in a social context. And it is primarily from this social context that human beings find meaning, usually through a collection of myths, symbols and rituals through which that meaning is asserted.

In this chapter, we will suggest another heuristic model for understanding evil and suffering in the religions of the world. We will begin to explicate this theory by making a distinction between the "general problem of evil" and the "specific problem of evil." When we use the term "general problem of evil," we mean what the religions of the world have to say about three sets of questions.[26]

These may be summarized this way:

1. How is evil to be defined?
2. What is the origin of evil?
3. What meaning can be assigned to evil?[27]

Many of the religions of the world may be seen on a continuum that looks like this:

Religions of Solution	Religions of Dissolution
Dualistic Religions	Monistic Religions
Zoroastrianism	Vedantic Hinduism
Mithraism	Hinayana Buddhism
Manicheanism	Christian Scientists

The religions on the left are each dualistic, in that they believe that there are two gods or two forces that make up metaphysical reality. In the ancient Persian religion Zoroastrianism, there are two gods. The good god's name is Ahura Mazda, while the bad god's name is Angra Mainya. All good comes from the good god, while all evil comes from the bad deity. Similar views can be seen in the two Roman religions listed above, Mithraism and Manicheanism. These religions are called Religions of Solution because the origin of evil can be established simply by saying it came from the bad god.[28]

The Religions of Dissolution, on the other hand, are called this because the adherents to these religions believe that all of reality is made of one substance, and that substance is divine.

For the Vedantic Hindu, all of reality is what he calls "Brahma," or ultimate reality. One's soul, or *atman*, is nothing more than an aspect of ultimate reality or *Brahma*. In fact, the ancient Indians had the expression "*tat tvan asi*," or "that you are," nothing more than an aspect of ultimate reality. If Brahma is all that there is, and Brahma is good, then it follows that there is no such thing as evil.[29] Thus, the Vedantic Hindus "dissolve" the problem of evil because, most fundamentally, evil does not exist. Now between the Religions of Solution and the Religions of Dissolution, we may find a third set of religions. We will call these "Religions of Paradox." These are the Monotheistic faiths, that is, Judaism, Christianity and Islam. These traditions are to be found halfway between the other two types. Thus, our continuum now looks like this:

Religions of Solution	Religions of Paradox	Religions of Dissolution
Dualistic	Mixed	Monistic
Zoroastrianism	Judaism	Vedantic Hinduism
Mithraism	Christianity	Hinayana Buddhism
Manicheanism	Islam	Christian Scientists

Figure i.[30]

The Religions of Paradox get their name because believers in these faiths ascribe to the following propositions:

1. God is All-Good.
2. God is All-Knowing.
3. God is All-Powerful.
4. Evil exist in natural, moral and metaphysical forms.[31]

These religions are called Religions of Paradox because there seems to be some sort of contradiction in terms of believing all four propositions are true at the same time. The Religions of Paradox are like the Religions of Solution because both traditions believe that evil is real. The Religions of Paradox are like the Religions of Dissolution because both traditions believe that all of reality comes from one source (God or Brahma), while at the same time, that source is All-Good.[32]

The Religions of Paradox include Judaism, Christianity and Islam because all three traditions assent to the beliefs that God, or Allah, is

All-Good, All-Knowing and All-Powerful, as well as the Creator of the Universe, out of nothing, simply by speech.

Over the history of Judaism, Christianity and Islam, the Religions of Paradox have developed various "Answers" or "Responses" to the specific problem of evil. The specific problem of evil is only a problem for the Religions of Paradox—Judaism, Christianity and Islam. In the next section of this first chapter, we shall look at many of these.

Responses and Answers to the Problem of Evil

In the history of Biblical materials, there have been eight major responses or answers to the issues of theodicy and the problem of evil. These may be divided into two types—deontological and teleological. In a deontological account of ethics, morality centers on one's ethical duties that are based on moral rules without exceptions. Deontological views of ethics are universal in both time and place.

In a deontological account of ethics, actions are seen as being intrinsically good or evil. Thus, telling the truth or keeping one's promises are intrinsically good actions, while murder and rape are, by their very natures, evil actions. The most famous deontological theories of ethics are the Ten Commandments and Immanuel Kant's theory of the categorical imperative. In both systems, a set of moral duties can be derived from universal moral rules.[33]

In the Biblical materials, four main deontological responses to the problem of evil have been employed. We will enumerate these here, and then discuss them one at a time. These four deontological theories are the following:

1. Retributive Justice (individual and collective)
2. The Free Will Defense
3. The Original Sin Perspective
4. The Influences of Demonic Forces Theory[34]

The Retributive Justice theory suggests that the reason human beings experience evil and suffering is because they, or their families, have done something morally wrong. Sometimes this theory is asserted in regard to individuals, and sometimes to a family, a clan, or even to a nation. These two theories of Retributive Justice are, most likely, the oldest answers about evil and suffering to be found in the Old Testament, or Hebrew Bible.

Indeed, often when human beings are visited with evil and suffering, they ask, "What have I done to deserve this?" The question itself seems to imply a theory about evil and suffering. That is, Retributive Justice. This theory may be found throughout both the Old and the New Testaments.[35]

The second Deontological Theory listed above is that of the "Free Will Defense." Proponents of this theory argue that much evil and suffering is the result of bad human choices or exercises of human free will. In this view, God gave humans free will as something that is morally good, but then they often misuse it to commit evil acts. This view also posits that a world in which humans have free will is better than one in which they do not.

The Free Will Defense has been employed in a number of places in the Bible, as well as in the history of Western philosophy in figures such as Augustin, Moses Maimonides, Thomas Aquinas, Gregory the Great, Rene Descartes, John Calvin, G. W. Leibniz, and many other thinkers. Passages that mention free will in the Bible include Genesis 2:16–17, Deuteronomy 30:19–20, Second Chronicles 9:7, Joshua 24:15, Isaiah 55:6–7, Proverbs16:9, and Ezekiel 18:30-32.

Verses of the New Testament that speak of the phenomenon of human free will include First Corinthians 10:13, Second Peter 2:9, Galatians 5:13, Romans 6:23, 10:9–10 and 13:2, the Gospel of John 1:12–13 and 7:17, and the Book of Revelation 3:20. In the Old Testament, the Free Will Defense goes by the name of the "Two *Yetzerim* Theory." The word *yetzer* is a classical Hebrew word that designates "inclination" or "imagination." The ancient Jews believed that God endowed every human with two *yetzerim*, one to the good or *tov*, and the other to evil, or *Ra'*. It is one's human free will that decides which of the two *yetzerim* is employed into action. The word *yetzer* is first used in the Hebrew Bible at Genesis 6:5 and 8:21.

In the first of these verses, the text tells us that "The Lord saw that every imagination [*yetzer*] of the thoughts of the heart [*leb*] was only evil [*ra'*] continually." At Genesis 8:21, after the flood, the text reveals that God brought the flood because "the imagination [*yetzer*] of man's heart is evil."

Among the ancient Jews, the seat of the self was to be found in the *Leb*, or "Heart." It was the organ of decision-making, while also playing the role of the organ in which the self is to be located. In more modern times, the organ of the self has become the brain. Other ancient cultures believed the self was located in the liver, the organ that made one "alive."

Our third deontological theory, Original Sin, holds that after Adam and Eve committed the first sin in Genesis 3, all humans after them inherit this Original Sin. This view suggests that human beings are morally and ethically corrupted due to the disobedience of Adam and Eve, our first parents. There are a number of passages in the Old Testament that have been interpreted in this manner. In the New Testament, Saint Paul also seems to have been a proponent of this explanation of evil and suffering.

Among the places in the Old Testament or Hebrew Bible where scholars have suggested that the Original Sin Theory may be found are Psalm 51:5, Ezekiel 18:4, Deuteronomy 1:39, Isaiah 59:2, Psalm 14:2–3, as well as various passages in the Book of Job, such as Job 5:7 and 25:4, for example. The former passage reveals that "Man is born in trouble, as sparks fly upwards," while the latter passage, the one at 25:4 asks, "How can man be righteous before God? How can he who is born of a woman be clean?" Psalm 51:5 also provides a presentative example of the Original Sin Theory in the Old Testament. It tells us:

> Behold, I was shaped in iniquity, and in sin did my
> mother conceive me.

Selections in the New Testament that imply the Original Sin Theory include Romans 2:14–15, 3:10–18, 5:12, 6:12, and 7:9–11, and Ephesians 2:1–3. Romans 3:10–18 tells us that "As it is written, 'There is none that is righteous, no, not even one.'" Romans 5:12 is, perhaps, the best New Testament passage on the Original Sin Theory. It reveals:

> Wherefore, as by one man's sin entered into the world,
> and death by sin; and so death comes to all men
> because all men sin.

The Influences of Demonic Forces Theory, our fourth deontological view, relates that much of human evil and suffering may be attributed to demonic figures in the Biblical materials. Specifically, this theory asserts that the Devil or Satan and his minions are responsible for much of the evil and suffering that is visited on human beings. Sometimes this view is tied to another explanation that is called the "Fallen Angels" narrative. This view is much more popular in Christianity and Islam, less so in ancient Judaism.[36]

Among Old Testament passages that endorse the Influences of Demonic Forces Theory, we will give three representative examples. These come at Leviticus 20:6, Job 4:15, and Isaiah 14:12–14. In the former, the texts speak of "mediums, wizards, and demons prostituting themselves to them." The Book of Job at 4:15 tells us that, "A spirit glided past my face, and the hair of my flesh bristled." Presumably, Job refers to some sort of demon. The passage from the Prophet Isaiah, at 14:12–15, we see a reference to Lucifer "who has fallen from the Heavens, oh Day Star, son of Dawn."

A variety of New Testament passages also posits a belief in the influences of demonic forces, such as at the Gospel of Matthew 12:45, First Peter 5:8, Second Timothy 2:25–26, and the Book of Revelation 16:14, to cite four representative examples. The passage from Matthew speaks of "seven evil spirits."[37] First Peter 5:8, refers to the Devil "who prowls around, looking for someone to devour." Second Timothy 2:25–26 refers to what it calls the "snares of the Devil." And the Book of Revelation 16:14 speaks of "the spirits of Devils." In addition to these four deontological theories on the issues of theodicy and the problem of evil, there also have been four teleological theories about the explanation of human evil and suffering. A teleological system of ethics is one that emphasizes consequences or outcomes rather than principles or moral duties. One way to distinguish deontological views of ethics as opposed to teleological views is that the former tend to be backward-looking, while the latter is forward-looking.[38]

The four teleological explanations for evil and suffering experienced by human beings are the following theories:

5. The Contrast View
6. The Test View
7. The Moral Qualities Approach
8. Divine Plan Theory[39]

The Contrast View, or theory number five, argues that in order to have an explanation of the concept of evil, one must also understand the idea of the Good. Proponents of this view maintain that one cannot have a notion of the Good without also having the idea of evil. When this view of evil and suffering is employed in Biblical materials, it is often discussed in the context of light and darkness.[40] A typical Old Testament passage that suggests the Contrast View is the Book of Job 17:12 that tells us:

> They make night out of day. The light they say is nearer
> to the darkness.

Job 24:14 provides another example of the Contrast Theory. This verse tells us:

> "The murderer rises in the darkness, that he might kill
> the poor and the needy. And in the night, he is a thief."

The overall perspective of the Contrast View, then, is that Good is such a valuable commodity, that evil must also exist so that we may more properly understand both of these moral ideas. We cannot have one without the other.[41]

Our second teleological view of the explanation of evil and suffering is called the Test View. Advocates of this view maintain that God frequently employs evil and suffering to test or to try the moral characters of human beings. This view is a way of determining if someone is as loyal to the Divine as he or she claims to be. The Book of Job is often suggested as an example of this sixth theory of theodicy.[42] At Job 7:18, for example, the verse tells us that God "visits people every morning and tests them at night." The opening line of the *Akedah* narrative that is Genesis 22:1 also advocates the Test Theory of evil and suffering.

The Moral Qualities Approach, our seventh theory, suggests that God often uses evil and suffering to chasten humans or to make their moral character better. This theory has the name "Moral Qualities" because certain moral qualities like patience and forbearance only can be developed fully in the context of evil and suffering. In the history of philosophy, this theory has been employed by second-century church father Irenaeus, and contemporary British thinker John Hick in his book *Evil and the God of Love*.[43]

At the Book of Job 5:17 and 20, we see two examples of the Moral Qualities Theory. The former speaks of God reproving people, while in the latter verse, He "will redeem you from death."

Both the Test View and the Moral Qualities Approach are employed in many passages in the Hebrew Bible or Old Testament. Many of these passages, as we shall see in a later chapter, can be found in the Book of Job. The Test View and Moral Qualities Approach are similar in that both theories speak of the moral characters of human beings, one theory that "tests" that character, and the other to improve it.

Both the Test and Moral Qualities theories are teleological because they both speak of the "outcomes" or consequences of God's employment of evil and suffering in His relationship with human beings. In this sense, both theories look forward to determining the testing, or the improvement, of human, moral character, or moral truth.

Finally, perhaps the most often used theory of evil and suffering in contemporary human life is what is sometimes called the Divine Plan Theory. Proponents of this view say that what appears to be examples of evil and suffering in the short-run, turn out to be part of some larger divine plan in the long run.

Advocates of the Divine Plan Theory often say things like "God's ways are not man's ways," or "Everything happens for a reason." Those who make such statements in contemporary life are committed to our eighth Theory—the Divine Plan Perspective. The Divine Plan Theory is often employed in both the Old and the New Testaments. The end of the Book of Job, chapters 38 to 41, for example, often has been interpreted that way.

At Proverbs 16:4, we see one example of where the Old Testament posits a belief in the Divine Plan Theory. This text tells us:

> The Lord has made everything for its purpose, even the
> wicked for the day of trouble.

Another Old Testament passage where the Divine Plan Theory is mentioned is in the Book of Isaiah 25:1. The Prophet relates:

> Oh Lord, you are my God, and I will exalt you. I will give
> thanks to your name. For you have worked wonders,
> plans formed long ago with perfect faithfulness.

At First Chronicles 28:12, we have a third Old Testament passage that indicates the Divine Plan Theory. It relates about God:

> And the plan of all that He had in mind, for the courts of
> the house of the Lord and all of the surrounding rooms,
> for the storehouses of the house of God and for the
> storehouses of the dedicated things.

The Divine Plan Theory also appears to be behind the meaning of Psalm 37:23 that relates, "The steps of a man are established by the Lord when He delights in his ways."

The Prophet Jeremiah also refers to the Divine Plan Theory at 29:11, where Jeremiah relates, "For I know the plans I have for you," declares the Lord, "plans for welfare and not for evil, to give you a future and a hope."

A final Old Testament passage that endorses the Divine Plan Theory is Psalm 33:11. This verse reveals that "The plans of the Lord stand firm forever, the purposes of his heart through all generations."

The Divine Plan Theory can also be seen in a variety of New Testament passages, as well. We will give four representative examples here. These come at Galatians 5:13, Ephesians 1:4–5, Romans 8:29, and two verses from the Acts of the Apostles, at 2:23 and 4:28. In the verses from Ephesians, 1:4–5, we find Paul observing that:

> Even as he chose us in him before the foundations of
> the world that we should be blameless before him. In
> love, he predestined us for adoption as sons through
> Jesus Christ, according to the purpose of His will.

Romans 8:29 also mentions the idea of predestination when Paul writes:

> For those whom He foreknew, He also predestined to
> be conformed to the image of His Son, in order that he
> might be the firstborn among many brothers.

In two places of the Acts of the Apostles, we also see references to the Divine Plan Theory. These come at 2:23 and 4:28, where we are told:

> This Jesus, delivered up according to the definite plan
> and the foreknowledge of God, you crucified and killed
> by the hands of lawless men.

And at Acts 4:28, the text speaks of doing "whatever your hand and your plan had predestined to take place." From this analysis, it should be clear that both the Old and the New Testaments often endorse the position we have called the Divine Plan Theory.

In addition to these eight answers and responses to the issues of theodicy and the problem of evil, two other points of view will be seen throughout this study. These are called the Hidden God Perspective and the Practical Approach to Evil and Suffering. In the former view, the believer thinks that God has deliberately hidden Himself, or His face, often when the believer is suffering.

As we shall see, this theory frequently can be found in both the Old and the New Testaments. For example, this view may be found at Deuteronomy 31:17 and 18, as well as 32:20. It can also be found in the major prophets, a few of the minor prophets, in the Book of Job at 13:20, 15:20 and 34:29.

The Hidden God Theory has also been employed by many of the Psalms, such as at Psalms 10:1, 13:1, 27:9, 55:1, 69:17, 89:46, 102:2, and 143:7. The Hidden God Theory also has been employed by Isaiah, Jeremiah and Ezekiel. Among the minor prophets, the Hidden God Theory also may be found in Micah 3:4, as well as Hosea 5:6 and Obadiah 1:6.

The Hidden God Theory can even be found in several passages in the New Testament, including Acts of the Apostles 26:26, as well as several passages in the Epistles of Paul, including three cases in First Corinthians at 2:7 and 4:5, and Second Corinthians 4:2.

The Practical Approach to Evil and Suffering is a theory that can only be found in the New Testament. As we shall see in later chapters, the Practical Approach, we shall argue, is a position that was often endorsed by the person of Jesus Christ and his handling of the issues of evil and suffering in the New Testament.

The Practical Approach to Evil and Suffering is not a theory to be found in the Old Testament. It does, however, frequently appears in the New Testament, including the four Gospels, as well as in the Epistles of Paul.

This brings us to a section in this first chapter on the vocabulary of words about evil and suffering that may be found in the writers of the books of the Old Testament, including the most often employed word for evil, *Ra'*.

Biblical Language for Evil

This brings us to the next task in this first chapter, the Biblical language of words for evil, misery, etc. in the Hebrew Old Testament and the Greek New Testament. We will begin with four classical Hebrew words for "evil" in the Old Testament. The first of these is the word *Ra'*, the normal Old Testament word for "evil." The word is employed hundreds of times in the Hebrew text. Some representative examples are at Genesis 2:9 and 17, 3:5 and 22, 6:5, 8:21, and 19:19.

A second Hebrew word from the same Semitic root is the word *Ra'aw*. It also usually designates "evil," such as at the Book of Job 8:20 that tells us:

> God will not reject a blameless person, nor will he take
> the hands of evildoers.

A third Hebrew word, *Ra'ah*, which is also from the same Semitic root, is employed to stand for "evil," as well as the verb, "to devour," and a noun for "harm." At the Book of Job 24:21, the text reveals:

> They harm [*ra'ah*] the childless woman, and do no good
> to the widow.

Another classical Hebrew word for "evil" is the term *dibbah*. The same word is also employed in the Old Testament to designate "infamy." For example, consider the Book of Numbers 13:32, that tells us:

> So they brought to the Israelites an unfavorable [*dibbah*] report of the land they had spied on.

The word *dibbah* is also used in the Old Testament to designate anything that is "unfavorable" or "unsavory." These four Hebrew words are used throughout the Old Testament to indicate evil actions or evil things. Another word employed in the Old Testament or Hebrew Bible to designate "harm" two times or "evil" is *ason*, that is used, for example, at Genesis 4:24 and Exodus 21, 22 and 23. In the former, *ason* is frequently rendered as "avenged," as in the New Revised Standard Version. At Exodus 21, 22 and 23, the same noun is used to imply "harm" two times.

Another classical masculine Hebrew noun, a word that designates "wicked" and "wickedness," is the word *reasha*. It is only employed seventeen times in the Hebrew Bible or Old Testament, such as Deuteronomy 9:27, Isaiah 58:6, Proverbs 4:17, Micah 6:10 and Ecclesiastes 7:25.

The classical Hebrew word *deraon* is employed many times in the Hebrew Bible or Old Testament. It is most often translated as "aversion," or "to be afraid of something." It is used, for example, at Isaiah 66:24 and the Book of Daniel 12:2. In the former, it is translated as "abhorrence," and in the latter, the New Revised Standard Version translates it as "shame."

Other classical Hebrew words for "shame" are all connected to the Semitic root BSH. These include *bosh*, *bosheth*, *boshah* and *boshnah*. Of these, the first is the most frequent word used to express "shame." It can be found at Genesis 2:25, Exodus 32:2 and the Book of Judges 3:25. *Bosheth* is the second most employed word in the Old Testament to mean "shame." It can be found at First Samuel 20:30 and Second Samuel 21:7. *Bushah*, the final word for "shame" is used less frequently in the Hebrew Bible or Old Testament. It can be found, however, at places like Psalm 89:45 and Ezekiel 7:18.[44]

Finally, the Hebrew word *A'ven* in the Old Testament or Hebrew Bible designates "wickedness." It is also used as a synonym for *buz* and *buzah*, the two classical Hebrew words for "contempt." Another word used for "contempt" is *bizzayon*. It is only employed once at Esther 1:18. All of these words for contempt come from the verb *bazah* that also sometimes indicates "disdain," such as at Genesis 25:43, Numbers 15:31 and First Chronicles 15:29.[45]

The Koine Greek of the New Testament has a much more extensive vocabulary of words related to evil actions, people or simply for the morally wrong. We will examine many of these terms next in this study of evil and suffering in the Bible.

Most of the words for bad and evil in the New Testament are related, in one way or another, to the word *kakos*, the normal Greek term for "evil," as well as for an "evildoer." Indeed, Koine Greek words related to *kakos* include *kakia*, "evil" or "malice." *Kakothia*, "evil" or "bad character." *Kakolegio*, "evil" or the verb "to revile." *Kakopathia*, a term that means both "evil" and "suffering."[46]

Other New Testament words related to *kakos* are *kakopatheo*, "evil" or "harmful." *Kakopoleo*, a word that stands for both "evil" and "injury." *Kakopios*, the normal term for "criminal," as well as another synonym for "evil." The term *Kakopolos*, both "evil" and "evildoer." In addition to these words related to *kakos*, four other Koine Greek terms are also employed to designate "evil," including the word *poneros*, one of the normal words for "evil." Another word *Rehe'mah*, is also used to speak of "evil." When the Greek term *adekena* is employed in the New Testament, it means "wrong," as much as it does "evil."[47]

Finally, two other Koine Greek words, words from which the English word "blasphemy" has come, are *blasphemo* and *blasphemia*. In addition to both of these words designating "blasphemy," they are also used to mean "wrong" or "evil."[48]

This brings us to one final task of this first chapter, in which we will establish in both the Hebrew of the Old Testament and the Greek of the New Testament, that God is purported to be All-Good, All-Knowing and All-Powerful, in addition to being the Creator of the universe. We turn, then, to the task of establishing the attributes of God in Biblical literature.

The Attributes of God in Biblical Literature

The main purpose of this final section of Chapter One is to show that God is believed to be All-Good, All-Knowing and All-Powerful in both the Old Testament and the New Testament. We will begin with an analysis of the Old Testament and then will turn to the attributes of God in the New Testament.

That the God of the Old Testament is Omniscient, or All-Knowing can be established at Psalm 147:4–5, Psalm 69:5, Psalm 139:1–6, Proverbs 15:2–3, and First Chronicles 8:9. In fact, at Psalm 147:4–5, we see a confirmation of God's omniscience, as well as His omnipotence. This couplet tells us:

> He determines the number of the stars. He gives to all of them their names. Great is our Lord and abundant in power. His understanding is beyond measure.

At the Book of Psalms 69:5, we see another indication of the omniscience of God:

> Oh God, You know my folly. All the wrongs I have done are not hidden from You.

A similar conclusion about God's omniscience can be seen at Psalm 139:1–6 that tells us:

> Oh Lord, You have searched me out and have known me. You know when I sit down and when I rise up. You know my thoughts from afar...Such knowledge is too wonderful for me. It is high, I cannot attain it.

The Book of Proverbs at 15:3 also speaks of the All-Knowing nature of God. The verse relates, "The eyes of the Lord are in every place, keeping watch on the evil as well as the good." From these examples, it should be clear that in the Old Testament, God is said to be Omniscient.

It is just as clear in the Hebrew Bible that God is understood as being Omnipotent, as well. Consider, for example, Jeremiah 10:12 and 32:17. In the former, the text relates, "It is He who made the Earth with His power, and who established the world by His wisdom, and by his understanding, He stretched out the Heavens." At Jeremiah 32:17, we find another reference to the omnipotence of God. The text relates:

> Ah, Lord God, it is You who have made the Heavens and the Earth by Your great Power, and by Your outstretched arm. Nothing is too hard for Thee.

In the Prophet Isaiah at 40:28, we find a reference to God's omnipotence, as well as his Eternality. The Prophet relates:

> The Lord is the everlasting God, the creator of the ends of the Earth. He does not faint or grow weary. His understanding is unsearchable.

At the Book of Job 11:7–8, we see another reference to God being omnipotent. The text asks, "Can you find out the deep things of God? Can you find out the limit of the Almighty? It is higher than Heaven—what can you do? Deeper than Sheol—what can you know?" In Genesis 17:1, God refers to Himself as, "I am God Almighty." And the Book of Deuteronomy, at 4:37–39, refers to God's "great power."

So far, in this section of Chapter One, we have established that in the Old Testament of the Hebrew Bible, God is said to be both Omniscient and Omnipotent. We will move next to the idea of His Omnibenevolence. In the Book of Psalms 18:30, it reveals that "The way of this God is perfect," presumably this means moral perfection. Not only is God perfect, Psalm 19:7 tells us that:

> The law of the Lord is perfect, reviving the soul. The testimony of the Lord is sure making wise the simple.

Even the name of God itself is morally good, as Psalm 54:6 relates, "With a freewill offering I will sacrifice to You, I will give thanks to Your name, for it is morally good." The Prophet Isaiah, as well, at 5:16, speaks of the Lord being perfect in Justice when it relates:

> But the Lord of Hosts is exalted in Justice, and the Holy God shows Himself holy in righteousness.

A few verses later, at Isaiah 5:20, the Prophet says more about the attributes of God. This verse confirms God's goodness and also may be an endorsement of the Contrast Theory introduced earlier in this first chapter. This text warns:

> Woe to those who call evil good and good evil, those
> who put darkness for light and light for darkness, and
> who put bitter for sweet and sweet for bitter.

One of the best ways to see that the writers of the Old Testament or Hebrew Bible believed that God is All-Good is to look at the Psalms. For example, this claim is made at Psalms 25:8, 27:13, 33:5, 34:6 and 8, 100:4 and 5, 143:10, and 145:5–7, among many other passages in the *Tehillim*, or Psalms. Finally, at Jeremiah 9:24, the text speaks of God's kindness, justice and righteousness, all in the same line. Jeremiah relates, "I am the Lord who practices kindness, justice, and righteousness in the Earth, for in the things that I delight." We now have assented to the views that in the Old Testament, God is seen as All-Good, All-Knowing and All-Powerful. It is just as clear that God also was the Creator of the universe in an *ex nihilo*, that is "out of nothing" style. This, of course, is established by the first two chapters of Genesis, as well as in passages like Psalm 8:1–3, that speaks of "the Heavens being the work of Your fingers."

The Prophet Isaiah, at 29:16, suggests a metaphor for understanding God's relationship to the universe. The Prophet asks, "Shall the Potter be regarded as the clay?" Isaiah employs this same metaphor at 45:9 and 64:8. For him, God is to the world, as the potter is to his clay.

In fact, at Isaiah 45:9, the Prophet extends the metaphor a bit. He relates:

> Woe to him who strives with his Maker, an earthen
> vessel with the potter. Does the clay say to Him who
> fashioned it, "What are you making?" or "Your work
> has no handles"?

The Psalmist, at 102:25–27, speaks of God, "laying the foundations of the Earth. And at Isaiah 44:24 and 45:18, we see two final references to God being the Creator of the universe. In the former, Isaiah has God say, "I am the Lord Who made all things," and at Isaiah 45:18, we find the text telling us:

> For thus says the Lord who created the Heavens, He is
> God, who formed the Earth and made it. He established

it. He did not make it a chaos. He formed it to be inhabited.

From our analysis so far in this section of Chapter One, we have established that in the Hebrew Bible, or Old Testament, God is said to be All-Good, All-Knowing and All-Powerful, in addition to being the Creator of the Universe out of nothing. We may find these same attributes in the New Testament, as well, as we shall see next.

To establish that the writers of the New Testament also assented to the view that God is All-Good, All-Knowing and All-Powerful, and the Creator of the Universe, we will give three passages that establish each of these four attributes of God, at least according to the New Testament.

In regard to the omniscience of God in the New Testament, First John 3:20 tells us that God "knows all things." The Gospel of Matthew appears to make the same claim when, at 10:30 we learn that "God has numbered all the hairs on your head." The Acts of the Apostles 1:24 suggest that "God knows what is in the hearts of all people." And First Corinthians 2:11 implies that the things that God knows no human being can know.

Many placers in the Psalms indicate that God is believed to be All-Knowing. These include Psalm 4:13, 44:21, 139:1–4, 145:7, and 147:4. The same idea also can be found at the Book of Isaiah 40:28 and 46:9–10, as well as First Kings 8:31.

That God is believed to be Omnipotent in the New Testament can be established by Matthew 19:6, Luke 1:37 and First Corinthians 4:20. In the passage from Matthew, we are told that "for God all things are possible." Similarly, Luke 1:37 tells us that "nothing is impossible for the Lord." In the passage from First Corinthians, the one at 4:20, Paul tells us:

> For the kingdom of God is not just a lot of talk, it is something that is living by the power of God.

That God is said to be All-Good in the New Testament may be established at Matthew 7:11, Acts 14:17, Romans 2:4 and Second Thessalonians 1:11. In the passage from Matthew 7, the author asks, "If you who are evil still give good gifts to your children, how much more does your Father in Heaven give out good things for those who ask Him?" The passage from Acts speaks of God being a witness, "for those who do the good." At Romans 2:4, Paul speaks of God's "kindness, forbearance, and patience." And Second Thessalonians 1:11 refers to the goodness of God and its relation to the faith of humans.

Other passages in the New Testament that speak of God's omnipotence include Luke 1:37 and 49, Acts of the Apostles 2:24, Matthew 10:27 and 19:26, Second Corinthians 4:7 and 6:18, and the Gospel of Mark 10:27, 14:31 and 14:62.

Finally, it is clear from Colossians 1:16, Romans 1:20, Acts 14:15 and Hebrews 11:3 that God is thought to be the Creator of the Universe in the New Testament. Colossians says that in Christ, "All things in the Heavens and on the Earth, both visible and invisible, were created by God." Paul speaks at Romans 1:20 of:

> Even since the creation of the world, his eternal power
> and divine nature, invisible though they are, have been
> understood and seen through the things that He has made.

Thus, we have established in this section of Chapter One that in both the Old Testament and the New Testament, God is said to be All-Good, All-Knowing and All-Powerful, as well as the Creator of the Universe, in an *ex nihilo*, or "out of nothing" fashion. Earlier in the chapter, we also have shown that both the Hebrew Bible and the New Testament make frequent references to the three types of evil described earlier—natural, moral and metaphysical.

What we have said about the Old and New Testaments in this chapter about the attributes of God, the three kinds of evil, and the idea that Allah creates the world out of nothing, also can be seen in the *Qur'an*. At Surah 46:33, we are told that Allah is All-Powerful. The same claim is made at Surah 35:44 that also speaks of God's omniscience in Islam.

In the Muslim Holy Book, Allah also creates the universe by speech, but he does not say, "Let there be light." Rather, the All-Mighty in Islam simply expresses the word *Kul*, or "Be!" This word is used eight times in *Al-Qur'an*. In all eight instances, it makes a reference to the creation of something by Allah.[49]

This brings us to the major conclusions we have made in Chapter One. In the second chapter of this study of evil and suffering in the Bible, we will explore many of the places of the Torah, the first five books of the Hebrew Bible, or Old Testament, to discover which of our theories in Chapter One may be found in the Torah, or Chapter Two.

Conclusions

We began this first chapter with an introduction to what has come to be known as the issues of theodicy or the problem of evil. An observation from the ancient Greek philosopher Epicurus was the first recorded version of expressing these issues. Next in Chapter One, we made a distinction between what we called the "general problem of evil" and the "specific problem of evil," a problem for the monotheistic faith—Judaism, Christianity and Islam.

In the second section of this first chapter, we offered a continuum of which the views of many of the religions of the world can be found, for the general problem of evil is a problem for any religion of mankind. Next, we introduced the idea of the specific problem of evil. If God is All-Good, All-Knowing and All-Powerful, then why is there so much evil and suffering in the world?

In the fourth section of Chapter One, we introduced and then discussed eight different responses or answers to the specific problem of evil. Four of these, as we have shown, are deontological responses: Retributive Justice, the Free Will Defense, the Original Sin Perspective and the Influences of Demonic Forces Theory. Each of these four theories looks backward to discover the origin or meaning of human evil and suffering.

This material was followed in this first chapter with an introduction and analysis of four teleological responses or answers to the specific problem of evil. These views were The Contrast View, the Test View, the Moral Qualities Approach, and the most often used Teleological View, the Divine Plan Theory. In the analysis of Chapter One, we have shown where in the Biblical texts these eight views of the issues of theodicy and the problem of evil may be found.

At the close of Chapter One, we have shown that God's omnipotence, omniscience and His Omnibenevolence can be shown in the contexts of both the Old Testament, or Hebrew Bible, and the New Testament. In this final section, we established the view that the four propositions for the establishment of the specific problem of evil all can be seen as existing in both Biblical testaments. In other words, we have shown at the end of Chapter One that God is purported to be All-Good, All-Knowing and All-Powerful in both the Old and the New Testaments.

Along the way in this chapter, we also introduced the idea of there being three separate kinds or flavors of evil in the Biblical material. We have labeled these kinds of evil as moral evil, natural evil and metaphysical evil.

The first variety of evil, moral evil, as we have shown, is human evil and suffering caused by moral agents, humans, angels or demons. Murder, rape, stealing, etc., are all examples of moral evil. The term "natural evils" refers to human evil and suffering that occurs by natural phenomena such as floods, storms and deadly diseases.

The third type of evil introduced in Chapter One, metaphysical evil, is that evil and suffering that principally goes on in the mind. This is the variety of evil into which we would place dread, anxiety and many other forms of mental suffering that often goes on in human beings.

We have also shown along the way that these three types or varieties of evil may be found in both the Hebrew Bible, or Old Testament, and the New Testament. Thus, the overall conclusion from Chapter One has been to establish that the four propositions of the specific problem of evil—that God is All-Good, All-Knowing and All-Powerful, and that evil exists in the Bible in moral, natural and metaphysical forms.

We shall now turn our attention to the phenomena of evil and suffering to be found in the Torah, or the first five books of the Old Testament—Genesis, Exodus, Leviticus, Numbers and Deuteronomy. These books contain some of the oldest Biblical views of what to make of evil and suffering in the Bible. We shall turn our attention to evil and suffering in the Torah, the first part of the Hebrew scriptures.

Chapter Two:
Evil and Suffering in the Torah and Historical Books

The human compulsion to deny death is exceeded only by a desire to absolve the deity of responsibility for injustice. In truth, the two motivating forces are integrally related to one another for death stands as the ultimate question mark attached to any defense of God. Why, one asks, were we fashioned from such stuff that we will eventually become food for worms?

—James Crenshaw, *Theodicy in the Old Testament*

Time and again, faith in Providence seems to have need of theodicy when disturbing and enigmatic upheavals in nature or human life threaten to put the orderly, divine guidance of all that takes place in question.

—Walter Eichrodt, "Faith in Providence in the Old Testament"

The portrait of the history and religion of ancient Israel has been radically altered in the last two centuries due to the influence of the Historical-Critical method. Yet, remarkable as it may seem, one feature of the old portrait has not been altered in the slightest. That is, the perception that, whether it is applied to Israel as a whole or its individual members, the relation between action and consequences is described in the Old Testament as being determined by the retribution of Yahweh.

—Klaus Koch, "Is There a Doctrine of Retribution in the Old Testament?"

Introduction

The ancient Jews divided their scriptures into three basic parts: the *Torah*, the *Nabiim*, and the *Kethuviim*, or the "Law," the "Prophets," and the "Writings." The main purpose of this second chapter is to review and to discuss what can be found in the Torah, as well as the historical books, about the questions about evil and suffering. Indeed, our task in this chapter is to analyze the issues of theodicy and the problem of evil as they appear in the first five books of the Hebrew Bible, or Old Testament. That is, Genesis, Exodus, Leviticus, Numbers and the Book of Deuteronomy, as well as the books from Joshua to Second Chronicles in the Old Testament or Hebrew Bible. In the five books of the Torah, we see several of the earliest examples of evil and suffering in the Bible. At Genesis 2:16 and 17, God punishes Adam and Eve for their disobedience; at Genesis 4:3 to 5, we see the first example of sibling rivalry that led to murder; God intentionally killed every man, woman, and child on the planet, with the exception of eight people, during the Flood.

God burns down an entire city, women and children included, at Genesis 19:23 to 24, simply because they were homosexuals. At Exodus 20:5 and 34:7, God punishes children for the sins of their fathers, unto the third and fourth generations. At Exodus 21:2 to 6, God seems to endorse slavery, and He appears to sanction the selling of daughters at Exodus 21:7. God also orders three thousand Israelites to be killed simply because they worshipped a golden calf.

We learn that disabled people were not allowed to approach the altar (Leviticus 21:16–23). God destroyed the Canaanites at Hormah, simply as a favor to the Jews (Numbers 21:1–3). God ordered Moses' army to "utterly destroy" sixty cities, killing all the women and children, at Deuteronomy 3:3–7. He ordered the Jews to kill the people of seven nations, and he told them to "show no mercy" to them, at Deuteronomy 7:12.

And Deuteronomy 23:2 tells us that a bastard child cannot attend services, "even to the tenth generation." Thus, even early in the Torah, we can see more than a dozen examples of evil and suffering in the Torah, or the Books of Moses. As we shall see in this second chapter, there are many examples of evil and suffering to be found in the historical books, as well.

We will begin Chapter Two by making some brief comments about the three major parts of the Old Testament. This will be followed by looking carefully at what the writers of the Tora have to say about evil and suffering. Indeed, we will analyze which of the responses or answers introduced in Chapter One can be found in the Torah. The second section of Chapter Two is the central section of the chapter. Before that analysis, however, we will make some observations about the idea of a *Berith*, or a "Covenant" in the ancient Near East and the Hittites and the ancient Jews, in particular. This idea of a Covenant is the most important category for an understanding of the God Yahweh's relationship to the ancient Jews.

This material will be followed by a careful analysis of the places in the historical books of the Old Testament, where the issues of theodicy and the problem of evil arise. By "historical books," we mean those texts from the Books of Joshua and Judges through Samuel, Kings and both books of Chronicles.

The Idea of a Covenant

The idea of a *Berith*, or a "Covenant," was a category in theology that could be found among the ancient Egyptians, the Mesopotamians, the Hittites and the ancient Jews. This idea is a simple way of describing a "Contract." The word *Berith* is employed in a variety of places in the Hebrew Bible, such as at First Kings 2:42–46, Second Kings 11:4, First Samuel 18:3–4 and Second Samuel 3:12–21, among many other passages.

The best way to comprehend the function of the *Berith* in the ancient Near East is among the Hittites, an ancient people who occupied Anatolia, or Asia Minor, beginning in the twelfth century BCE. The Hittites had contracts between gods and their people that had five principal parts. These were the following:

1. Introduction of the Contractual Parties
2. History of the Relationship between those parties
3. The New Agreement

4. Blessing and the Curses
5. Sealing Ceremony[50]

The first of these parts simply identified the contractual parties with words like "I am King so and so and you are my people, the So and Soites." The second part of the contract reviewed the past relationship between the two parties. The third part outlines the provisions of the New Agreement. Part four of the Hittite Contract described what will happen if the contract is not kept. This was most often a catalog of blessings and curses, depending on whether the contract was kept or not.

The final part of the Hittite Contract was the "Sealing Ceremony, a ritual that shows what will occur if the contract was not kept. It involved the splitting of important farming animals, putting one side to the right and the other to the left. A representative of the human party to the contract then would pass between the pieces of the animals with a lighted torch. The understanding was that if the contract was not kept, then the humans would wind up in a condition like the animals.[51] The use of the torch was thought to make it easier for the gods to see the contract, even from Heaven.

We mention this phenomenon of the Hittite Contract because the ancient Jews seem to have borrowed the idea from their neighbors. Consider Genesis 15, where Abraham makes a *Berith* or contract with *Yahweh*, the God of the ancient Jews. Genesis 15:7–11 is the introduction to the contractual parties, as well as the history. The New Agreement can be found at verses 12–16. The Sealing Ceremony and the Blessings and Curses appear in verses 13 to 21.

Another *Berith* can be seen in the 24th chapter of the Book of Joshua. Verses 1 to 13 are the identification of the parties and the history. Verses 25 and 26 are the New Agreement. The Blessings and the Curses can be found at verses 19, 20 and 25.

A number of other elements were sometimes included in ancient Jewish covenants. We will mention five of these. First, the *Berith* often was written down (see Joshua 24:26–28). Second, there were witnesses to the contract (see Joshua 24:22 and 27–28). Third, there often was a sharing of a meal (see Genesis 26:28–30). Fourth, there often was the taking of an oath (see Genesis 26:28). And finally, there may have been an exchanging of clothes that can be seen at First Samuel 18:4, for example.

One way to understanding the earliest views of the ancient Jews on the issues of theodicy and the problem of evil is to explore how well they appear to have kept their *Berith*, or Contract with Yahweh. When things were going well with the agreement, the nation as a whole was blessed. When things were not good between God and Israel, the nation was cursed.

Other contracts between Yahweh and the Israelites were Tribal Covenants, such as at Genesis 21:22–32, Genesis 26:26–31, and Genesis 31:43–54. Other references to tribal covenants can be found at Leviticus 2:13 and Second Chronicles 13:5. This brings us to some general comments on the three parts of ancient Hebrew scriptures—the Law, the Prophets, and the Writings—the topic of the next section of this second chapter.

Comments on Torah, Prophets and Writings

As we have indicated earlier, the ancient Jews conceived of their scriptures as having three parts—Torah, Prophets and Writings. For the most part, the oldest parts of the scriptures come in the Torah and the historical books mentioned earlier—Joshua, Judges, the books of Samuel, Kings and Chronicles. Most of this material was written most likely between 1,000 BCE and 800 BCE, except the books of Chronicles that are dated between 500 and 400 BCE.

The major prophets' writings, Isaiah, Jeremiah and Ezekiel most likely were completed from the eighth to the sixth century BCE. The *Kethuvim*, or the "Writings," contains material that is very old, some of the Psalms, for example, were completed from the sixth century BCE to the middle of the second century BCE.

By the year 150 BCE, then, the Hebrew Bible, or the Old Testament, pretty much looked the way it does today. Thus, we may record the history of attitudes toward phenomena like evil and suffering simply by looking at what the text says about those issues at any given time of the history.

As we shall see in this chapter and throughout this study, attitudes among the ancient Jews about fundamental theological issues changed over time. The views on the issues of theodicy and the problem of evil may have been very different by the time we arrive at the major or the minor prophets.

Similarly, what books of the writings like Proverbs or the Book of Job have to say about evil and suffering, for example, may be very different than what was written in the Torah, the historical books, or even in the *Nabim*, or the prophets.

One other preliminary remark about the issues of theodicy and the problem of evil is in order in regard to the Hebrew Bible, or the Old Testament. To wit, in many Old Testament texts, there is frequently a combination of theories to explain or to respond to evil and suffering among the ancient Jews. In the Torah, for example, we often see the combining of individual and collective forms of the Retributive Justice Theory with what we have called the Test View or the Moral Qualities Theory back in Chapter One.

To cite another example, among the major prophets—Isaiah, Jeremiah and Ezekiel—we find a number of verses that assent to the Collective Retributive Justice Theory. But we also find a number of passages that reject this theory, such as at Jeremiah 31:29–31, Ezekiel 18:23 and Isaiah 45:15.

The Book of Job, as we will argue in a later chapter of this study, is a compendium of views on the problem of evil and theodicy, even though the opening line of the book tells us that the patriarch *Iyyov*, or Job, is *tam va yashar*, or "blameless and upright." In the rest of the book, as we shall see, we will find many of the other answers and responses we have introduced in the opening chapter of this study on evil and suffering in the Bible.

Indeed, among those theories we will see in the Book of Job are Retributive Justice, Collective Retributive Justice, Free Will Defense, Original Sin Theory, Influences of Demonic Forces Theory, Test View, Moral Qualities Theory, Contrast Perspective, and, of course, Divine Plan Theory.

This brings us to the central section of this second chapter in which we will explore the places in the Torah, where the text appears to have something to say about the issues of theodicy and the problem of evil. As we shall see in the next section, there are also a variety of theories on evil and suffering to be found in the Torah, as well.

Evil and Suffering in the Torah

In the first five books of the Hebrew Bible or Old Testament, there are a variety of words that are employed to stand for "avenge," "vengeance," and "punishment." These words are all used to express what we have called the Retributive Justice Theory from Chapter One. Two of these words come from the Semitic root NQM. These are *naqam* and *naqamah*. The former may be found at Leviticus 26:25, where it means "punishment." It also can be found at Deuteronomy 32:35, 41, and 43, where it means "vengeance." In the last of these, *naqam* is used in the future tense, an indication that vengeance will come later, as part of a Divine Plan.

The word *naqamah* is used in the Torah and the historical books at Numbers 31:2, 3, and 7, as well as Judges 11:36 and Second Samuel 4:8. At Numbers 31:2, it means "avenge," at 31:3, "vengeance," and at 31:7, it implies "killed" rather than vengeance.[52]

The classical Hebrew word *darash* is another term to signify "avenge." It is used at Genesis 25:22, Deuteronomy 23:21 and 22, as well as at First Chronicles 10:14. In the passage from Genesis, *derash* means "avenge," as it does at First Chronicles 10:14. But the word is employed twice at Deuteronomy 23:21 and 22. In the first instance, it means "guilt," while in the second, it means "avenge."

In the following verse, at Deuteronomy 23:23, the text tells us this, "Whatever your lips utter you must diligently perform, just as you have freely vowed to the Lord your God with your own mouth." Thus, this appears to be an example of the Free Will Defense.[53]

A fourth word in the Hebrew Bible or Old Testament to designate "revenge" is the seldom-used term *shillumah*. One example of the word's use can be found at Psalm 91:8, where it seems to mean "punishment." This text tells us, "You will only look with your eyes and you will see the punishment of the wicked."[54]

A final Hebrew word related to vengeance and retribution is the term *Goel*, which means a "blood avenger." This is the word for "Redeemer" in the famous passage in the Book of Job at 19:25 and 26 that Handel's *messiah* has made famous. The word *Goel* is employed in many places, including Psalm 19:14 and 78:35, as well as Proverbs

23:11 and Isaiah 41:14. The word *Goel* usually implies a family's representative that is required to "avenge the blood" of his own family.

We begin with these words related to vengeance and retribution because, in most cases in which they are employed, they come in the context of a "pay back" of some sort, usually the collective kind.

Indeed, for the most part, the earliest views in the Torah on the issues of theodicy and the problem of evil tend to be related to Retributive Justice, as well as Collective Retributive Justice. This can be established by looking at a dozen or so key passages in the Hebrew Bible. Consider, for example, these three verses: Deuteronomy 8:18–19, 11:13–17 and 28:1–6.

In the first passage from Deuteronomy 8:18–19, the text tells us:

> You shall remember the Lord your God, for it is He who gives you the power of wealth that He may confirm His covenant which He swore to your fathers, as at this day. And if you forget the Lord your God and go after other gods and serve them and worship them, I solemnly warn you this day that you shall surely perish.

In the above passage, we find belief in polytheism, as well as Collective Retributive Justice. A few chapters later at 11:13–17, God again tells us this about keeping His commandments:

> If you obey my commandments which I commanded you this day, to love the Lord your God, and to serve Him with all your heart and with all your soul, He will give the rains to you in its season...But take heed, lest your heart be deceived, and turn aside and serve other gods...and the anger of the Lord will be kindled against you, and He will shut up the Heavens, so there is no rain.

Again, the writer of this text appears to combine belief in polytheism, the possibility of belief in other gods, the use of the *Yetzerim* Theory, with the mentions of "heart" and "soul," in verse 13, and Collective Retributive Justice. In the final passage from Deuteronomy, the one at 28:1–6, the Lord again speaks of following, or not following His commandments. If one follows them, the "Lord your God will set you high above the other nations." This is followed by a series of blessings as the consequences for following the commandments in verses 2–6.

At Leviticus 26:14–20, we find a similar passage in regard to the welfare of the ancient Jews and their relationship to their God Yahweh. This text relates:

> But if you will not hearken to me and will not do all of these commandments. If you spurn my statutes and in your soul you abhor my ordinances, so that you will not do all of My Commandments, while breaking My Covenant, I will do this to you. I will appoint over you sudden terror, consumption, and fever, that waste the eyes and cause life to pine away.

The word for "soul" in verse 15 is the noun *nefesh*. It is often also used as a synonym for the Self in classical Hebrew. At times, it also means something close to the modern notion of the term, with its mind-body dualism in many languages.

It should be clear in these verses that the keeping of the Covenant by the ancient Jews is to be blessed, while not keeping the *Berith* with Yahweh was to be cursed. Thus, this is an aversion of Collective or National Retributive Justice. Many other passages from the Torah also endorse both Individual and Collective Retributive Justice. Consider, for example, the Book of Numbers 16:26 that advises us, "Depart, I pray you, from the tents of wicked men, and touch nothing of theirs, lest you be swept away with all their sins." This verse also implies a Collective form of Retributive Justice. "Stay away from the tents of the wicked, lest you will be destroyed along with them."

Many of the narratives in the early chapters of Genesis are versions of the Retributive Justice Theory. We see this theory, for example, in the punishment of Adam and Eve in Genesis 3:11 to 19, in the story of Cain and Abel in Genesis 4, as well as in the destruction of Sodom and Gomorrah in chapters 18 and 19 of Genesis. Another example of the Retributive Justice Theory may be found at Genesis 18:25. At this place in the Torah, the author tells us,

Far be it from you to do such a thing, to slay the righteous with the wicked, so that the righteous fare as the wicked. Far be that from you. Shall not the Judge of all the Earth do what is just?

Perhaps the most famous passages about the Retributive Justice Theory in the Old Testament are to be found at Exodus 21:23–25 and at Exodus 34:7. The beginning of the former passage tells us this:

If any harm follows, then you shall give life for life, eye for eye and tooth for tooth, hand for hand and foot for foot, burn for burn, wound for wound, stripe for stripe.

At Exodus 34:6–7, the writer again speaks of the issues of theodicy and the problem of evil from the standpoint of Collective Retributive Justice. This text relates:

The Lord passed before him and claimed, "The Lord, the Lord, a God merciful and gracious, slow to anger and abounding in steadfast love and faithfulness, and keeping steadfast love for thousands, forgiving iniquity and transgression and sin, but who will by no means clear the guilty to the third and fourth generations."

Another passage from the Torah, this one at Deuteronomy 31:16–18, the writer of the text speaks of the consequences in breaking the Covenant with Yahweh. This text relates:

And the Lord said to Moses, "Behold you are about to sleep with your fathers. Then this people will rise up and play the harlot after the strange gods of the land, where they go to be among them, and they forsake Me and break My Covenant, which I had made with them. Then My anger shall be kindled against them in that day, and I will forsake them and hide my face from them. And they will be devoured, and many evils and troubles will fall upon them, so they will say in that day, 'Have not these evils not come upon us, so they will say in that day, 'Have not these evils come upon us because

our God is not among us?' And I will surely hide My face
on that day on account of all the evils which they had
done because they had turned to other gods."

In another passage in Deuteronomy, this one at 29:28–29, the
writer combines Retributive Justice with the Divine Plan Theory. In
these verses, we learn:

And the Lord uprooted them from their land in the
anger and fury and great wrath, And cast them into
another land, as at this day.

Many other Torah passages are narratives about examples of evil
where everything turns out for the Good in the end. The Sacrifice of
Isaac narrative of Genesis 22, the flight from Egypt narrative, the story
of the ten plagues, and many other narratives have been interpreted
over the centuries, in both Judaism and Christianity, as examples of the
Divine Plan Point of View. Rabbi Avi Weiss wrote an article in January
8, 2018, for the *Devar Torah*, for example, in which he argues that the
Divine Plan View is the best way to interpret the narrative of the ten
plagues. Rabbi Weiss writes:

As creation was carefully carried out by God for a world
that was potentially "very good" (Genesis 1:31), so too
were the plagues a carefully designed plan by God to
undo part of that creation which had gone wrong.[55]

Rabbi Weiss (b. 1944) is an American Orthodox Rabbi. He is
head of the Hebrew Institute of Riverdale in The Bronx, New York.
He writes on a variety of topics in his job, as well as freelance
pieces.

So far, this looks like the Collective Retributive Justice Theory,
but then at Deuteronomy 29 we see the following, "The secret things
belong to the Lord, our God, but the things that are revealed belong
to us and to our children forever, that we may do all the words of this
law." The "secret things" sound more like the Divine Plan Theory than
like the Retributive Justice Theory.

At several places in the Torah and the historical books that argue
against the Collective Retributive Justice Theory, such as Deuteronomy

24:16 and 32:3–5, as well as Second Chronicles 25:4. In the first of these, the writer tells us:

> Parents should not be put to death for their children,
> nor should children be put to death for their parents.

At Deuteronomy 32:5, the text speaks of "degenerate children who have dealt falsely with God." And at Second Chronicles 25:4, the writer makes the same judgment in Deuteronomy. The Chronicles passage relates:

> The parents should not be put to death for their children, nor should the children Be put to death for their parents.

Several passages to be found in the Torah also ascribe to the Test View, as introduced in Chapter One. Among these many texts are Genesis 22:1, the beginning of the Akedah Narrative, Deuteronomy 8:2 and 14, as well as Deuteronomy 29:3. The last of these speaks of "great trials." The opening verse of Genesis 22:1 tells us that, "After these things, God put Abraham to a test." At the Book of Deuteronomy 8:2, the text refers to God "testing humans, so He knows what is in their hearts." Thus, we might add the Test View to the collection of responses or answers in the Torah to the issues of Theodicy and the Problem of Evil.

Another example of the Test View to be found in the Torah comes at the Book of Numbers 20:20, which tells us God "has put me to the test these ten times and have not harkened me to my voice."

This same view can also be seen in various passages in the historical books, which we shall see in the next section of Chapter Two. It is enough to say now, however, that many of these may be found in the Book of Judges. For two examples, see Judges 2:22 and 3:1–4.

One way to see that the writers of the Torah assented to a belief in the Free Will Defense is to look at some of the verbs in Genesis and Deuteronomy that appear to establish the claim of Free Will. Deuteronomy 30:19–20 tells us to "Choose life." At Genesis 2:16–17, the Lord God tells Adam and Eve which trees in the Garden they were allowed to eat, and He does this with the implication that the first parents had to use their Free Will to decide what to do next.

Similarly, at Deuteronomy 11:26–28, the Lord God tells the Jews that they have the choice to obey, or to not obey His commandments, as well as what the consequences would be is they did not keep them. And if they have that choice, then they must possess Free Will. At Exodus 32:7–8, the text speaks of the retributive consequences for worshipping the golden calf. God says, "My wrath may burn hot against them, and I may consume them, but of you I will make a great nation."

Another way we can see the application of the Free Will Defense is in the many uses of the word *yetzer* in the Torah, including Genesis 6:5 and 8:21. Other examples of the use of the word *yetzer* in the Torah and the historical books may be found at Deuteronomy 31:21 and two places in First Chronicles at 28:9 and 29:18. In these latter two verses, the word is often translated as "intentions," again suggesting a belief in Free Will.

Not all the cases of Retributive Justice are of the collected variety. At Deuteronomy 7:10, for example, the text relates, "And He requites to their faces those who hate him, by destroying them. He will not be slack with him who hates Him. He will requite him to his face." In this verse, the theory behind it is Individual Retributive Justice, rather than Collective Retribution. This same theory is employed in a variety of other passages in the Torah, as well as the historical books. Another Torah verse that employs Individual Retributive Justice can be found at Deuteronomy 22:21, where the subject matter for discussion is the treatment of a young woman who has lost her virginity before her marriage. Ultimately, by verse 21, the text tells us what was to be done with the young woman in question. The text relates:

> Bring out the young woman to the door of her father's house, and the men of the city shall stone her to death with stones because she wrought folly in Israel by playing the harlot in her father's house. So you shall purge the evil from the midst of you.

In the same chapter at 21:12 and 13, the writer again expresses a version of the Retributive Justice Theory. This text relates:

> Whoever strikes a person mortally shall be out to death.
> If it was not premeditative, but came about by an act

of God, then I will appoint for you a place to which a
killer may flee. But if someone willfully attacks and kills
another by treachery you should take the killer from
my altar for execution.

This passage points to a fact in the Torah that not all killings are
murder in the first five books of the Bible. Some murders in the Torah
are given the name *bi-shagagah*, a word that suggests "unintentional,"
"accidental," or even "inadvert." In these acts in the Torah, there is
no *mens rea*, or "evil intent," as they say in English and American law.

The Hebrew expression *bi-shegagah* is used many times in the
Torah. Such as at Leviticus 4:2, 22, and 27, as well as 5:15 and 18,
and 22:14 and 24. The idea of "unintentional" also can be found at
Numbers 15:24–29. It can also be found at Numbers 35:11 and 15, as
well as Joshua 20:3 and 9. *Bi-shegagah* also can be found in two verses
in the Book of Ecclesiastes at 5:6 and 10:5.

There was still, however, a good amount of ambiguity about this
law. Was an exile to a city of refuge considered as a way of protecting
the accidental killer, or was it itself another form of punishment, not the
death sentence that would have applied to one who had intentionally
killed?

Recall that Adam and Eve were exiled from Eden after their sin.
After killing Abel, Cain was told that he "would be a restless wanderer
on the face of the Earth." In the daily prayers for Orthodox Jews, there
is the line, "Because of our sins, we were exiled from the land." In the
Book of Numbers 35:25 to 27, we are given the rules about a "City of
Refuge" in the Torah.

Another Torah passage that also suggests Individual Retributive
Justice can be found at the Book of Leviticus 17:24, where the text
reveals that the Lord says that "bloodguilt shall be imputed to any man
who has shed blood, and that man shall be cut off from his people."

Even in occasional passages in the Torah, the writers seem to
imply a belief in the Original Sin Theory, such as at Deuteronomy 1:39.
This text advises:

Moreover, your little ones, which you said should be
a prey, and your children, which in that day had no

knowledge between good and evil, they shall go in
thither, and unto them shall I give it, and they shall
possess it.

Many in the Christian tradition, of course, see the narrative of
Genesis 3 to be an example of the Original Sin Theory, particularly in
the consequences given to Adam and Eve in verses 16 to 19.

A number of passages in the Torah also speak of those who
worship demons, like Leviticus 20:6 that advises, "If a person turns to
mediums, wizards, and demons, playing their harlot after them, I will
set my face against that person and against his family, and I will cut
them off from among his people." This is an obvious reference to the
Influence of Demonic Forces Theory.

Another passage in the Torah where the Influences of Demonic
Forces can be seen is at Deuteronomy 32:17, where the text relates,
"They sacrificed to demons which were no gods, to gods they have
never known." Another Torah passages where demons are mentioned
is at Leviticus 17:7, where the text relates:

Therefore, they shall no more slay their sacrifices to
demons (or satyrs) after whom they pray the harlot.
This shall be a statute forever to them throughout their
generations.

The plural, masculine noun for "demons" in this verse is *seydim*.
This Hebrew term is a borrowed word from the Assyrian *Sedu*. It is
only employed one other time in the entire Hebrew Bible. This verse
comes at Psalms 106:37, which we shall discuss in the later chapter
devoted to evil and suffering in the Psalms.

Another classical Hebrew word to designate the demonic is the
plural noun *se'irim*, that is used, for example, at Leviticus 17:7. The
Revised Standard Version translates this noun as "Satyrs," as it does
throughout the Torah.

Another term to designate the demonic in the Torah is the expression,
"the spirit of jealousy," which is employed at the Book of Numbers 5:14
and 5:30. Sometimes the word *Ruah*, or "Spirit," is also used in the Torah
to indicate a spirit entity with evil intentions or actions.

Certainly, we must add to these passages about the Influences of Demonic Forces in the Torah, the appearance of the *nachash*, or serpent, in Genesis 3:1 and 14. Traditionally in Christianity, this serpent has been identified with Satan and the Demonic.

Finally, the very first two references to "Light" in the Torah appear to be examples of what we have labeled the Contrast View in Chapter One of this study of evil and suffering in the Bible. The first of these comes at Genesis 1:4, where Yahweh "saw that the Light was Good, and God separated the Light from the Darkness." In the second reference to Light in the Bible, which comes fourteen verses later at 1:18, the narrator of Genesis tells us that the making of the Sun and the Moon was "to govern the night and the day, and to separate the light from the darkness, and God saw that it was Good."

From our analysis of the issues of theodicy and the problem of evil in the first five books of the Old Testament, or the Torah portion of the Hebrew Bible, we have seen the application of the following theories on evil and suffering as introduced in Chapter One of this study:

1. Individual Retributive Justice
2. Collective Retributive Justice
3. The Free Will Defense
4. Original Sin Theory
5. The Influence of Demonic Forces View
6. The Contrast View
7. The Test View
8. The Moral Qualities View
9. Divine Plan Theory[56]

Back in Chapter One, these were all the traditional responses and answers that were introduced to respond or to answer the issues of theodicy and the problem of evil. There we introduced four deontological answers and four teleological responses. Precisely, the ones we have enumerated here in Chapter Two of evil and suffering in the Bible.

Finally, there are several passages in the Hebrew Bible or Old Testament where the Hidden God Theory may be found. One illustrative example of this theory can be found at Deuteronomy 32:10, where Yahweh relates, "I will hide My face from them…" At Deuteronomy 31:17, Yahweh again tells us:

> Then My anger will be kindled against them in that day,
> and I will forsake them and hide My face from them.

In the very next verse, Deuteronomy 31:18, Yahweh again related, "But I will surely hide My face in that day because of all the evil that they will do, for in the process they will turn to other gods." At Deuteronomy 32:20, Moses speaks of God, who said, "I will hide My face from them, and I will see what their end will be." The Hidden God View is another theory that may be discovered throughout both the Old and the New Testaments. More will be said of this theory later in this study.

At this point, however, we may point to two other examples of this theory at Leviticus 5:2 and Deuteronomy 30:11. The former text tells us this:

> Or if a soul touches any unclean thing, whether it be
> a carcass or an unclean beast, or a carcass of unclean
> cattle, or the carcass of unclean creeping things, and it
> be hidden from him, he also shall be unclean and guilty.

At Deuteronomy 30:11, we find another illustration of the Hidden God Theory. This text relates:

> For this commandment which I command to you this
> day is not hidden from you, and neither is it far off.

We also find the opposite of God hiding His face in the Torah. One such passage can be found in the Book of Numbers 6:24–26, where the text reveals:

> The Lord bless you and keep you.
>
> The Lord makes His face shine upon you and be gracious
> to you.
>
> The Lord lift up His countenance upon you and give you
> peace.

This brings us to the issues of theodicy and the problem of evil in the historical books of the Hebrew Bible, or Old Testament. By that term, we mean the books from Joshua and Judges to the books of Samuel, Kings, and First and Second Chronicles, the topic of the next section of Chapter Two.

Evil and Suffering in the Historical Books

The range of responses and answers to the issues of theodicy and the problem of evil in the historical books of the Old Testament or Hebrew Bible is considerably smaller than what we have seen in the Torah in the second chapter. For the most part, the answers and responses in the historical books are mostly related to the following theories as introduced back in Chapter One:

1. Retributive Justice (both individual and collective)
2. The Free Will Defense
3. The Influences of Demonic Forces View
4. The Test Theory
5. The Hidden God Theory
6. Divine Plan Point of View[57]

At Joshua 23:12–13, in the context of ancient Jews marrying women of surrounding nations, the writer of Joshua seems to assent to the Collective Retributive Justice Theory. The text in question tells us this:

> For if you turn back and join the remnant of these nations left here among you, and make marriages with them, so that you marry their women and they yours, know that the Lord your God will not continue to drive out these nations before you. But they shall be a snare and a trap, a scourge on your sides, and thorns in your eyes, until you perish from off the good land that God has given you.

Clearly, God is against the idea of intermarriage with other nations near the ancient Jews, and because of the practice, Yahweh brings punishment to the Chosen People by making them "perish from the land that has been given to them. Thus, we have an example of Collective Retributive Justice.

Similarly, Second Kings 17:18, after the text speaks of "provoking God to anger," goes to say that, "The Lord was very angry with Israel, and removed them out of His sight, and none was left but the tribe of Judah." By verse 23 of the same chapter, the writer again speaks of "removing Israel out of His sight," and, as a consequence, Israel was exiled from their land and taken to Assyria. Again, this is a version of the Collective Retributive Justice Theory.

At Second Samuel 24:10–17, and particularly at verse 15, again, we see the God Yahweh punishing the nation of Israel. The text relates in verse 15:

> So the Lord sent a pestilence upon Israel from the morning until the appointed time. And there died many of the people from Dan to Beersheba, seventy thousand men.

Many other passages in the historical books also assent to both Collective, as well as Individual forms of the Retributive Justice Theory. Sometimes the object to the retribution is an individual, and at other times it is the nation of Israel as a whole.[58] Second Kings 18:12 is another place in the historical books where we see Retributive Justice at play. The text relates:

> Because they did not obey the voice of the Lord their God but transgressed His Covenant, even all that Moses the servant of the Lord commanded. They neither listened nor obeyed.

This is followed directly by punishment for the disobedience, making the passage another example of the Collective Retributive Justice Theory. Again, in the historical books, we find many references to the Retributive Justice Theory, applied to individuals, as well as to the nation as a whole.[59] First Samuel 25:29 and 2:6 also ascribe to the Retributive Justice Theory. In the former passage, the writer makes reference to one who follows the Lord and one who does not. Yahweh says, "If men rise up to pursue you and to take your life, the life of your

Lord shall be bound up in a bundle of the living…and the lives of your enemies will be slung out as from the hollow of a sling-shot."

At First Samuel 2:6, the writer again relates God's relationship to the faithful and the evildoer when he says, "The Lord kills and brings life, He brings some down to Sheol, and others He raises up." The word Sheol, of course, is the classical Hebrew term for the underworld. It is the place that the shades go after death.

The writer of Second Samuel 3:39 also speaks of Yahweh's treatment of the evildoer. This verse tells us:

> The Lord requites the evildoer according to the wickedness he has done.

This, of course, is another direct reference to the Individual Retributive Justice Theory. Indeed, this is one verse among many in the Books of Samuel, where this theory appears to be beneath these various passages.

There are also places in the historical books of the Old Testament where Retributive Justice of an individual, or a nation, appears to be called into question. Consider, for example, the Book of Judges 6:13–14, that tells us this:

> And Gideon said to him, "Pray, if the Lord is with me, why then has this befallen all of us. And where are all of His wonderful deeds that our fathers have recounted to us, saying, 'Did not the Lord bring us up from Egypt?' But now the Lord has cast us off, and given us into the hand of Midian."

The author of Judges, at both 15:8 and 16:28, also speaks of Retributive Justice in the context of "avenging" some of the nation of Israel's enemies. Again, beneath these two passages, the Retributive Justice Theory clearly can be found.

A similar view may be found at Second Chronicles 25:4 that tells us the following:

> The parents shall not be killed for the children, nor should the children be put to death for their parents, but all shall be put to death for their own sins.

This appears to be an argument against familial sin, as well as one in favor of the Individual Retributive Justice Theory. The exact same argument is made at Deuteronomy 24:16 and 32:3–5.

The Free Will Defense may also be seen in the historical books in places such as Joshua 24:15. This text gives us the advice, "now that you are unwilling to serve Yahweh, choose this day whom you will serve…" This reference to choice is clearing an indication of the Free Will Defense.

Another way the Free Will View may be seen in the historical books are the many places where the word *yetzer* is employed in those books. We will cite two examples to establish the claim. These come at First Chronicles 28:9 and 28:18. In the former the text relates:

> And you, my son Solomon, know the God of your father
> and serve him with a single mind and a willing heart.
> For the Lord searches every mind and understands
> every plan and thought.

The word for "mind" here is *yetzer*. The verse also employs the word *leb*, or "heart," where the thought is to be found. A few verses later, at First Chronicles 28:18, we see a reference to a "plan" (*yetzer*) in the mind of God. The same word appears in the next verse, as well. It refers to the plan (*yetzer*) of His works.

In several places in the historical books, we also can find the application of the Test Theory that was introduced in Chapter One. Consider two examples, the Book of Judges 2:22 and 3:1–4. In the former, we see Yahweh say, "That by them I may test Israel, whether they will agree to walk in the way of the Lord, or not."

At Judges 3:1–4, we see two references to the same theory. At verse one, we are told, "Now these are the nations which the Lord left, to test Israel by them, that is, all of Israel who had experience." At verse four, still speaking of these same nations, the text relates about them, "They were for the testing of Israel, to know whether Israel would obey the commandments of the Lord which he commanded their fathers through Moses."

Many episodes in the historical books of the Old Testament, or Hebrew Bible, show the God of the Israelites "testing" his people. Such as holding water from the Jews in Joshua 2. A number of other verses among the historical books also indicate belief in the Test Theory. This brings us to a number of places in the historical books of the Old Testament, where the Influences of Demonic Forces Theory appears to be at work as an explanation for why people suffer or experience evil in those books.

At Second Chronicles 11:15, for example, the text reveals:

> And He appointed His own priests for the high places, and for the demons, and for the calves which He had made.

First Chronicles 21:1–2 gives us the clearest example of the Demonic Forces Theory in the historical books. The text in question relates:

> Satan stood up against Israel and incited David to number the Israelites. So David to Jo'ab and to the commanders of the Army...

First Kings 22:21 uses language about a "lying spirit," suggesting another example of the Influences of Demonic Forces Theory in the historical books of the Hebrew Bible, or Old Testament.

First Chronicles 29:8, and again at verse 18 of the same chapter, employs the Hebrew term *yetzer*, perhaps an argument for the use of the Free Will Defense in the historical books. And various passages in Second Kings at 8:7–10 and 23:33, for example, are likely to be uses of the Divine Plan Point of View. First Kings 9:4–5 speaks in the future tense about God "establishing a royal throne over Israel forever," again another indication, perhaps, of a belief in the Divine Plan Theory, some with the use of future-tense verbs.

At Judges 7:4 and Second Chronicles 32:31, we may find two other examples of the Test View in the historical books. The former uses the word *tsaraph*, a word that frequently is applied to the "testing" of metals in the Old Testament. The latter passage employs the verb *Nacah*, or "to test," as it is used here.

From this analysis of the theories in the historical books of the Old Testament, we have suggested that examples of the following theories have been employed by the writers of the books from Joshua to Second Chronicles: Retributive Justice Theory, both Individual and Collective, the Free Will Defense through the use of the word *yetzer*, the Influences of Demonic Forces Theory in First and Second Chronicles, as well as verses in First Kings, several examples of the Test Theory, as well as a few passages that seem to indicate the Divine Plan Theory.

There are also a number of references in the historical books of the Hebrew Bible to the use of the classical Hebrew noun *Berith*, or "Covenant." In the next section of this second chapter, we shall carefully look at some of these in the historical books of the Old Testament.

Berith (Covenant) in the Historical Books of the Old Testament

The word *Berith*, or "Covenant," appears dozens of times in the historical books of the Old Testament. In the books of Joshua and Judges, the word occurs in three different contexts. The first of these is in reference to the Ark of the Covenant, the first piece of tabernacle furniture for which precise directions were delivered in Exodus 25. The word "Covenant" is employed in this context at Joshua 2:3–6 and 11–17, 4:18, 6:6–8 and, 8:33, as well as the Book of Judges 20:27.

The second context in which the word *Berith* appears in the books of Joshua and Judges are those verses that speak of the possibility of a transgression of the Covenant that Yahweh made with patriarch Abraham in Genesis 15. Examples of this context include Joshua 7:11–15 and 23:6, as well as Judges 2:20.

The third context in which the word Covenant is used in Joshua and Judges is where reference is made to the making or breaking of a *Berith*. Examples of this third context in the books of Joshua and Judges may be seen at Joshua 9:6 and 24:25, as well as at Judges 2:1.

At Joshua, we see the Gibeonites making a covenant with Joshua. The leader of the Gibeonites says, "We have come from a far country, so now make a covenant with us."

The other passage from Joshua that speaks of making a covenant comes at Joshua 24:25. This text speaks of Joshua making a covenant "with the people that day, and then made statutes and ordinances for them at Shechem." This covenant between Joshua and the people is written down on a stone that becomes "a witness" to the covenant in question.

In the Book of Judges 2:1, the text speaks of the relationship between Yahweh and the Chosen People. God says, "I brought you up from Egypt into the lands to which I swore to your fathers." Another indication of the Divine Plan Theory is that God delivers what He had promised earlier. But then this is followed by these words by Yahweh:

> I will never break my covenant with you, and you shall
> make no covenants with the inhabitants of this land,
> and you shall break down their altars.

The idea of a *Berith*, or "Covenant," is employed in four different contexts in the two books of Samuel, as well. Again, the first of these is references to the Ark of the Covenant at First Samuel 4:3–5 and Second Samuel 15:24. The second context for uses of *Berith* in Samuel are instances where Jonathan wishes to make a Covenant with David. At First Samuel 18:3 and 23:18, the word "Covenant" is used. One interesting feature of the first of these is that it uses the exchange of clothing in the course of the contract.

The idea of "making a covenant with one's servants" is the third context of the use of the word *Berith* in Samuel. The heads of households, it is suggested, has the same kind of contract with his servants that God has with the Israelites, complete with the ideas of keeping or not keeping the contract and the subsequent blessings and curses to be incurred.

The fourth context in the Books of Samuel, where the idea of a *Berith* appears, is where Nahash, the King of the Ammonites, wishes to make a Covenant with the Jews. This can be found at First Samuel 11:1–2, where Nahash says, "Make a treaty [*Berith*] with us, and we will serve you." Again, the normal stipulations of an ancient Near Eastern contract would pertain to such an agreement.

In the two books of Kings, we find three separate contexts where the word *Berith* is employed. The first is like Joshua, Judges and Samuel, where it refers to the Ark of the Covenant, such as at First Kings 3:15 and 6:19, for example. The second context is when some leader attempts to make a *Berith* with the Jews, or where King Solomon makes a Covenant with King Shim'ei, which he does at First Kings 2:42–46.

At Second Kings 11:4 and 17, King Jehoi'ada wishes to make a *Berith* with the ancient Jewish nation. And Ben-Hadad also desires to make a contract with King Ahab and the Jews at First Kings 20:34.

The third context in which the word *Berith*, or "Contract," can be seen, may be found at Second Kings 17:15, 35 and 38. In each of these three verses, Yahweh complains that the Jews appear to hate the covenant and statutes that He made with their fathers. And in this, Yahweh was "provoked to anger" in each of them.

The word *Berith* also appears a number of times in the two books of Chronicles. All told, there are thirty separate uses of the word *Berith* in the two books. About half of these are mentions of the Ark of the Covenant. These may be found at First Chronicles 15:25–26 and 28–29; 16:6 and 37, 17:1, 22:19, and 28:2 and 18. Also, at Second Chronicles 5:2, 7 and 10, all of which refer to the Ark of the Covenant.

Most of the other uses of the word *Berith* in the books of Chronicles come in the context of referring to the Covenant made with "the Fathers." Among these are First Chronicles 16:16 that refers to the *Berith* made "with Abraham." The verse before 16:16 that gives some advice that "One should be mindful of the everlasting Covenant." Second Chronicles 15:12 uses the same language. At Second Chronicles 6:14, the writer speaks of the fact that Yahweh "keeps His covenant with steadfast love."

Additionally, at Second Chronicles 23:1, 3 and 16 speak of Yahweh "making a covenant with the tribes of Israel." Second Chronicles 29:10 also describes Hezekiah's desire to make a covenant with the Lord.

Finally, Second Chronicles 13:5 refers to something it calls a "Covenant of Salt." The expression "a Covenant of Salt" occurs three times in the Hebrew Bible or Old Testament. The other two references are at Leviticus 2:13 and the book of Numbers 18:19. There is also a fourth verse at Ezra 4:14 that refers to the "Salt of the Palace." In ancient Israel, salt was regarded as a necessary ingredient in a daily meal, so it is very easy to see a connection between salt and covenant-making. When people ate together, they became friends and hospitality to one another cemented the idea of friendship.

Salt was also a preservative in the ancient world. Thus, it would be easy to see a Salt Covenant as one that was everlasting, or one that lasted a very long time. Thus, as Numbers tells us at 18:19, "a Covenant of Salt forever before Yahweh." In regard to the reference at Second Chronicles 13:5, David received his Kingdom forever from Yahweh "by a Covenant of Salt.

In the Gospel of Mark at 9:50, Jesus tells his disciples, "Have salt in yourselves, and be at peace with one another." It is likely he means something like, "Be true to yourselves forever and ever." This brings us to the conclusions we have made in this second chapter.

In the third chapter of this study of evil and suffering in the Bible, we shall turn our attention to the places in the major prophets: Isaiah, Jeremiah and Ezekiel, where these Biblical prophets have made observations on the issues of theodicy and the problem of evil.

Conclusions

We began this second chapter with a summary of the three parts of scripture in the Hebrew Bible, or Old Testament—*Torah, Nabim* and *Kethuvim*, or "Law," "Prophets" and "Writings." This was followed by a description of the important phenomenon of the *Berith*, or "Covenant," as background material for understanding evil and suffering in the Torah and the historical books.[60]

This was followed by some very basic observations about the Torah, prophets and the writings. We then moved to an analysis of many of the places in the Torah where the issues of theodicy and the problem of evil can be found. From this analysis, we have suggested that, at times, the first five books of the Bible endorse the Individual and Collective Retributive Justice Theory, Free Will Defense, Original Sin Theory, Influence of Demonic Forces theory, Test View, Moral Qualities Perspective, as well as the Divine Plan Theory.

Next in Chapter Two, we analyzed and discussed the places in the historical books of the Old Testament, where questions about evil and suffering arise. At the close of this analysis, we have concluded that the writers of the historical books of the Hebrew Bible have endorsed both forms of Retributive Justice, the Free Will Defense, mostly using the theory of the two *Yetzerim*, the *yetzer ha ra* and the *yetzer tov*, or the evil and the good imaginations or inclinations.[61]

We also suggested in Chapter Two that the writers of the historical books of the Old Testament also have endorsed, or assented to, the Influence of Demonic Forces Theory, the Test Perspective, and the Divine Plan Theory. In the final section of this second chapter, we introduced and discussed the places in the historical books of the Old Testament, where the category of the *Berith*, or the Covenant, appears in the books of the Old Testament from Joshua and Judges to the books of Samuel, Kings and Chronicles. In that material, we have seen that the idea of the Covenant has played a vital role in all of these books of the Hebrew Bible.[62]

Indeed, we have shown at the close of Chapter Two that the idea of the *Berith* first established between Yahweh and the patriarch Abraham, as the representative of the nation of Israel, was a foundational idea of all subsequent understandings of evil and suffering throughout the historical books, and beyond. This brings us to Chapter Three, in which the subject-matter of that chapter principally will be the way that the three major prophets of the Old Testament—Isaiah, Jeremiah and Ezekiel—have dealt with the questions of theodicy and the problem of evil. It is to the major prophets, then, that we turn next.

Chapter Three:
Evil and Suffering in the Major Prophets—
Isaiah, Jeremiah and Ezekiel

The existence of evil, in its variegated aspects, is an important philosophical and religious issue, as evil has implications with regard to human life, nature, and religious faith in Divine Providence. The existence of evil presents a particularly difficult religious issue for monotheism, in which God is the exclusive creator of the world and the exclusive God, as in Judaism.

—Bilha Nitzan, "Evil and its Symbols in the Qumran Scrolls."

Thus, the essential dividing line is not between men who sin and men who do not sin, but between those who are pure in heart and those who are impure in heart. Even the sinner whose heart becomes pure experiences God's goodness as it is revealed to him. As Israel purifies its heart, it experiences that God is good to it.

—Martin Buber, "The Heart Determines"

Despair over the earthly or over something earthly is really a despair about the eternal over oneself, in so far it is a despair for this is the formula for all despair...He thinks he is in despair over something earthly and constantly talks about what he is in despair over, and yet he is in despair about the eternal.

—Soren Kierkegaard, *Fear and Trembling*

Introduction

The purpose of this third chapter is to analyze and discuss the many ways that the major prophets in the Hebrew Bible, or Old Testament, have dealt with or responded to the questions of theodicy and the problem of evil in their books. The "major" prophets—Isaiah, Jeremiah and Ezekiel—are called major because these books are longer than those of the minor prophets.

We will begin Chapter Three with an introduction to Isaiah, Jeremiah and Ezekiel. In this opening section, we also will point to several aspects of the books of the major prophets that Isaiah, Jeremiah and Ezekiel have in common. This will be followed by separate sections on each of the three major prophets, one after the other, beginning with Isaiah, then Jeremiah, and finally, Ezekiel. The purpose of these three sections is to explore and to discuss what Isaiah, Jeremiah and Ezekiel have to say about the issues of evil and suffering.

In their texts, chapter four, as we shall see, primarily will center on what the minor prophets believed and wrote about the issues of theodicy and the problem of evil.

Introduction to the Major Prophets

The major prophets in the Hebrew Bible, or Old Testament, are Isaiah, Jeremiah and Ezekiel. Many contemporary scholars on these three books argue that they are very different from each other, but in this analysis, we shall maintain that they are actually quite similar in many ways. Although the three wrote in different centuries—Isaiah in the eighth century BCE and Jeremiah and Ezekiel in the sixth century, the three, nevertheless, have at least eight major similarities among them.

First, throughout the books of Isaiah, Jeremiah and Ezekiel, a careful reader will notice the theme of "Judgment on Judah" (Isa. 1–12, Jer. 1–29 and Ezek. 1–24). A second element that the three have in common is that all three contain "oracles against other nations" (Isa. 13-23, Jer. 46–51 and Ezek. 25–32). A third common element in the major prophets is the "Future Restoration" of the Nation of Israel (Isa. 40:55, Jer. 30–33 and Ezek. 33–48). Often this use of future-tense verbs, as we have shown, is a signal for the Divine Plan Theory.

A fourth aspect that the major prophets share is a call to the "People of Judah to Repent."

And finally, the themes of evil and suffering frequently may be seen to arrive in the books of Isaiah, Jeremiah and Ezekiel, as we shall see in this third chapter. In a similar fashion, the overarching message of each of the three major prophets was a call for the people of Judah, the Southern Kingdom, to repent and to turn away from idolatry of various forms. While this message was frequently rejected, the promises of God continued to come.

Sixth, this message was brought to all three of the major prophets through judgment and through discipline, and the message was received by each within the context that there would be a restoration, as well as an ultimate culmination in a glorious eschatological restoration of the Nation of Israel.

A seventh aspect of the prophecies of Isaiah, Jeremiah and Ezekiel is that all three seem to end their books by pointing to the hope that was found in the promise of God, Who was faithful to His Chosen People. God would establish Himself as the Restorer in each of these three prophetic books, where a renewed life, hope and great future was to come. To the Kingdom of Judah. A final similarity among the books of Isaiah, Jeremiah and Ezekiel is a reliance on certain images and metaphors that appear in all three books. For example, the image of a vineyard at Isaiah 5:7 and Ezekiel 19:10 or an olive tree at Jer. 11:16, refers to the pruning or removing of certain features of the vine or the tree. A variety of other images and metaphors are shared by the three major prophets.[63]

Although these eight themes remain constant in the three major prophets, the contexts in which the three operated were very different. Isaiah's ministry lasted through the course of King Uzziah until the reign of Hezekiah. Jeremiah and Ezekiel worked during the reigns of Jehoiakim through Zedekiah.

In conclusion, each of these eight aspects of the books of Isaiah, Jeremiah and Ezekiel, the imagery used among them, as well as the messianic and eschatological emphasis in each book, demonstrates a consistency among them, while at the same time demonstrate specific differences in their prophecies. When placed side by side, however, each of the three attests to the interweaving and unity of Old Testament Prophecy.

This brings us to the description of a timeline of "Rule and Prophecy among the Ancient Jews." This timeline will aid us in placing each of the three major prophets in the political and religious contexts in which they were placed.

Timeline of Political Rule and Prophecy in Ancient Israel

The purpose of the following timeline[64] is to place each of the major prophets in the political, historical and religious contexts in ancient Israel:

1250 to 1200 BCE	Hebrew tribes settle in Canaan.
1250 to 1150 BCE	Many Canaanite towns destroyed by Israelites.
1213 to 1203 BCE	First reference to Hebrews in Egyptian records.
1180 to 1010 BCE	Saul becomes first King of Israel.
1035 to 970 BCE	David, second King of Israel.
950 BCE	Solomon builds the First Temple.
841 BCE	Israel pays tribute to Assyria.
791 to 740 BCE	Uzziah rules Judah.
740 to 685 BCE	The time of Isaiah.
728 to 686 BCE	Hezekiah rules Judah.
722 BCE	Israel conquered and exiled by Assyrians.
721 BCE	The upper class of the Northern Kingdom is exiled by the Assyrians.
640 to 609 BCE	Josiah rules Judah. He enacts religious reforms.
627 to 580 BCE	The time of Jeremiah.
612 BCE	The Babylonians, the Chaldeans conquer and destroy Nineveh (Assyria).
605 BCE	Babylonians invade Judah and exile the Jews.
605 to 530 BCE	Daniel, prophet in exiled Judah.

597 BCE	Second invasion by Babylonians.
593 to 570 BCE	Ezekiel, prophet of exiled Judah.
586 BCE	Fall of Jerusalem to Babylonians. Much of population exiled. Temple in Jerusalem destroyed.
539 BCE	King Cyrus II, Cyrus the Great of Persia, captures Babylon and establishes empire.
538 BCE	First return of exiled Jews to Jerusalem under King Zerubbabel.
516 BCE	Construction of the Second Temple begins.

This timeline suggests that the Hebrews first entered Canaan around 1250 BCE. By 1180, Kingship had begun, and around 950, the First Temple had been built. For much of the next three centuries, the Assyrians to the north and Egyptians to the south battled over the possession of Canaan/Israel. Regarding the major prophets, using this timeline, it is clear that the Prophet Isaiah worked from the middle of the eighth century BCE into the early seventh century. Jeremiah, the second major prophet, wrote and worked in the late seventh century BCE to the first two decades of the sixth century BCE. And the prophet Ezekiel wrote from the exiled Judah in the opening three decades of the sixth century BCE.

Each of the three major prophets completed their books in times of great turmoil. Isaiah, when the Assyrians constantly threatened the Jews; Jeremiah, during the period of religious reforms in Israel brought by King Josiah; and Ezekiel completed his book of prophecy, in exile, after the second invasion by the Babylonians in the early sixth century BCE. Indeed, it is likely that the prophet Ezekiel was among those who were exiled to the Kingdom of the Babylonians.

With this timeline, we can now understand each of the three major prophets in the political and religious contexts in which they operated. We will now move to each of the three, beginning with the Prophet Isaiah, to discuss what they had to say about the questions of theodicy and the problem of evil in their Hebrew books.

Isaiah on Evil, Suffering and Theodicy

The first of the major prophets, Isaiah, wrote his book from 740 to around 681 BCE, in the Southern Kingdom of Judah, after the nation of Israel was divided under the rule of King Rehoboam. In Isaiah's day, Judah was stuck between two powerful and aggressive enemies—Assyria and Egypt. Thus, the leaders of Judah spent much of their time trying to appease and curry favor with the two superpowers. Nevertheless, Isaiah spent much of his book criticizing the leaders for relying on human help, rather than repenting from their own sin, and turning back to their God, Yahweh.

At chapter 57:1 of his book, the Prophet Isaiah raises the issues of theodicy and the problem of evil, when he wrote:

> The righteous man perishes, and no one lays it to heart.
> Devout men are taken away while no one understands.
> For the righteous man is taken away from calamity, he
> enters into peace, they rest in their beds and walk in
> their uprightness.

Indeed, throughout his book, Isaiah frequently commented on the issues of evil and suffering. In fact, of the three major prophets of the Hebrew Bible, Isaiah wrote far more on these issues than either Jeremiah or Ezekiel. Of the chapters of the Book of Isaiah, the prophet mentions or assents to six of the theories introduced in Chapter One, as well as a seventh theory we have not seen so far in this study. We will begin our analysis of Isaiah's views with this seventh theory we shall call the "Hidden God" Perspective that appears a number of times in the book.

Two representative examples of the Hidden God Theory may be seen at Isaiah 45:15 and 59:2. In the former, Isaiah tells us this: "Truly, You are a God who hides Yourself, Oh God of Israel, Our Savior." At 59:2, Isaiah relates to the people of Judah:

> But your iniquities have made a separation between
> you and your God, and your sins have hidden His face
> from you, so that He does not hear.

Another example of the same theory can be seen at Isaiah 45:3, where Isaiah tells us that God says, "I will give you the treasures of darkness and the hoards in secret places that you may know that it is I, the Lord, the God of Israel, who calls you by your name." The same view also can be seen at Isaiah 8:17, 54:8 and 64:7, and in each of these, God "hides His face" from the Israelites.

The six theories and responses introduced in Chapter One that can be found in Isaiah's book, besides the Hidden God Theory, are the following: Individual Retributive Justice, Collective Retributive Justice, the Influences of Demonic Forces Theory, Original Sin Theory, the Contrast View, and the Divine Plan Perspective.

Among the examples of the Individual Retributive Justice Theory are Isaiah 2:18–21, 9:18–20, 13:11–13, 45:9–11, and 59:18. In the first of these, Isaiah speaks of the phenomenon of idols and their place in the nation of Israel. The Prophet relates:

> And the idols shall utterly pass away.
> And men shall enter the caves of the rocks
> and the holes in the ground,
> from before the utter terror of the Lord,
> and from the glory of his majesty
> when he rises to terrify the earth.
> In that day, men will cast forth,
> their idols of silver and of gold,
> which they made for themselves to worship
> to the moles and to the bats,
> to enter the caverns of the rocks
> and the clefts of the cliffs
> from before the terror of the Lord
> and from the glory of his majesty
> when he rises to terrify the earth.

Several verses in chapter nine of Isaiah also assent to the Retributive Justice Theory, such as verses 13–17 and 18–20. The latter speaks of the fate of evildoers. The text relates:

> For wickedness burns like a fire
> It consumes briars and thorns.

It kindles the thickets of the forest
and they roll up in a cloud of smoke.
Through the wrath of the Lord of hosts
the land is burned.
And the people are like fuel for the fire.
No man spares his brother.
They snatch on the right, but are still hungry
and they devour on the left, but are not satisfied.
Each devours his neighbor's flesh...
For all his anger is not turned away
And His hand is stretched out still.

At 13:11–13, Isaiah is even more explicit about the fate of the wicked:

I will punish the world for its evil,
and the wicked for their iniquity.
I will put an end to the pride of the arrogant
And lay low the haughtiness of the ruthless...
Therefore, I will make the heavens tremble
And the earth will be shaken out of place
At the wrath of the Lord of hosts
In the day of His fierce anger.

The Prophet Isaiah also gives a warning to those who struggle against the Lord at 45:9, when the text informs us, "Woe to him who strives with his Maker." But then immediately after this line, Isaiah provides a metaphor that looks more like the Divine Plan Theory. The text asks:

Does the clay say to him who fashions it, "What are you
    making?"
Or "Your work has no handles."
Thus says the Lord, the Holy One of Israel and his Maker
"Will you question me about my children,
Or make commands to me concerning the works of my
    hands?"

In this metaphor, God plays the part of the sculptor and humans the part of the clay or the pot. Should the pot ask questions of the potter? Isaiah adds in verse 12, "I made the Earth and created man upon it. It was my hands that stretches out the heavens when I commanded all their hosts."

Finally, at 59:18, Isaiah again shows that he is an advocate of the Retributive Justice Theory when he observes:

> According to their deeds, so will He repay,
> wrath to His adversaries, requital to His enemies,
> to the coastlands He will render acquittal.

Psalm 7:11 gives us another example of the Retributive Justice Theory. The Psalmist tells us, "God is a righteous Judge. He is a God of indignation every day." And a few verses later, at 7:15 and 16, we see another example of retribution, not unlike the tragic hero and his *hubris* in Greek tragedy. Verses 15 and 16 speak of, "Men who make a pit, and after digging it out, fall into the hole they have made."

At Isaiah 34:8, the prophet employed the verb *shillum* that usually indicates some sort of retribution or requital. He also employed the words *leb* and *lebah*, both that stand for "heart." One of these uses comes at Isaiah 6:10. The same verse contains the word *yetzer*, which here is generally rendered as "mind."

The Prophet Isaiah also often uses the masculine noun *naqam* that generally means retribution or vengeance. Among the passages in Isaiah where we see the use of this word are 34:8, 35:4, 47:3, 59:17, 61:2 and 63:4.

The Prophet Isaiah also assents to the Collective version of the Retributive Justice Theory in several places in his book, such as at 14:21 and 59:21. In the former, we find the advice from the prophet:

> Prepare the slaughter for his sons
> because of the guilt of their fathers...

At Isaiah 59:21, we see another example of Collective Retributive Justice. The prophet relates:

> And as for me, this is my covenant with them, says the
> Lord. My spirit which is upon You, and the words which
> I have put in your mouth, shall not come out of your
> mouth, or out of the mouths of your children, or out of
> the mouths of your children's children, says the Lord,
> from this time forth and forevermore.

The Prophet Isaiah also appears to endorse the Influences of Demonic Forces Theory in several places, such as at the opening of chapter twenty-seven, when He refers to "Leviathan, the twisting serpent."[65] Leviathan, in the Old Testament, is often used as an embodiment of evil. And 13:11 that may be a reference to storm demon.[66] The only use or possible use of the Original Sin Theory in the Book of Isaiah comes at 59:3–4. This text speaks of:

> For your hands are defiled by blood and your fingers with
>   iniquity.
> Your lips have spoken lies and your tongue mutters wick-
>   edness.
> No one enters suit justly
> No one goes to law honestly.
> They rely on empty pleas, they speak lies,
> They conceive mischief and they bring forth iniquity.

Several Christian exegetes, beginning with the Early Church Fathers and continuing to thinkers like Thomas Aquinas and Albert the Great, and many others, have interpreted this couplet in Isaiah 59 as a version of the Original Sin Theory. No Jewish scholar, however, has interpreted 59:3–4 that way.[67]

Another text of the major prophets that have been associated with the Original Sin Theory in the Christian Church is Ezekiel 18:20. This text relates, "The one who sins is the one who will die." Augustine says since all sin, all will die, and the reason that all sin, he says, is because everyone suffers from Original Sin, or *peccatum originale*, in Augustine's vocabulary. These words are followed by an argument against Collective Retributive Justice when Ezekiel says:

> The child will not share the guilt of the parent, nor will
> the parent share the guilt of the child. The righteousness
> of the righteous will be credited to them. And the
> wickedness of the wicked will be charged against them.

Thus, this passage appears simultaneously to be an argument against Collective Retribution and an argument for the Individual Retributive Justice Theory, with the righteous being credited and the wicked man's actions being "charged against" him.

This is immediately followed in Ezekiel 18:23 and 24, by another discussion of the prophet's view of Collective Retribution. At the opening of the same chapter, Ezekiel 18:2–4, the prophet argues against the old adage, "The parents have eaten sour grapes, and the children's teeth are set on edge." "As I live," says Ezekiel, "this proverb should no longer be used in Israel."

There are also many passages in the Book of Isaiah that also appear to endorse what we have called the Contrast View in Chapter One of this study. Some of these come at 5:20, 9:2, 45:7 and 59:9. The first of these has become the object of much debate. It relates, "Woe to those who call evil good, and good evil, who puts darkness for light and light for darkness, who put bitter for sweet and sweet for bitter."

Many of the passages that suggest the Contrast View in the Old Testament indicate that light stands for the good and darkness for evil, such as in the above passage. Another example can be seen at Isaiah 9:2, which tells us, "The people who have walked in darkness have seen a great light. Those who dwell in the land of deep darkness on them has the light shined." A similar view and metaphor can be observed at Isaiah 45:7. This text also has been controversial, for it seems to suggest that God is responsible for "weal and woe."

The Book of Isaiah 45:7 tells us that God relates:

> I form light and create darkness.
> I make weal and create woe.
> I am the Lord who does all these things.

The Prophet Isaiah also appears to endorse the Divine Plan Theory in many passages in his book. One of these comes at Isaiah 14:24 that tells us, "The Lord of hosts has sworn, 'As I have planned, so shall it be, and as I have purposed, so shall it stand.'" At chapter 13:19, Yahweh appears to tell the future about Babylon, and thus the Divine Plan Theory when He remarks:

> And Babylon, the glory of kingdoms
> The splendor and pride of the Chaldeans,
> will be like Sodom and Gomorrah
> when God overthrew them.

The several opening verses of chapter 43 of Isaiah also adopts a version of the Divine Plan Theory where many of the verbs are in the future tense. Consider, for example, verse two that relates, "When you pass through the waters, I will be with you, and through the rivers, they shall overcome you. When you walk through the fire, you shall not be burned, and the flame shall not consume you."

In the Book of Isaiah, his dedication to the Divine Plan Theory most clearly can be seen at 55:8–9. Isaiah tells us:

> For my thoughts are not your thoughts, nor are your
> ways my ways, says the Lord. For as the heavens are
> higher than the earth, so are my ways higher than your
> ways, And my thoughts than your thoughts.

Indeed, any mention of God's ways not being man's ways are direct references to the Divine Plan Theory. God knows, while human beings do not know. This same view, as we shall see later in this chapter, is expressed throughout the major prophets.[68] At 58:11 of his book, the Prophet Isaiah again speaks of God and Israel in the future tense. The verse tells us:

> And the Lord will guide you continually
> and will satisfy your desires with good things
> and will make your bones strong.
> And you shall be like a watered garden.

Finally, the opening verse of chapter sixty-one of the Book of Isaiah also seems to be an assent to the Divine Plan Theory when it says, "The Spirit of the Lord is upon me because the Lord has anointed me to bring good tidings to the afflicted. He has sent me to bind up the broken-hearted, to proclaim liberty to the captives, and the opening of the prison to those who are bound."

If the Lord has given these instructions to the Prophet Isaiah, then it should be clear that God and the prophet were both sure that these things will come about through the ministry of the Judean prophet, Isaiah. One final aspect of the Prophet Isaiah and his views of evil and suffering had to do with the prophet's vocabulary, particularly in regard to chapter 59. In that chapter alone, Isaiah uses ten different words related to evil and suffering. The Revised Standard Version renders these terms this way:

> wrath (v. 18)
> vengeance (17)
> oppression (13)
> iniquity (2, 3, 6, and 7)
> transgression (12, 12, 13, 20)
> sin (2)
> lies (4)
> mischief (4)
> evil (7)

Indeed, the Prophet Isaiah had a far more sophisticated and nuanced view of classical Hebrew words connected to evil and suffering than either of the other two major prophets, Jeremiah and Ezekiel, or any of the minor prophets, as well, for that matter.

Isaiah uses the Hidden God Theory much more often than the other major prophets. It can be found at 18:17–18, 45:15, 54:8 and 57:17, to cite four examples of many other passages in Isaiah. At Isaiah 54:8, the text has God saying, "In an outburst of anger, I hid my face from you for a moment." A few chapters later, at 57:17, Isaiah again quotes Yahweh:

> Because of the iniquity of his unjust gain,
> I was angry and struck him.
> I hid my face and was angry.
> And he went on turning away
> In the ways of his heart.

This brings us to the views of the Prophet Jeremiah on the issues of theodicy and the problem of evil, the subject matter of the next section of chapter three.

Jeremiah on Evil, Suffering and Theodicy

Like Isaiah, the Prophet Jeremiah served Judah, the Southern Kingdom. As a prophet, he ministered from 626 until 585 BCE, which means he was present during the destruction of Jerusalem at the hands of the Babylonians in 586 BCE. In addition to the Book of Jeremiah, the prophet is also ascribed the Book of Lamentations, as well. In our analysis, we will speak of the two books of Jeremiah together.

At the opening verse of chapter twelve, Jeremiah speaks of the problem of evil to God, the prophet relates:

> Righteous are You, o Lord
> When I complain to You.
> Yet, I would complain to you
> And I would plead my case before You.
> Why does the way of the wicked prosper?
> Why do all who are treacherous thrive?

For the next several chapters of Jeremiah, the prophet speaks of Yahweh bringing destruction to Judah and the Babylonians. Finally, at 20:7–9, Jeremiah addresses God and asks:

> O Lord, You have deceived me, and I was deceived.
> You are stronger than I and You have prevailed
> I have become a laughing- stock all the day.
> Everyone mocks me.
> For whenever I speak, I cry out.
> I shout, "Violence and destruction!"
> For the Lord has become for me
> A reproach and a derision all day long.
> If I say I will not mention him
> Or speak anymore in His name,
> There is in my heart as it were a burning fire
> Shut up in my bones

And I am weary in holding it in
And I cannot.

Jeremiah seems to be concerned that it is often the case that the righteous man suffers, while the evil man prospers. This raises in his mind, the value of the covenant that Yahweh made with Abraham as the representative of Israel and God's Chosen People. By chapter 31:29–31, Jeremiah expresses an answer to this conundrum. It is there that he reveals:

> Behold the days are coming, says the Lord, when I will make a new covenant with the house of Israel and the house of Judah, not like the covenant that I made with their fathers, when I took them by the hand to bring them out of the land of Egypt, my covenant which they broke, though I was their husband says the Lord.

Thus, Jeremiah suggests that Yahweh will make a new covenant with Israel and Judah, a covenant not like the one that He made with their fathers. Along the way, in both Jeremiah and in Lamentations, the prophet makes nearly fifty different comments about the issues of theodicy and the problem of evil. In some of these, he endorses the Retributive Justice Theory, and in others, he criticizes it.

Additionally, Jeremiah regularly employs the Two *Yetzer* Theory, as introduced in Chapter One, as the ancient Jewish version of the Free Will Defense. Occasionally, Jeremiah appears to assent to the Moral Qualities Perspective, the Test Theory, the Contrast View, as well as the Influences of Demonic Forces Theory. Finally, in both books, Jeremiah 15:1 endorses a version of the Divine Plan Point of View.

In regard to the Retributive Justice Theory, we find mention of it at Lamentations 2:22, as well as Jeremiah 23:12, 48:12 and 46, 50:33, and 51:39 and 55, among many other examples.

At Lamentations 1:20, we are told by Jeremiah that he is concerned that reward and punishment do not always work the way they should when he says:

> Behold, O Lord, for I am in distress,
> my soul is in tumult.

My heart is wrung within me
because I have been very rebellious.
In the street the sword bereaves;
In the house, it is like death.

Jeremiah appears to be in distress because the good people are punished, while the bad are rewarded. And beneath this worry, of course, is the Retributive Justice Theory. At Jeremiah 23:12, we find another example of the Retributive Justice Theory. Jeremiah tells us in the passage:

Therefore, their way shall be to them
Like slippery paths in the darkness
Into which they shall be driven and fall,
For I shall bring evil upon them
In the year of their punishment, says the Lord.

At Jeremiah 48:12, Jeremiah speaks of Retributive Justice in relation to the god Chemosh of the Moabites. Jeremiah relates:

Therefore, behold the days are coming, says the Lord, when I shall send to him tilters who will tilt to him and empty his vessels, and break his jars into pieces. Then Moab shall be ashamed of Chemosh, as the house of Israel was ashamed of Bethel, their confidence.

It should be clear that the use of the future-tense verbs, "are coming," "shall send," and "shall be ashamed," are an indication of the Divine Plan Theory, for Jeremiah believes he will see a restoration of the Jewish Nation in the time to come.

The god Chemosh mentioned in the above passage is the principal deity to which the Moabites offered human sacrifice. Jeremiah suggests that in the future, Moab will be embarrassed of Chemosh.

At Jeremiah 50:33–34, Jeremiah's attention turns to the fate of the Babylonians. He tells us:

Thus says the Lord of hosts, the people of Israel are oppressed and the people of Judah are with them. All who took them captive have held them fast. They

refuse to let them go. The Redeemer is strong. The Lord
of Hosts in his name. He will surely plead their cause,
that he may give rest to the Earth, but unrest to those
of Babylon.

At Jeremiah 51:55–56, Jeremiah again speaks of the Retribution
Theory and the Kingdom of Babylon. The prophet relates:

> For the Lord is laying Babylon to waste
> And stilling her mighty voice
> Their waves roar like many waters
> The noise of their voice is raised.
> For a destroyer has come upon her
> Upon Babylon. His warriors are taken
> Their bows are broken into pieces.
> For the Lord is a God of recompense,
> He will surely requite.

The prophet not only endorses Retributive Justice, at times, he
also criticizes that view. At Lamentations 5:7, for example, Jeremiah
relates: "Our fathers sinned and now are no more, and now we bear
their iniquities." At Jeremiah 31:29, the prophet again is critical of
Collective Retributive Justice when he relates:

> In those days they shall no longer say, The Fathers have
> eaten sour grapes, and the children's teeth are set on edge.

This verse comes just before the notion of the new covenant
spoken by Jeremiah earlier in this third chapter. At any rate, the second
major prophet appears to be against the idea of familial Collection
Retribution.

In nearly a dozen passages, Jeremiah uses the word *yetzer*, or
"inclination," or "imagination," in his book. Some of these occur at
Jeremiah 3:17, 7:21, 9:14, 11:8, 13:10, 16:12; 18:12, and 23:17. Each
of these uses of the word *yetzer* tied it to the noun *leb*, or "heart," the
seat of the self and decision-making among the ancient Jews. Thus,
Jeremiah endorses the Free Will Defense in regard to the issues of
theodicy and the problem of evil, as well.

At Jeremiah 17:10, the prophet combines the Test View with the *Yetzerim* Theory, and the Retributive Justice Theory when it relates:

> I the Lord tests the mind and search the heart to give all
> according to their ways, according to the fruit of their
> doings.

The Test View, of course, is indicated by the use of the verb "to Test." The use of "mind" and "heart" indicates the *Yetzerim* Theory, and the "according to the fruits of their doings" implies the Retributive Justice Theory.[69]

The second of the major prophets also appears to endorse the Influences of Demonic Forces Theory at Lamentations 2:16 and Jeremiah 8:17. In the latter passage, Yahweh says, "Behold, I am sending among you serpents and adders which cannot be charmed, and they shall bite you." In Christianity, this verse often has been interpreted as referring to the Demonic, particularly in the Early Church and Medieval Period.[70]

At Lamentations 2:16, Jeremiah speaks of his enemies, "hissing and gnashing their teeth," and again, many Christian have found this to be a reference to the Devil, or to Satan and his minions.

Something close to the Moral Qualities View, as well as the Test Theory, may also be seen in Jeremiah's books. Two representative examples can be seen at Lamentations 4:6 and 3:40. In the latter passage, Jeremiah suggests:

> Let us test and examine our ways and thereby return
> to the Lord.

At Lamentations 4:6, Jeremiah speaks of the "Chastisement of the daughter of my People has been greater than the punishment of Sodom that was overthrown in a moment, with no hand being laid upon it." The idea of chastisements and chastening traditionally has been associated with the Moral Qualities Point of View.

Finally, in both the Book of Lamentations and Jeremiah, the prophet appears to assent to the Divine Plan Theory with respect to the issues of theodicy and the problem of evil. We find something like this theory, if not the theory itself, at Lamentations 3:19–21 and 37–38, as well at Jeremiah 1:5, 29:11, 32:42 and 34:13. We shall examine the passages from Lamentations first, followed by the verses in Jeremiah that seem to endorse the Divine Plan Theory.

At Lamentations 3:19–21, the Prophet Jeremiah relates:

> Remember my afflictions and my bitterness
> the wormwood and the gall.
> My soul continuously thinks of it
> And is bowed down within me.
> But this I call to mind,
> And, therefore, I have hope.

At the end of verse 24 of the same chapter, the prophet again reveals, "Therefore, I will hope in Him." And at verses 37 and 38, again in chapter three of Jeremiah, the prophet asks:

> "Who has commanded and it came to pass, unless the
> Lord has ordained it? Is it not from the mouth of the
> Most High that Good and evil come?

Jeremiah 1:5 tells us about Yahweh speaking to Jeremiah:

> Before I formed you in the womb, I knew you;
> And before you were born, I consecrated you.
> I appointed you a Prophet to the nations.

It should be clear that in the Prophet Jeremiah's view, his life unfolding had been to that point, and would continue to be, a small part of the Grand Plan that God has fashioned from long before the life of Jeremiah and the writing of his books had been in existence. Yahweh, according to the prophet, had planned it that way. The Prophet Jeremiah also employs the Hidden God Theory in several passages of his book. Jeremiah 33:5 is a good representative example. Speaking of the Jews, Jeremiah relates:

> While they are coming to fight with the Chaldeans and
> to fill them with the corpses of men whom I have slain,
> in My anger and in My wrath, I have hidden My face
> from this city because of all the wickedness.

This brings us to an analysis of the views of the Prophet Ezekiel on the questions of theodicy and the problem of evil—the subject matter of the next section of chapter three.

Ezekiel on Evil, Suffering and Theodicy

The Prophet Ezekiel was born in the land of Israel to his father, Buzi, a Hebrew prophet in his own right. In the year 586 BCE, Jerusalem was conquered by the Babylonians, as we have shown earlier in this chapter. The Jews were then exiled to Babylon, where Ezekiel spent the remainder of his life. Ezekiel's prophecies are unique because they were experienced in Babylon. He became a prophet back in Israel, but he continued in Babylon in exile. Ezekiel appears to have begun his life as a prophet in 597 BCE.

In Babylon, Ezekiel and the other Jewish exiles were settled on the banks of the Cedar River, and it was here that the message came from God to Ezekiel:

> The word of the Lord came expressly unto Ezekiel, the priest, the son of Buzi in the land of the Chaldeans, by the River Chebar, and the hand of the Lord was there upon him.[71]

Ezekiel's call in Babylon came in "the fifth year of the Exile," or 592 BCE. The only other facts we know of the Prophet Ezekiel's life is that he was married, and his wife died of a stroke.[72] The last date that Ezekiel mentions is in the twenty-seventh year of the captivity. Thus, his public ministry appears to have lasted for twenty-two years.

Ezekiel was uniquely qualified to give a defense of the Justice of God because he was both a priest and a prophet. Although he was trained to be a priest at the age of thirty, Yahweh interrupted his priestly life and ordained Ezekiel as a prophet. The views of Ezekiel on the issues of theodicy and the problem of evil begin in chapter two of his book, verses one to seven. Earlier in his book, in chapter one, God manifested Himself in a chariot of fire, perhaps to get the prophet to understand that the Lord was serious.[73]

In this experience, Ezekiel saw an outward vision of the Heavenly throne of God, in the form of the chariot, which was on the move.

Judgment was coming to Israel. When Ezekiel saw the chariot/throne, he fell on his face, "And when I saw it, I fell upon my face, and then I heard a voice that spoke."[74]

The Divine voice tells the prophet that what was going on in Babylon is part of a providential judgment of God upon Israel because of the rebellion of Israel. Next, God required something very unusual from Ezekiel. He was to eat a scroll of a book. At Ezekiel 2:8–9, God tells the prophet:

> But you, son of man, hear what I have to say to you. Don't be rebellious like the rebellious house, but open your mouth and eat what I give you. And when I looked behold a hand was stretched out to me, and a written scroll was in it. And he spread it before me, and it had writing on the front and the back, and there was written on it works of lamentation and mourning, and woe.

Although Ezekiel expected the scroll to taste bitter, in fact, it turned out to be sweet. How could words of woe and doom be sweet? More than anything else, perhaps, this is an application of what we have called the Contrast View back in Chapter One of this study. The Prophet Ezekiel also employed a variety of the other answers and responses on evil and suffering that we cataloged back in the opening chapter.

Consider, for example, the narrative at 5:5–17, which appears to combine the Retributive Justice Theory and the Divine Plan Point of View. At verses 5 to 11 of this narrative, the text speaks of the Jews not following the ordinances of God. Beginning in verse twelve, however, the narrator begins to speak of the restoration of Israel, principally by using verbs in the future tense, as if speaking of a Divine Plan for the future.

At times, however, the Prophet Ezekiel appears definitively to be against the idea of Collective or familial Retribution. Consider, for example, Ezekiel 14:14 and 20. These verses tell us:

> Even if these three men, Noah, Dan'el, and Job, were alive today, they would only be able to save their own righteousness.[75]

At Ezekiel 14:20, Ezekiel mentions the same three patriarchs a second time, and that, "They would deliver neither their son nor daughter, they would deliver but their own lives by their righteousness." In the narratives of these patriarchs, of course, each was able to save his own children by his righteousness. But now this will no longer be possible. Thus, this appears to be a rejection of the Collective Retributive Justice Theory and an endorsement of the Individual Retribution Theory.

At Ezekiel 18:2–4, the prophet again returns to Collective Retributive Justice when he asks:

> What do you mean by repeating the proverb concerning the lands of Israel, 'The fathers have eaten sour grapes, and the children's teeth are set on edge?' As I live, says the Lord-God, this proverb will no longer be used by you in Israel. Behold all souls are mine, the soul of the father as well as that of the son is mine. The soul that sins shall die.

Clearly, at Ezekiel 18:2–4, the prophet again appears to be against the idea of Familial or the Collective Retributive Justice Theory. Ezekiel advises the Jews to no longer use the proverb in question in the same way that Job, Noah and Dan'el can only save themselves and not their children. At Ezekiel 18:20, the prophet makes the same point about the individual nature of the consequence of sin, and against the idea of Familial, or Collective Sin. Thus, by chapter 18 of his work, Ezekiel appears to be against the idea of Collective Retributive Justice.

The use of future-tense verbs may also be detected in chapter 47, near the end of the book. About returning to Israel, God speaks of dividing up the land. At verses 13–14, he says, "shall divide." Verses 15, 18 and 19 employ "shall be," as does verse 20. Verse 21 employs "shall divide" again. At verses 22 and 23, we find "shall alot" and "shall assign." And all of this is in the context of returning to the Promised Land after the Babylonian captivity.

The Prophet Ezekiel also uses the "Hidden God" Theory at 39:24. At that verse, Ezekiel tells us, "According to their uncleanness and according to their transgressions, I dealt with them, and I hid My face from them." Ezekiel also mentions the Hidden God Theory again in the same chapter, at verse 39, where God says, I will not hide My face any more from them, when I pour out My Spirit upon the house of Israel."

Ezekiel also employs the theory of the two Yetzerim. One place where he does this is at 36:26–27, where the word *yetzer* is used two times in relation to the *leb*, or "heart." At 18:30, God tells Ezekiel that the people should "repent and turn away from their transgressions," suggesting again that the Jews have power over their own free will.

So far in our analysis of the book of the third major prophet, Ezekiel, we have suggested that regarding the issues of theodicy and the problem of evil, Ezekiel assented to the Retributive Justice Theory, the Divine Plan Perspective, the Hidden God Theory, the Contrast View, and the Free Will Defense.

At Ezekiel 18:21–24, we find a curious collection of comments on evil and suffering. The text in question at verses 21 and 22 tells us this:

> But if a wicked man turns away from all of his sins that he has committed and then keeps My statutes, and does what is lawful and right, he shall surely live. None of the transgressions which he has committed shall be remembered against him, for in the righteousness he has done, he shall live.

So far, this looks like a total endorsement of the Retributive Justice Theory. But then the tone of Ezekiel's voice changes with these words:

> Have no pleasure in the death of the wicked, says the Lord, and not that he should turn his own way and live? But a righteous man may turn away from his righteousness and commit iniquities and does the same abominable things that the wicked man does, shall he live? None of the righteous deeds he has done shall be remembered, for the treachery of which he is guilty, and by the sins he has committed, he shall die.[76]

These verses that begin in God taking no pleasure in the death of the wicked transforms into a discussion of the fates of the wicked who turn to God and the good who turn to evil.

In the end, however, the prophet again seems to endorse the traditional Retributive Justice Theory. A number of other verses in the Prophet Ezekiel's book also endorse the Divine Plan Theory. One representative passage is the couplet found at chapter 47:13–14. Again, using future tense verbs, the writer contemplates what life will be like when the Jews would return from the Babylonian captivity. Indeed, whenever Ezekiel employs future tense verbs at the end of his book, they are almost always to indicate the return of the Jews to the Promised Land, which Yahweh, their God, had pre-ordained for them.

At 21:13 of Ezekiel's book, the prophet refers to what it calls a "testing," a word that comes from the Hebrew verb *nasah* meaning "to try" or "to test." This is the only time the verb appears in Ezekiel, but it is frequently employed throughout the Torah in places like Genesis 22:1; Exodus 15:25, 16:4 and 17:7; Numbers 14:22; and Deuteronomy 4:34, 6:16 and 13:3. At any rate, we may add the Test View to our answers and responses in the Book of Ezekiel. Ezekiel does not, however, use the verb *bachan* or "to Test" as does Jeremiah at 6:27, 9:7 and 17:10.[77]

In regard to the views of Ezekiel on the issues of theodicy and the problem of evil, some interpreters suggest that chapter 28:11 to 19 are a reference to the influences of Demonic Forces Theory. Matthew Henry, as well as a number of other scholars, have suggested that this narrative refers to the Fallen Angels Narrative and that verses 11 to 19 is nothing more than a description of the creation of the angels and the fall of Satan and his minions. More modern and contemporary interpreters, however, have been dissuaded from suggesting this point of view.

Some Christian interpreters, such as Thomas Aquinas and John Calvin, believe that Ezekiel 18:20 is a proof text for original sin. The text relates, "He who sins shall die."[78] Both Aquinas and Calvin relate that all sin, because all suffer from original sin, and all die because of the sin of Adam.[79]

At any rate, from our analysis, we may conclude that the sixth-century BCE major prophet Ezekiel endorsed, consented to, or possibly believed in the following theories on answers with regard to the issues of theodicy and the problem of evil:

1.   Retributive Justice Theory (Individual and Collective)
2.   The Hidden God View

3. The Free Will Defense (*Yetzerim* Theory)
4. The Contrast View
5. The Influences of Demonic Forces Perspective
6. The Test Theory
7. Original Sin Theory
8. Divine Plan Theory[80]

In addition, the Prophet Ezekiel also employs the Hidden God Theory in several places in his book. One of these comes at Ezekiel 39:24. In this verse, the prophet speaks of Yahweh's relationship with the Jews. He tells us, "According to their uncleanliness and according to their transgressions, I dealt with them and hid My face."

This brings us to the major conclusions we have made in this third chapter. The subject matter of Chapter Four of this study is the issues of theodicy and the problem of evil among the minor prophets.

Conclusions

We divided this third chapter of this study of views on evil and suffering in the Bible into five sections. In the first of these, we have introduced and discussed the backgrounds of the three major prophets of the Old Testament, or Hebrew Bible—Isaiah, Jeremiah and Ezekiel.

In that section, we have shown that Isaiah and Jeremiah prophesized in Judah, the Southern Kingdom, while Ezekiel came from Israel, and mostly wrote during the Babylonian captivity.

In the second section of Chapter Three, we provided a timeline of ancient Israel and Judah, from the time that the Hebrews entered the land until the Persian period. In this timeline, we also set each of the major prophets in their historical and political contexts.

The remaining three sections of this chapter have been devoted to views of evil and suffering by first Isaiah, then Jeremiah, and finally, Ezekiel. In the first of these sections—the one on the Prophet Isaiah—we suggested that Isaiah endorsed, mentioned or assented to the Hidden God Theory, both forms of Retributive Justice, the Influences of Demonic Forces Theory, possibly the Original Sin Perspective, the Contrast View, and the Divine Plan Theory, as outlined in Chapter One.

We also suggested in the section on Isaiah's views on the issues of theodicy and the problem of evil that the first of the major prophets had a much more extensive and subtle vocabulary with regard to classical Hebrew words related to evil and suffering. In the section of this third chapter on the views of the Prophet Jeremiah on evil and suffering, we have argued that in chapter 12, Jeremiah raises the issue of why the righteous suffer, and he continued to speak of that question, through chapter 20, and onto the suggestion of a new covenant between God and the nation of Israel, to be established in the future, in chapter 31:29 to 31.

Since both the books of Lamentations and Jeremiah have been assigned to the prophet, we have treated the two books together to ascertain Jeremiah's understandings of the issues of theodicy and the problem of evil.

Indeed, in the section on Jeremiah, we have shown that he endorsed both forms of Retributive Justice, though, at times, he seems to have been critical of the Familial or Collective Form of Retributive Justice. Along the way, we have also shown that Jeremiah employed the Two *Yetzerim* Theory, and thus endorsed the Free Will Defense. He may have made references to the possibility of the Influences of Demonic Forces Theory, and he assuredly, as we have shown, was a firm believer in the Divine Plan Perspective.

Perhaps the most significant aspect of Jeremiah's views on evil and suffering was his suggestion of the idea of a new covenant, sketched out in chapter 31 of his book, and the idea that this new covenant would replace the one made with the patriarch Abraham in chapter 15 of the Book of Genesis.

In this section of this third chapter on the views of the Prophet Ezekiel on the questions of theodicy and the problem of evil, we have maintained that the third of the major prophets had a much more inclusive view of these problems in that he employed nearly all of the answers and responses we had introduced and discussed back in Chapter One.

In fact, in the section of Ezekiel's perspectives, we suggested that the prophet often endorsed both forms of Retributive Justice, though he criticized the familial variety. He refers to the Hidden God

Theory; to the Two *Yetzerim* Theory, the ancient Jewish version of the Free Will Defense; to the Contrast View; the Test and Moral Qualities Perspectives; possibly to the Influences of Demonic Forces Theory; the Original Sin Perspective and, above all, like the other major prophets, to the Divine Plan Theory.

This brings us to the views on the issues of theodicy and the problem of evil of the minor prophets, the subject matter of the fourth chapter of this study on views of perspectives on evil and suffering in the Bible. It is to the minor prophets, then, to which we turn next.

Chapter Four:
Evil and Suffering in the Minor Prophets

The idea of righteousness is the expression of a worldview spread throughout the ancient Near East from Egypt to Mesopotamia. According to this belief, the world is arranged in an encompassing order...comprising nature, justice, wisdom, war, cult, and kingdom.

—Hans Heinrich Schmid, *History of Wisdom*

All the children of the light are ruled by the Prince of Light and walk in the ways of Light. But all the children of darkness are ruled by the Prince of Darkness and walk in the ways of Darkness.

—The Dead Sea Scrolls (1Qs 3:20–21)

Evil in the world is a terrible reality. One will look in vain for a comprehensive, handy definition of evil, but, unfortunately, none is to be found.

—-Dietmar Wyrwa, "Augustine and Luther on Evil"

Introduction

The purpose of this fourth chapter is to describe and to discuss the views of the minor prophets of the Old Testament, or Hebrew Bible, on the issues of theodicy and the problem of evil. We will begin the chapter with an introduction to the minor prophets, followed by several sections of the chapter in which we will explore the perspectives on the issues at hand, beginning with the pre-exilic minor prophets, Jonah and Amos, followed by the exilic prophets, Hosea, Obadiah, Micah, Nahum, Habakkuk and Zephaniah. These sections of Chapter Four will proceed to two final sections of the chapter on the post-exilic prophets of Haggai, Zechariah, Jonah and Malachi and what they had to say about evil and suffering.

The prophetic tradition in the Old Testament is divided between the major prophets and the minor prophets. These books first received these names sometime in the fourth century around the time of Saint Augustine. These books have their names because the books of the major prophets are longer, while those of the minor prophets are considerably shorter.

There are twelve minor prophets. These books are:

- Jonah
- Obadiah
- Micah
- Amos
- Nahum
- Habakkak
- Hosea
- Zephaniah
- Haggai
- Zechariah
- Malachi
- Joel.[81]

The minor prophets vary in size, from the single chapter of Obadiah to Hosea and Zechariah that are both fourteen chapters long. The twelve books range in time from Hosea and Amos that both date from the mid-eighth century BCE to portions of the Book of Zechariah and Malachi that most likely come from the fourth century BCE.

A number of themes are shared by the twelve minor prophets. Some of the most important of these are the questions, "What does God demand of human beings? How do historical events signify the words of God?" And, most importantly, for our purposes, "What do the minor prophets tell us about the phenomena of evil and suffering among the Jews in ancient Israel and Judah?"

It is not known when these short works of the minor prophets were transferred and collected to a single scroll. The first evidence we have for the twelve as a collection comes from the writings of Jesus ben Sirach around the year 190 BCE.[82] Other evidence found among the Dead Sea Scrolls suggests that the order of the twelve we have in modern times had been established by the year 150 BCE.[83]

Some scholars have suggested that the first six of the twelve originally were together, and later the other six were added. The two groups seem to complement each other, with Hosea through Micah forming the first group, bound together by questions of iniquity, and Nahum to Malachi proposing responses or resolutions to those iniquities.

Many modern scholars agree that the editing process that produced the book of the minor prophets reached its final form in the city of Jerusalem, during the Achaemenid period, from 538 until 332 BCE. However, there are disagreements about whether it was early or later during that time. Contemporary scholar Katharine Dell suggests that the final form of the minor prophets came in the Hellenistic period from 332 to 167 BCE.[84]

In general, each of the twelve books of the minor prophets includes three separate kinds of narratives. These are the following: autobiographical materials, first-person narratives from these *Nabiim*, or prophets. Biographical materials, third-person narratives, suggesting they were edited by someone other than the original writers. Oracles or speeches ascribed to the prophets, often in poetic form, and drawing from a wide variety of genres, including covenantal lawsuits, oracles against other nations, judgments against the Jews and other nations, messenger speeches (angels and other prophets), songs, hymns, symbolic actions, vision sayings and ecstatic visions.[85]

In the Masoretic Text of the Hebrew Bible, these twelve works were counted as one scroll. The twelve minor prophets are now studied together, with the same order among Jewish, Protestant and Catholic Bibles. Among many Orthodox Christian Bibles, the minor prophets are ordered according to the Septuagint version. Among the Orthodox versions, the order of books is:

- Hosea
- Joel

- Amos
- Obadiah
- Jonah
- Micah
- Nahum
- Habakkuk
- Zephaniah
- Haggai
- Zechariah
- Malachi[86]

In the Roman Catholic liturgy, the minor prophets are read as part of the Tridentine Breviary during the fourth and fifth weeks of November. In Year One of the modern Lectionary, Haggai, Zechariah, Jonah, Malachi and Joel are read. In Year Two, Amos, Hosea, and Micah are read.[87] The twelve books of the minor prophets are collectively commemorated in the Calendar of the Saints of the Armenian Apostolic Church on the thirty-first of July every year.[88] This brings us to an analysis of Hosea and Joel on evil and suffering.

Evil and Suffering in Hosea and Joel

The Book of Hosea is the first of the minor prophets. According to the text, Hosea began his prophetic activity during the reign of Jeroboam the Second, who ruled from 786 until 746 BCE. Hosea appears to have been active until near the fall of the Northern Kingdom in the year 721 BCE.[89]

The Prophet Hosea appears to have been a native of the Northern Kingdom since he shows familiarity with the history and topography of the land (see: 4:15, 5:1 and 13, 6:8–9, 10:5, 12:11–12, and 14:6, for examples). If Hosea was from the north, then along with Jonah, he was the only prophet writing from the Northern Kingdom of Israel. Indeed, it has been said that Hosea was to the Northern Kingdom what Jeremiah was to the Southern Kingdom of Judah.[90]

Hosea looked forward to the Assyrian captivity of the Northern Kingdom, just as Jeremiah looked forward to the Babylonian captivity of the Kingdom of Judah. Hosea's prophetic activity is closely related to that of the Prophet Amos. He was a younger contemporary of Amos, and the careers seem to have overlapped. There is much similarity, for example, in the sins that they condemn.

The Book of Hosea may be divided in a number of ways. One way is to say that chapters one to three are about the agonies of his personal life, while chapters four to fourteen are more about the tragedy of an unfaithful people. In fact, this second part is more like a series of sermons or homilies that sketch out the sins of the people in relation to the character of God.

Regarding the questions of evil and suffering, Hosea's comments are many and often about these issues. In the theories and responses we have outlined in chapter one of this study, the Prophet Hosea appears to mention, or assent to, the following points of view:

- Retributive Justice Theory
- Original Sin Theory
- The Moral Qualities Perspective
- Divine Plan Theory

At times, Hosea also combines these theories, such as at 10:5–6, where he links the Retributive Justice Theory with a Divine Plan that God has for the future. Hosea combines the same two theories, in the same manner, at 1:10–11, as well. In the latter, the text uses verbs like "shall be gathered" and "shall appoint," while in 10:5–7, the text employs verbs like "shall wail," "shall be carried," and "shall be put to shame." And all of these verbs appear in the context of the punishment of sins and the possibility of a new and better time to come, a restoration of the Kingdoms of Israel.

At chapter 2:6, Hosea again uses the Collective Retribution Theory, for he speaks of the whole nation when he puts in the mouth of God:

> Therefore, I will hedge up her way with thorns
> And I will build a wall against her,
> So that she cannot find her paths.

At both 4:7 and 5:9, the Prophet Hosea provides two other examples of the Retributive Justice Theory. The former relates, "The more they increased, the more they sinned against me, and I will turn their glory into shame." At 5:9, Hosea tells us, "Ephraim shall become a desolation in the day of punishment among the tribes of Israel. I declare what is certain."

Several verses in chapter eight of Hosea also speak of the Retributive Justice Theory, such as at verses 1:13–14. The opening verse of the chapter says:

> Set the trumpet to your lips, for a vulture is over the
>   house of the Lord,
> Because they have broken my covenant and have trans-
>   gressed my laws.

Several verses later, at 8:13–14, Hosea speaks of the bad behavior of the Jews and their consequences in the future. Hosea writes:

> They love sacrifices. The sacrifice flesh and eat it; but
> the Lord has no delight in them. Now he will remember
> their iniquity and punish their sins. They shall return
> to Egypt. For Israel has forgotten its Maker and built
> palaces. And Judah has multiplied fortified cities, and it
> shall devour its strongholds.

The Prophet Hosea, at 9:9 of his book, again refers to the Retribution Theory when he writes, "They have deeply corrupted themselves as in the days of Gib'e-ah. He will remember their iniquity; He will punish their sins." In the following chapter, at 10:4, Hosea again speaks of the sins of the Jews and the consequences to follow them:

> They utter mere words.
> With empty oaths they make covenants.
> So judgment will spring up like poisonous weeds
> In the furrows of the field.

A few verses later, at 10:13, Hosea makes clear the connection between sin and punishment, "You have plowed iniquity, and you have reaped injustice. You have eaten the fruit of lies." At 13:11, Hosea informs us, "I have given you kings in My anger, and I have taken them away in my wrath." And at the opening verse of chapter 14, Hosea speaks of the relation of stumbling to iniquity. Hosea tells us:

> Return, O Israel, to the Lord your God,
> For you have stumbled because of your iniquity.

In addition to the two forms of the Retributive Justice Theory, the Prophet Hosea also may be making a reference to the Original Sin Theory. The prophet says there, "But at Adam they transgressed the covenant, and the dealt faithlessly with them." The prophet may be referring to the sin in the Garden of Eden, to the inherited sin afterward, or to both at the same time. Many Christian interpreters, like Augustine of Hippo, for example, saw the verse that way.[91]

In at least two places, 7:12 and 10:10, the Prophet Hosea may be using the Moral Qualities Perspective. In the former passage, he writes, "...I will chastise them for their wicked deeds." And at 10:10, the Prophet Hosea again employs the verb "chastise" twice, at 10a and c. The classical Hebrew word in question is *yacer*, which is often used among the major prophets, as well, such as at Ezk. 23:38, Jer. 46:28, and Isa. 28:26.[92]

In addition, the Prophet Hosea also regularly employed a version of the Divine Plan Theory, often in the context of the restoration of both kingdoms of ancient Palestine to be made into one Israel. As we have shown earlier in this section of Chapter Four, these plans of God come in context of sin, followed by punishment and then restoration. Among these verses in Hosea are 3:4:5:10, 10:7–8; 11:5–6 and 13:15–16.

The Book of Joel, the second of the minor prophets, is a book that contains no historical events. In the early modern period, the book was believed to be dated between 835 and 800 BCE. More recent scholarship, however, places the Book of Joel sometimes between the late seventh century and early sixth century BCE. The protagonist of the book cannot be identified, with any precision, with any of the other twelve people named Joel in the Hebrew Bible with that name.

The Prophet Joel is not mentioned outside the book under his name and a passage in the Acts of the Apostles, at 2:16, in the New Testament. Verse 1:1 of the Book of Joel tells us that his father's name was Pethuel, who does not appear elsewhere. Judging by his many references to Judah and the city of Jerusalem (see: 2:32, 3:1, 6, 8 and 16–20), it seems likely that Joel came from the Southern Kingdom.

The Book of Joel has a number of linguistic parallels to the Hebrew of Amos, Micah, Jeremiah and Ezekiel. Many have suggested that the writer of Joel borrowed these prophets. Other scholars suggest some common sources that the writers and the readers of these books might have shared.[93]

The Book of Joel contains an immense infestation of locusts, or *arbeh*, in classical Hebrew. The locusts are a harbinger to the "great and dreadful Day of the Lord" at 2:31. The locusts are also mentioned at 1:4 and 2:25. Confronted with the appearance of the locusts, Joel calls on the people to repent, including the old and the young (1:2–3), the drunkards (1:5), farmers (1:11), and priests (1:13).[94]

The Prophet Joel describes the locusts as "Yahweh's Army," and he relates that their appearance is a reminder that the Day of the Lord is close at hand. Joel does not, however, voice the popular belief at the time that the day will be a time of judgment.

The autobiographical portion of the Book of Joel comes at 1:2 to 2:11. The call to repentance, at 2:12–17. And the restoration of Judah, at 2:18–27. All of chapter three is more about the Day of the Lord, with the nations around the Jews being judged at 3:1–16, and Yahweh's final blessing about renewal described at 3:17–21.

The writer of the Book of Joel speaks of the Retributive Justice Theory at 1:15, 2:1, 2:12–15, and 2:23, among many other places. He also seems to endorse the Divine Plan Theory with his use of many future tense verbs at 2:24–25, 2:30–32 and 3:18–21. Thus, Joel's references to evil and suffering are not all that different than those of Hosea. This brings us to the perspectives of Amos and Obadiah, the subject matter of the next section of this fourth chapter.

Amos and Obadiah on Evil and Suffering

The Book of Obadiah is the shortest book in the Old Testament, or Hebrew Bible, a mere twenty-one verses. It purports to be what it calls the "Vision of Obadiah." Nothing is known of the life of the prophet except for his name, which means "Servant of Yahweh."[95]

The name "Obadiah" appears to have been a common name of his time (see: First Kings 18:3–16, First Chronicles 3:21 and Ezra 8:9, where the name is used).

The date and place of composition are matters of some dispute. These issues are mostly a matter of determining how verses 11 to 14 of Obadiah are related to two specific historical events: The rebellion of Edom against Judah during the reign of Jehoram from 853 to 851 BCE (see: Second Kings 8:20–22 and Second Chronicles 21:8–15). In this case, Obadiah would be a contemporary of Elisha. The Babylonian attacks on Jerusalem were from 605 to 586 BCE. In this case, Obadiah would be a contemporary of the Prophet Jeremiah. The second alternative seems more likely. Although the date of the text is not decided, we know the book is tied to the Edomite assault on Jerusalem that is described in verses ten to fourteen. The Prophet Obadiah appears to have written his book just shortly after the attack.

There are striking parallels between verses one to six of Obadiah and Jeremiah 49:9–10 and 14–16. This has caused some scholars to argue that the two books share a common source not otherwise known to us.

The Book of Obadiah may be divided into the following three parts:

- Title and Introduction (1:1)
- Judgment on Edom (1:2 to 14)
- The Day of the Lord (1:15 to 21)[96]

For the most part, the writer of the Book of Obadiah combines the Retributive Justice Theory with the idea that the Jewish kingdoms will be restored some time in the future. This is made explicit in 1:2–4. Where Obadiah relates:

> Behold I will make you small among the nations, you shall be utterly despised. The pride of your heart has deceived you, you who lives in the cleft of the rocks, whose dwelling is high, who say in your heart, "Who will bring me down to the ground?" Though you soar aloft like the eagle, and though your nest is set among the stars, there I will bring you down.

At verse 8 of Obadiah, the prophet speaks of the treatment of Edom, when he writes, "Will I not on that day, says the Lord, destroy the wise men of Edom and understanding out of Mount Esau." Edom, of course, was populated in ancient times by the people of Esau. In fact, verse 10 refers to the relation of Esau to Jacob: "For the violence brought to your brother Jacob, shame shall cover you, and you shall be cut off forever."

By the time we get to verse 15 of Obadiah, the text begins to speak of the Day of the Lord and Restoration when it says, "For the Day of the Lord is near upon all of the nations. As you have done, so shall it be done to you, and your deeds shall return to you on your own head." Again, the use of these future tense verbs would seem to indicate a belief that God has a Divine Plan of restoration in mind.

Indeed, by the very end of the book, the Lord tells us that, "Saviors shall go up to Mount Zion so that they may rule Mount Esau, and the Kingdom will then be ruled by your God, Yahweh."

The Book of Amos is the fourth of the books of the twelve. Amos was a Judean prophet from a village called Tekoa. He was active in the Northern Kingdom of Israel, during the reign of Jeroboam the Second (786 to 746) The Book of Amos is considered to be one of the earliest of the prophetic books. He earned his living from the flock and the sycamore-fig grove (1:1 and 7:14–15). It is not clear whether he was the owner or a hired hand. Given his vocabulary, however, it is unlikely that he was a peasant.

Although his home was in Judah, he was sent to announce Yahweh's judgment on the Northern Kingdom of Israel. For the most part, it is likely that his ministry was at Bethel, which at the time was Israel's main religious sanctuary, where the rich of the Northern Kingdom worshipped.[97]

The dominant theme of the Book of Amos is stated clearly at 5:24. This verse tells us:

> But let justice roll down like waters
> and righteousness like an ever-flowing stream.

The Prophet Amos saw himself as an instrument in the hands of Yahweh, who was going to judge his unfaithful, disobedient and covenant-breaking people, His Chosen People. According to Amos, this response from Yahweh will not be simply to warn; rather it will be total destruction. So Amos calls for Israel to repent so that the Lord God might have mercy on the remnant (see:5:4–5 and 14–15).[98]

The God for whom Amos speaks is not simply the God of Israel. He also pits one nation against another to carry out His Divine purposes (6:14). Yahweh is a great King who rules the entire universe (see: 4:13, 5:8 and 9:5–6). Although Amos' message is primarily one of doom, Israel's neighbors do not escape Amos' attention.

The Book of Amos may be divided into the following parts:

- Title and Introduction (1:1)

- Introduction to Message of Amos (1:2)

- Oracles Against Nations, including Judah and Israel (1:3 to 2:16)

- Oracles Against Israel (3:1 to 5:17)

- Announcements of Exile (5:18 to 6:14)

- Visions of Divine Retribution (7:1 to 9:10)

- The Restoration (9:11 to 15)

Like the prophets before and after him, Amos often combines the idea of Retributive Justice with the use of future-tense verbs that point to the Restoration. We see this combination at 3:11, 9:8–10, and 9:13–15, for example. At times, Amos employs both the Collected and the Individual forms of the Retributive Justice Theory, such as at 1:3–5 and 7–8, 2:9, 3:6 and 14, and 4:9, 10 and 11.

Occasionally, Amos seems to assent to the theories we have called the Influences of Demonic Forces View, the Contrast Theory, as well as the Free Will Defense. We will provide one example of each of these theories in the writing of the Prophet Amos. At 5:19, the text refers to a "serpent who bit him." In Christianity, this has been interpreted to mean the influence of the Demonic Forces Theory, as has 9:3 that informs us:

> And though they hide from My sight at the bottom of the
>   Sea,
> there I will command the Serpent, and it shall bite them.

In the Christian tradition, among thinkers such as Gregory the Great, Thomas Aquinas and John Calvin, these two verses from chapters 5 and 9 of Amos have been seen as references to the works of the Devil and his minions.[99] The word for serpent in Amos is *nachash*, the same term employed to speak of the serpent in Genesis 3, where the same noun is used four times. Two other classical Hebrew nouns designate a "serpent." The first is *sareph* that came be found at Numbers 21:8. There it means a "fiery serpent." The other word is *tannim* that stands for a sea monster, like leviathan, for example, such as at Exodus 7:9 and 10.

At 5:18 and 20, the Prophet Amos speaks of the Day of the Lord as "darkness and not light," and at Amos 4:5, the writer tells us to:

> Offer a sacrifice of thanksgiving of that which is leavened
> and proclaim free will offerings, publish them,
> for so you love to do, O people of Israel.

The idea of a "Free Will offering," or *Ne'dabah*, in classical Hebrew is a sacrificial offering that is done spontaneously and voluntarily. The same word is employed throughout the Old Testament, or Hebrew Bible, such as at Deuteronomy 16:10 and 23:23; Leviticus 7:16–18, 22:18, 21 and 23; as well as at Psalm 119:108.[100] One also sees the Prophet Amos' endorsement of the Free Will Defense at 4:9–11. All of these passages use the phrase, "and yet to did not return to me." This would assume that the Jews had the ability to return, or not to return, to Yahweh, suggesting again the Theory of the Free Will Defense.

In addition to the many passages in which the Prophet Amos employs future-tense verbs to point to the Restoration, he also appears to assent to the Divine Plan Theory in passages such as 5:8, where the prophet seems to combine the Divine Plan Theory with the Contrast View. Amos tells us:

> He who made the Pleiades and Orion and turns darkness
>   into morning, and

> darkens the day into night, and who calls for the waters of
>   the sea, and pours
> them out upon the surface of the Earth. The Lord is His
>   name.

This verse begins with a description of Yahweh's creation of the universe, followed by the contrast of light and darkness, night and day. This verse is quickly followed by a clear example of the Retributive Justice Theory that tells us, "The Lord is His name. He makes destruction flash forth against the strong…"[101]

One final aspect of the Prophet Amos' views on evil and suffering is his extensive vocabulary of words related to evil and suffering, as well as his many employments of the word, *Ra'*, or "evil" itself. Amos uses the word "evil" at 5:13–15, 6:3, 9:4, 9:10, and a variety of other places as well.[102] This brings us to an analysis of prophets Micah and Nahum, among the minor prophets, in terms of the issues of theodicy and the problem of evil—the topic of the next section of this fourth chapter.

Micah and Nahum on Evil and Suffering

The Book of Micah stands sixth among the minor prophets, but it is third in the Septuagint version of the Old Testament. The Prophet Micah ministered during the reigns of Jotham (742 to 735 BCE), Ahaz (735 to 715 BCE), and Hezekiah (715 to 687 BCE). Since chapter 6 of Micah is addressed to Israel and chapter 1 speaks of the downfall of Samaria, Micah's prophetic career must have begun sometimes before 722 BCE.[103]

Assyria at the time was the great power to the north. Many of Micah's earliest messages were addressed to the people of Israel, often about the Assyrians. The Prophet Micah lived among the poor and sympathized much more with them because of their hard lot. Indeed, no other writer in the Old Testament is more indignant than Micah over the ways in which the rich and powerful used every chance to exploit the powerless and the weak.[104]

At times, Micah proclaims in the boldest of terms things like:

> Hear this, you leaders of the house of Jacob…who built
> Zion with bloodshed and Jerusalem with wickedness…

> Therefore, because of you, Zion will be plowed like a
> field, yea, Jerusalem will become like a heap of rubble.[105]

Although there are seven chapters in the Book of Micah, only chapters 1, 2 and 3 are attributed by most modern scholars to be written by the Prophet Micah. In Chapter 4, the book is more often quoted than any other chapter. This chapter looks very much, both linguistically and in terms of theological content to chapter 2 of the Book of Isaiah.[106]

Another notable passage in the Book of Micah is found at 6:6–8. Here we find a statement of prophetic religion at its best:

> And what does the Lord require of you? To act justly
> and to love mercy, and to walk humbly with your God.

Here the Prophet Micah points out that the God of the Jews, Yahweh, desires that his followers exhibit certain moral qualities rather than the making of sacrifices and burnt offerings to the Lord. Nowhere else in the Hebrew Bible, or Old Testament, can a more exalted conception of the nature of true religion and the moral qualities than the religion of Israel is deigned to foster in its followers.

In the Book of Micah, the prophet refers to a variety of answers and responses in regard to the issues of theodicy and the problem of evil. Among these views are Retributive Justice, both Individual and Collective; the Contrast View; possibly, the Influences of Demonic Forces Theory; and Divine Plan Theory as it applies to future tense verbs and the restoration of Judah and Israel.

The mention of the Demonic Forces Theory can be found at Micah 7:17, where the text relates, "And they shall lick the dust like a serpent, like the crawling things of the Earth." Although this text does not say that the serpent is evil, the line has been interpreted that way, mostly in Early and Medieval Christianity. This is precisely the way that Gregory the Great and Albert the Great have understood the verse in question.

Two passages in Micah's book also seem to indicate the Contrast View as introduced in Chapter One of this study. These come at 3:6 and 7:8. The first of these tells us:

> Therefore, it shall be night for you, without vision
> And darkness to you, without divination.

Micah 7:8 tells us, "When I sit in darkness, the Lord will be a light to me." The negative connotation of the word darkness is contrasted with the "light of Yahweh." At verse 9, he adds, "He will bring me forth to the light, and I shall behold His deliverance." The Prophet Micah refers to something close to the Collective Retributive Justice Theory when he writes:

> Behold, against this family, I am devising evil
> from which you cannot remove your necks,
> and you shall not walk haughtily.[107]

The Divine Plan Theory may be detected in the Book of Micah at 4:1, 4:10 and 5:7. And Micah employs future-tense verbs that also point to a restoration of Judah and Israel sometimes in the future. Among these verbs are "shall not walk," at 2:4; "will gather" and "will set" at 4:12; "will make" at 4:7; and "will bear," "will bring," "will cover," and "will gloat," in 7:9–10. In each of these, the Prophet Micah points to a time when the relationship between Judah and Israel and Yahweh, their God, will be a far better one.

Like some of the other minor prophets we have examined so far in this chapter, the Book of Micah has an abundance of Hebrew words for evil and suffering, including sin at 1:5, 6:13 and 7:9; transgressions at 12:5 and 3:8; shame at 2:7; 4:10 where travail may be found; evil at 2:1, 3, 3:2 and 4. Wickedness, which is used at 2:1, 6:10, and 6:11; lies and lying at 2:11 and 6:10. Deceitfulness can be found at Micah 6:12. And finally, "indignation" that is used at 7:9.

Nahum, the next of the minor prophets, principally wrote in his book about the end of the Assyrian city of Nineveh. Little is known about Nahum's personal life. His name means "comfort" or "comfortable" in classical Hebrew. The text tells us that he was from the town of Alqosh (1:1), which scholars place either in Northern Iraq or in the Northern part of Galilee.

Assyria had been the scourge of the ancient Near East for nearly three centuries. They conquered the city of Samaria in 722 BCE, and twenty years later, the Assyrians invaded Jerusalem. It is not surprising, then, that at 3:19, Judah is shown as joining in the general outburst of joy over the destruction of the city of Nineveh.

Nahum asserts Yahweh's moral government of the world. The destruction of Nineveh is evidence that God stands against oppression and the abuse of power. Nahum saw it as Divinely ordained, an act of Divine Justice. Indeed, Nineveh finally fell in 612 BCE. After the Assyrian king, Ashurbanipal, died in 632, the empire was in disarray, and it finally crumbled in 612 BCE.[108]

At 3:8–10, Nahum speaks of the fall of Thebes, which happened in 663 BCE, as if it had already occurred. It is likely then that Nahum delivered his prophecies between 663 and 612 BCE, most likely near the end of that period. Some of the proclamations of Nahum are directed to Judah (see 1:12–13 and 15), but most of his words are directed at Nineveh (see 1:11 and 14, 2:13, and 3:5– 17.

Nahum's book consists of mostly judgment oracles made up of strong, poetic discourses, with frequent use of metaphor and simile, vivid word pictures, and often staccato repetition (see 3:1–3). The book is filled with rhetorical questions, as well as a marked stress on moral indignation and an emphasis on the fate of the poor and the downtrodden.[109]

The main focus of the entire book is Yahweh's judgment on Nineveh because of her oppression, cruelty, idolatry and overall wickedness. In fact, the book ends with the total destruction of the city. The Ninevites were the greatest anti-Semites of the ancient world. They were ruthless in their treatment of their smaller neighbors.

The Book of Nahum may be divided into four main parts. These can be summarized this way:

Part I: Yahweh's Terrifying Appearance (1:2–8)

Part II: Nineveh's Judgment and Judah's Restoration (1:9 to 2:1)

Part III: The Attack on Nineveh (2:2 to 3:7)

Part IV: Nineveh's Inescapable Fate (3:8 to 19)

Regarding the phenomena of evil and suffering, the Prophet Nahum makes a number of comments. Many of these are related to the Retributive Justice Theory, but there are also scant references to the Divine Plan Theory when he mentions restoration directly or through the use of future-tense verbs.

Four examples of Retributive Justice may be found at Nahum 1:2–3; 1:12, 1:14, 2:13 and 3:19, which speaks of the fall of Nineveh. The first of these tells us, "Yahweh is a jealous God and avenging. Yahweh is avenging and wrathful. Yahweh takes vengeance on His adversaries and keeps wrath for his enemies. The Lord is slow to anger and of great might, and He will by no means clear His enemies.

The Prophet Nahum returns to his use of the Retributive Justice Theory a few verses later at 1:12 and 14. Speaking of the Assyrians, Nahum says at verse 12:

> Although they be strong and many, they will be put off
>   and pass away
> Although I have afflicted, I will afflict you no more.

At 1:14, the Prophet Nahum relates:

> The Lord has given commandments about you.
> No more shall your name be perpetrated
> From the house of your gods I shall cut off
> the graven image and the molten image.
> I will make your grave, for you are vile.

Here the Prophet Nahum condemns the idolatry of the Assyrians for worshipping false gods, as well as a prediction of the future destruction of the city of Nineveh that ultimately came about in 612 BCE.[110]

At 2:13 of his book, the Prophet Nahum is explicit about Yahweh's treatment of the Assyrians. He tells us:

> Behold I am against you, says the Lord of hosts, and I
> will burn your chariots in smoke, and the sword shall
> devour your young lions...

The "young lions" are an obvious reference to the young soldiers of the Assyrian Army, as well as its use of chariots. At the very end of his book, at 3:18–19, Nahum speaks of the destruction of Nineveh. Indeed, he addresses their king directly:

> You shepherds are asleep,
> O king of Assyria.

Your nobles slumber,
Your people are scattered on the mountains
with none to gather them.
There is no assuaging your hurt,
your wound is grievous.
All who hear the news of you,
clap their hands over you
For upon whom has not come
your unceasing evil.

The Prophet Nahum refers to the Divine Plan Theory directly, as at 2:2, or indirectly by using future-tense verbs about the Restoration. At 2:2, Nahum tells us, "For Yahweh is restoring the majesty of Jacob as the majesty of Israel, for plunderers have stripped them and ruined their branches."

Nahum also employs future-tense verbs in several places to indicate God's plan of the future in such places as 2:13; 5:5, 6, 7 and 11, for example. Verse 2:13 uses "will burn" and "will cut off." "Will lift up" and "will look" at 3:5. "Will throw" is employed at 3:6, and "will bemoan" at 3:7. And finally, "will be dazed" and "will seek" at 3:11. And in all of these, Nahum clearly speaks of the Restoration of the Jews, as well as the freedom from the yoke of the Assyrians. This brings us to the Prophets Habakkuk and Zephaniah and their views on evil and suffering.

Habakkuk and Zephaniah on Evil and Suffering

The Prophet Habakkuk also worked in the Kingdom of Judah around 600 BCE, just before the Babylonian captivity. He was one of the first Hebrew prophets that raises the issue of why the innocent suffer, and evil people are often rewarded. Is it fair that those who are evil often seem to win out over the righteous? In chapter two of Habakkuk, he provides the Divine response to this question. That is, in time, the evil will be punished and, in the meantime, believers should patiently endure their current state.[111]

The Prophet Habakkuk was a contemporary of the Prophet Jeremiah who also warned that an invading nation, the Chaldeans, would become the instrument of Yahweh against Judah. This can be seen in Habakkuk 1:6ff and Jeremiah 6:22–23.

Habakkuk's main prophecies were directed at the kingdoms of Babylon, Persia and Media, who all were growing into world powers. He was a wealthy man. He owned several properties that he inherited. In fact, Habakkuk remained in the Promised Land, even after the Exile.

Habakkuk's book is also noteworthy because a commentary on the book was among the first manuscripts found among the Dead Sea Scrolls, along with a complete manuscript of the Book of Isaiah, and a text called "The Manual of Discipline," also known as the "Rules of the Community. These texts were discovered in the caves at Qumran in 1947 by a Bedouin shepherd named Muhammad ed-Dhib. [112]

The Book of Habakkuk uses a number of literary devices not seen in some of the other minor prophets. These include the complaint (1:2–4 and 13–17), prophetic oracles (1:5–11 and 2:2–5), prophetic woes (2:6–19), and a lengthy psalm (3:1–15). The simplest way to understand the book is as a dialogue between Habakkuk and Yahweh. Habakkuk makes a complaint to God, and then He responds to the complaint.

This pattern can be seen thusly:

- First Complaint (1:2–4)
- God's Answer (1:5–11)
- Second Complaint (1:12–17)
- God's Answer. (2:2–5)[113]

At chapter 1:3–4, Habakkuk raises the issues of theodicy and the problem of evil. He tells us this:

> Why dost thou make me see wrongs and look upon
> trouble?
> Destruction and violence are before me, Strife and
> contention arise.
> So the law is slacked, and justice never goes forth,
> for the wicked surround the righteous
> so justice goes forth perverted.[114]

Yahweh's response to Habakkuk is to point out the looming of the Chaldeans, "that bitter and hasty nation." He calls them "full of dread and terror" (verse 7), and the Chaldeans "all come for violence." God tells us that the Chaldeans, "laugh at every fortress," and that they, "sweep by like the wind," and "their own might is their god."[115]

Habakkuk responds with another complaint. This one comes at 12:12–17. The prophet begins by asking, "Are You not the everlasting, O Lord my God, my Holy One?" Next, the prophet makes a comment that seems to combine the Divine Plan Theory with the Moral Qualities Perspective. Habakkuk tells us:

> O Lord, thou hast ordained them as a judgment;
> And Thou, o Rock, has established them for chastisement.
> You who are of purer eyes than to behold evil and cast no
>   look on wrong.
> Why do you look upon faithless men and are silent when
>   the wicked are
> swallowed up the man more righteous than he?

Yahweh responds to Habakkuk's second complaint at the beginning of chapter two. At 2:2–4, the Lord relates:

> And the Lord answered me:
> Write the vision, make it plain upon some tablets, so he
>   may run who reads it.
> For still the vision awaits its time, it hastens to the end—it
>   will not lie.
> If it seems slow, wait for it.
> It will surely come, it will not delay.
> Behold, he whose soul is not upright in him shall fail,
> But the righteous shall live by his faith.

Ultimately, then, the Prophet Habakkuk appears to endorse the Divine Plan Theory, which he argues for with the uses of future-tense verbs in relation to the Divine's scheme. Some Christian scholars, such as Matthew Henry and John Calvin, for example, find a reference to the Influences of Demonic Forces Theory at Habakkuk 3:14. This verse reveals the prophet saying:

> Thou did crush the heads of the wicked,
> laying him bare from thigh to neck.

This is most likely a reference to Yahweh defeating the evil beast Leviathan by the chopping off of his seven heads. In ancient Israel, as well as early Christianity, Leviathan was a symbol or reification of evil. And this may be the reference here as well. A variety of other Old Testament passages refer to the same theme.[116]

Ultimately, however, the Prophet Habakkuk falls back on the Divine Plan Theory when he remarks:

> I will quietly wait for the day of trouble
> To come upon the people who invade us.[117]

The Prophet Zephaniah worked on his book around 625 BCE, making him a contemporary of Jeremiah. The most significant aspect of his personal history is that he is a member of royalty from the royal line of Judah. His great grandfather was Hezekiah, one of Judah's greatest kings. When Hezekiah died, however, the throne was taken over by Zephaniah's great uncle, Manasseh, who became a very corrupt king.[118]

Zephaniah's prophecies took place during the reign of Josiah, who was eight years old when he came to power. Josiah later became responsible for the most thorough, religious reforms in Judah. Josiah began these reforms very late in his reign, not because there was a lack of the will, but rather because there were no copies of the Torah for the reforms to go by.[119]

In his book, the Prophet Zephaniah makes harsh remarks of the worship of certain gods in Jerusalem, such as the Great Baal and Milcom. He also is critical of wearing "foreign dress" at 1:8. King Josiah reigned from 640 until 609, with his religious reforms in the late 620s. Worldwide, Assyria was now in decline. The Persians and the Babylonians were on the rise. King Josiah met his death, however, while trying to hinder Pharaoh the Second from helping the Assyrians to overcome the Jews.[120] King Josiah was succeeded by King Jehoahaz, who eventually was deposed by Pharaoh. Thus, Jehoahaz was the first Jewish king to die in exile.

In his book, Zephaniah follows a certain pattern that looks like this:

- Rebellion. The people rebel against the teachings of Yahweh.

- Yahweh exacts retribution or judgment against them.

- Repentance. The people see the error of their ways, leading to repentance.

- Restoration. Yahweh responds to the repentance by restoring the Kingdom.[121]

Of all the minor prophets, the Book of Zephaniah provides the widest response to the issues of evil and suffering. Indeed, the following theories introduced in chapter one of this study all can be detected in Zephaniah's book:

- Individual Retributive Justice

- Collective Retributive Justice

- The Contrast View

- The *Yetzerim* Theory, or Free Will Defense

- The Influences of Demonic Forces Theory

- Divine Plan Theory. Divine Plan Theory using future-tense verbs.

Zephaniah combines the Collective Retributive Justice and Divine Plan Theory at 1:8–9, where the prophet informs us that Yahweh says:

> And on the Day of the Lord's sacrifice, I will punish the officials and the king's sons
> and all who array themselves in foreign clothes.
> On that day, I will punish anyone who leaps over the threshold
> and those who fill their master's house
> with violence and fraud.

In his book, the Prophet Zephaniah also endorses the Divine Plan Theory with his many uses of future-tense verbs that look forward to repentance and the reestablishment of the kingdom. At 1:10, he employs, "will be heard." At 1:12, "will search" and "will punish." At 1:18, Zephaniah uses "shall be able to deliver" an "shall be consumed." Similar future-tense verbs are employed in chapter two, as well, such as at 2:9–12. Most of these uses of future tense verbs, of course, are also a Collective form of Retribution Theory.

At Zephaniah's 3:19, we find an explicit reference to what we have labeled the Contrast Perspective in Chapter One of this study. At 3:19c, Zephaniah relates, "And I will change their shame into praise and be renown in all of the Earth." This is followed a few verses later with a mention of the Restoration at 3:20, "When I restore your fortunes before your eyes, says the Lord," an obvious reference to part IV of the pattern described earlier.

Two passages of Zephaniah's book have been interpreted as verses that imply the Devil or his minions. These come at 2:15 and 3:13. The former speaks of, "Everyone who passes by her hisses and shakes her fists," while 3:13 talks about a "deceitful tongue." Both of these verses are seen by Gregory the Great and Thomas Aquinas as examples of the Influences of Demonic Forces Theory.[122] The word for the verb "hisses" is *sharaq* that also may be found at Job 27:23 and Zechariah 10:8.

Along the way, in Zephaniah's book, the prophet uses an extensive vocabulary of words related to evil and suffering. The Day of the Lord, for example, is used seventeen times in the book of Zephaniah. Other words for evil may be found at 1:12, 15 and 18; 3:5, 8, 13 and 15.[123] This brings us to an analysis of the Prophets Haggai and Zechariah on the issues of theodicy and the problem of evil, our next topic in this fourth chapter.

Evil and Suffering in Haggai and Zechariah

The Prophet Haggai wrote in the period immediately after the return of the Jews from the Babylonian captivity. He has two major goals for his prophecies. First, that the Jews had forgotten their God during the Exile while choosing instead to act in their own self-interest. So, the Prophet Haggai suggests that it is now time to "reconsider the ways of the Lord." The second goal of the Book of Haggai is to get the Jewish people to rebuild the Temple at Jerusalem. The Prophet Haggai makes this second claim at 1:7, and continually refers to the same phenomenon throughout the book.

Chapter two of Haggai's book is framed by a discussion of Yahweh's relationship to the Jews. At 2:5, the Lord reminds His people that He was the God who led the Jews out of Egypt. At 2:19, Yahweh blesses the whole nation. And at 2:23, the end of the book, Yahweh reasserted that He has chosen Judah as His nation.

Like the other minor prophets, the Prophet Haggai uses a series of future-tense verbs, such as at 2:5–9 and 21–23. Yahweh employs "will shakes," and "shall be greater," in 2:5–9. He employs "will bless" at 2:19, and "will take" is employed at Haggai 2:23. Indeed, Haggai ends the book by simply declaring, "For I have chosen you," says the Lord of Hosts.

In regard to responses to evil and suffering in the Prophet Haggai's book, in the context of the people of Israel turning away from Yahweh after the Exile, the Lord refers to some Retributive Theory punishment. Yahweh tells us:

> And I have called for a drought upon the land of the hills, upon the grain, the new wine, the oil upon what the ground brings forth, upon men and cattle and upon all their labors.[124]

The Prophet Haggai again uses the Retributive Justice Theory in the context of the treatment of dead human bodies. The prophet relates:

> If one who is unclean by contact with a dead body touches any of these, does it become unclean? Then the priest answers, "It does become unclean." Then Haggai said, "So it is with the people, and with this nation before me," says the Lord; and so with every work of their hands, and what they offer is unclean.

In addition to the use of the Divine Plan Theory through future-tense verbs and the Retributive Justice Theory, the Prophet Haggai at times employs some unusual Hebrew verbs and nouns, such as his use of the word *chushim*, at 2:23, that designates a "signet ring." This variety of ring is only worn by certain Jewish kings. It stands for a special Divine favor, as Jeremiah 22:24 also mentions. Other mentions of the *Chushim* can also be seen at Daniel 6:17, Esther 8:10, and Exodus 28:11 and 39:30.[125]

The Prophet Zechariah is the second of the post-exilic minor prophets. He worked during the reign of Darius the Great and was a contemporary of Haggai, after the fall of Jerusalem in 586 BCE.[126] It is most likely that both Ezekiel and Jeremiah were sources for the writing of the Book of Zechariah.

Many modern scholars believe that the Book of Zechariah was written by two, and possibly three, authors. Those who hold this view divide the book into chapters 1 to 6, 7 to 8, and 9 to 14. The first of these three parts contains a series of eight visions given to the prophet. Chapter seven and eight of Zechariah raises the question of whether the Jews should any longer mourn the destruction of the city of Jerusalem.

Chapters nine to fourteen consists of two Oracles, chapters 9 to 11 and 12 to 14. The first of these, like the other minor prophets, gives an outline of the course of Yahweh's Providence, down to the time of the coming of the Messiah.[127] The second oracle, chapters twelve to fourteen point out the glories that await Israel in the "latter days," and the final triumph of the Kingdom of Yahweh.[128] Indeed, many of the verbs employed in the second oracle of Zechariah are in the future tense, suggesting the Divine Plan Theory.[129]

The Prophet Zechariah also uses a variety of other responses to the issues of theodicy and the problem of evil. For example, the Prophet Zechariah speaks of Satan at 3:1–4, where he tells us:

> Then he showed me Joshua the high priest standing before the angel of the Lord and Satan standing at His right hand to accuse him. And the Lord said to Satan, "The Lord rebukes you, O Satan The Lord who has chosen Jerusalem rebukes you. Is not this a brand plucked from the fire?"

At Zechariah 13:2, the prophet again appears to employ the Influences of Demonic Forces Theory, when Zechariah speaks of "removing prophets and unclean spirits." In his book, at Zechariah 4:10, he uses the verbal form of *Satan*, which generally means "despise" or "accuse," among the minor prophets. Zechariah, at 10:8, uses the term *sharaq* to stand for "hisses." Thus, this verse has also been pointed to as an example of the Influence of Demonic Forces Theory.

Like most of the other minor prophets, Zechariah also employs a number of future tense verbs to indicate that God has a Divine Plan to come in regard to the Jews. These future tense verbs can be found at 14:2–3, 5–6, 8–11, among a number of other verses in the Book of Zechariah. Most of these, of course, indicate that Yahweh has a Divine Plan for "the remnant of our God."[130]

There are also a number of verses that suggest Zechariah's use of the Retributive Justice Theory, such as 11:17, for example:

> Woe to my worthless shepherd
> who deserts his flock!
> May the sword smite his arm
> and his right eye.

The Prophet Zechariah also uses the Retributive Justice Theory in regard to the treatment of other nations by the God Yahweh. At 7:14, for example, the prophet relates:

> And I scattered them with a whirlwind among all the nations which they had not known. Thus, the land was left desolate, so that no one went to and fro, and the pleasant land was made desolate.

This brings us to the final two of the minor prophets, Jonah and Malachi, the subject matter of the final section of Chapter Four. This will be followed by the conclusions to this chapter, and then on to Chapter Five, an analysis of the perspectives on evil and suffering to be found in the Book of Job.

Jonah and Malachi on Evil and Suffering

The Book of Jonah is unlike the other works of the minor prophets in one important way. It is entirely narrative, with the exception of the poem in chapter two. Ostensibly the book is set in the time of Jeroboam in the eighth century BCE. More modern scholarship, however, places the Book of Jonah in the late fifth to the early fourth century BCE.[131]

The book does not identify its author. Tradition has ascribed it to the prophet himself. The book has many similarities to the narratives of Elijah and Elisha, and most likely came from the same circle of prophetic writing. One similarity shared by the three is the extension of their ministries to foreign lands (see Fist Kings 17 and Second Kings 8:7–15), in addition to Jonah preaching to Nineveh and the Ninevites.

The entire narrative has been compressed by the author into forty verses, with eight additional verses of poetry devoted to Jonah's prayer of thanksgiving. The climax of Jonah's narrative is that "Salvation comes from Yahweh."[132]

The narrative of the story of Jonah is fairly simple. Yahweh tells Jonah to go to the city of Nineveh, the place that has the strongest anti-Semites of the ancient world. Jonah refuses and chooses instead to take a ship to Tarshish, a city most likely in the south of Spain, as far away from Nineveh as he could go. While on the ship, a great storm comes up and the ship's captain, after casting lots, decided that Jonah is responsible. Thus, Jonah is cast into the sea, and the sea calms.[133]

A short time later, Jonah is swallowed by a great fish. For three days, he stays in the belly of the fish, and then he is spewed from the belly of the fish. Whereupon Yahweh again tells Jonah to travel to Nineveh and to minister to them. In chapter three, Jonah arrives in the Assyrian city, and he tells the people there that in "forty days they will be destroyed."[134] The king of the city orders the people to wear sackcloth and to repent their sins.

Afterward, Yahweh forgives the Ninevites because they had turned away from their sins. Jonah, however, was angry about the matter, and he asks Yahweh to take his life from him. Then Jonah left the city, and he built a booth for himself to keep out of the sun. And Yahweh then appoints a plant to arise so that Jonah might have more shade from the sun. Jonah was happy about the shade, and then the following morning, Yahweh sends a worm to gnarl at the base of the plant, which then withers.[135]

This causes Jonah again to ask for death at 4:8, for he is angry at the plant. Then Yahweh asks Jonah why he is angry at the plant, and

Jonah again asks for death, at 4:9. Yahweh then scolds Jonah for being perturbed at the Ninevites, who are 120,000 people, as well as their cattle. And the narrative comes to a close at that point.[136]

In regard to the issues of evil and suffering, the Book of Jonah employs a number of the responses outlined in Chapter One. At 2:9, the writer tells us that "deliverance belongs to the Lord," an example of the Moral Qualities View. The entire narrative of the Book of Jonah may be considered a version of the Divine Plan Theory, for it is clear that Yahweh had the end of the story in mind from the very beginning.

The author of the Book of Jonah does not, however, use many future-tense verbs, as most of the other minor prophets have done. He does employ a classical vocabulary about words related to evil and wickedness. He uses the word *Ra'* five times, and one of the words for wickedness once, at 1:2.[137]

The writer of the Book of Jonah also likens the three days in the belly of the fish to being in "the belly of Sheol," where the "bars are closed forever." This is a reference to the Gates of Sheol that can be seen in places like Jeremiah 17:27 and the Book of Job's 38:17, elsewhere in the Hebrew Bible, or Old Testament.

Finally, the twelfth and final, of the minor prophets, Malachi, is also the final book of the Hebrew Bible, or Old Testament. The book offers no identifying characteristics about the author, for the book says nothing of his family, nor the leaders of his day. The book does employ a Persian word for "Governor," suggesting that the period may have been between 538 and 333 BCE.[138]

We also can be sure that the Prophet Malachi delivered his message in the Kingdom of Judah. Among modern scholars, his book is called an "Oracle." The prophet mostly comments on the treatment of his people in relationship to Yahweh, their God, often in the most negative of terms.

- In the four chapters of his book, the Prophet Malachi employs five of our theological responses, as introduced in Chapter One of this study. These five theological approaches are:
- Individual Retributive Justice Theory
- Collective Retributive Justice Theory

- The Moral Qualities Approach
- The Influences of Demonic Forces Theory
- The Divine Plan Theory (using future-tense verbs)

The Retributive Justice Theory may be seen at Malachi 1:4–5 where the text tells us:

> If Edom says, "We are shattered but we will rebuild the ruins," the Lord of hosts says, "They may build but I will tear down, until they are called the wicked country, the people with whom the Lord is angry forever." Your own eyes shall see this, and you shall say, "Great is the Lord, beyond the borders of Israel."

The Prophet Malachi turns to the Collective Retributive Justice Theory, when he relates at 1:3:

> Behold, I will rebuke your offspring, and spread dung upon your faces, the dung of your offerings, and I will put you out of my presence.

At 3:3, Malachi speaks of the Lord being a "refiner and purifier of silver, purifying the sons of Levi." This verse could be construed as either the Moral Qualities View or the Test Perspective. At 3:5, Malachi speaks of those who "swear falsely," and may have had demons in mind. Thus, a possible nod in the direction of the Influences of Demon Forces Theory. The same line speaks of *Kashaph*, or "sorcerers," a word related to the verb "to whisper," something often employed by the Demonic.

Finally, the Prophet Malachi regularly employs future-tense verbs to speak of the Divine Plan that Yahweh has in store for the Jewish people, such as at 4:1, 3, and 5, where we find "shall turn," "shall tread down," and "will turn."

Along the way, the writer of the Book of Malachi uses words related to "evil" and "abomination," six times. The "Day of the Lord/ Fear of the Lord," twice at 3:16 and 4:5. He employs the word for Covenant (*berith*) five times, at 2:4–5, 2:8, 2:10 and 3:1. The Prophet Malachi also uses a number of words to signify "curse," such as at 1:14, 2:2, 3:5 and 3:9, two times.

This brings us to the conclusions of Chapter Four on the minor prophets. The subject matter of the following chapter are the places in the Book of Job where the issues of theodicy and the problem of evil are discussed.

Conclusions

We began this fourth chapter with a brief introduction to the minor prophets in the Hebrew Bible, or Old Testament. This was followed by six separate sections on the many views of the minor prophets on the issues of evil and suffering. We have divided these sections into pairs. Thus, there were sections on Hosea and Joel, Amos and Obadiah, Micah and Nahum, Habakkuk and Zephaniah, Haggai and Zechariah, and Jonah and Malachi.

In each of these six sections, we have seen extensive commentary on the questions of theodicy and the problem of evil, some more extensive than others. The Prophet Hosea, for example, employs the Retributive Justice Theory, Original Sin, the Moral Qualities View, and Divine Plan Theory with his extensive uses of future-tense verbs that point to the restoration of the kingdoms of the Jews.

Of the minor prophets, Zephaniah has the fullest use of answers and responses, as outlined in Chapter One of this study. As we have shown, Zephaniah employs both forms of the Retributive Justice Theory; the Contrast View; the Free Will Defense, with the Two *Yetzerim* Theory; the Influence of Demonic Forces View; and Divine Plan Theory, again with the use of future-tense verbs.

We have also seen extensive analyses in the sections of this chapter of Haggai and Zechariah, one of the longest of the minor prophets. As we have shown, both often suggest the Divine Plan Theory through the use of future-tense verbs, as well. We also have maintained that the Prophet Zechariah often employs the Retributive Justice Theory, both Individual and Collective Retribution, regarding the Jewish Nation as a whole.

We also have suggested that the entire Book of Jonah is nothing more than a narrative form of the Divine Plan Theory, with Yahweh knowing in the beginning how the entire story will turn out in the end, and the author of Jonah does it in a mere forty-eight verses.

Finally, we have shown that the final of the twelve minor prophets, the Book of Malachi, employs six of the answers or responses to evil and suffering, as outlined in Chapter One of this study. Malachi endorses, we have shown, Individual Retribution Theory, Collective Retributive Justice Theory, the Moral Qualities View, the Influence of Demonic Forces Theory, and Divine Plan Theory, including the use of future-tense verbs.

We also pointed out that many of the minor prophets, such as Malachi, for example, often have extensive vocabularies in classical Hebrew for words related to evil and suffering. This is also true of Zephaniah, Hosea and Amos, for other examples. This brings us to Chapter Five, the book in the Old Testament that contains the most extensive and comprehensive treatment of the issues of theodicy and the problem of evil—the Biblical Book of Job.

Chapter Five:
Evil and Suffering in the Book of Job

By all means, let Job the patient be your model so long
that it is possible for you, but when equanimity fails, let
the grief and anger of Job the impatient direct itself and
yourself toward God, for only with encounters with Him
will the tensions of suffering be resolved.

—David Clines, *Job 1-20*

Perhaps the first thing he [Job] discovered concerned
the mistaken reason for Job's quest. The consuming
passion for vindication suddenly presented itself as
ludicrous once the courageous rebel stood in God's
presence.

—James Crenshaw, *Old Testament Wisdom*

A peculiar aura of veneration tinged with diffidence
surrounds the whole Book of Job. This issue, in all prob-
ability, is a misapprehension of the way in which it was
composed.

—Samuel Terrien, *Job: Poet of Existence*

Introduction

More than any other book of the Bible, the Book of Job offers the
most comprehensive and deep responses to the issues of theodicy and
the problem of evil. We shall begin this fifth chapter with a lengthy
introduction to the book, followed by an extensive analysis of the many
answers and responses to the issues of evil and suffering that may be

found in the Man From Uz and his book. We also will examine the views on the evil and suffering of the major characters in the book. We next turn, however, to an introduction to the Book of Job.

Introduction

The Biblical Book of Job is the most extensive treatment of the issues of theodicy and the problem of evil in the Old Testament, or Hebrew Bible. It is a curious book because the first two chapters and the final ten verses of the book are written in prose, while the rest of the book is in poetry. It is likely that the prose parts of the book are older than the poetry. The prose is probably from somewhere near 1000 BCE, with the poetry about four to five hundred years later.[139]

In fact, the Job that appears in the prose sections of the book might be called the Patient Job, while, at the same time beginning in chapter 3, where Job protests the day of his birth, the patriarch who appears in the poetic sections of the book might be called the Angry Job. Similarly, the God of the prologue and epilogue seems very different from the God Who speaks from the Whirlwind in chapters 38 to 41. The former is very anthropomorphic, while the latter is much more mystical and ethereal.

The Book of Job begins with alternating scenes on earth and in heaven. The earthly scenes are about Job, a blameless and upright man who fears God and shuns evil."[140] Job has vast wealth, ten children, and a house fit for a wealthy man in the ancient Near East. The narrative then shifts to a debate in heaven between God and Satan about the genuine goodness of Job.[141] The result is that God gives Satan permission to touch anything of Job's but his person.

In the Book of Job, the word *Satan* always appears with the definite article *ha*. Thus, when he is mentioned, it is *ha Satan*. This figure, however, is not yet the demonic figure he will become later in Judaism. The word *Satan* comes from the STN Semitic root that generally means "adversary" or "opponent."

This is followed by the second scene on earth, where Job loses everything—his house, his children, the destruction of his livestock. But through all of this, Job remains faithful.[142]

Next, the book turns to another scene in heaven, another exchange between God and the Satan. Again, they argue about the authenticity of Job's faith. The result is that Satan is now given permission to touch Job's body, so Satan administers a disease that consisted of boils from the top of his head to the bottom of his feet, but God tells the Satan he could not kill the patriarch. Job's response to all this is his comment, "If we accept good from God, ought we not also to accept evil?"[143]

Chapter 3 of the Book of Job begins the poetic dialogue, a series of exchanges between Job and three of his friends, Eliphaz, Bildad and Zophar. These exchanges begin in the third chapter and continue for three rounds, ending at the close of chapter 31, Job's final discourse. It is in these dialogues that the views of Job and his three friends on the issues of evil and suffering may be found.[144]

Chapter 28 of the Book of Job is a curious one. The first half of the chapter is concerned with the activities in mines of miners. The second half of the chapter is an ode to the concept of *Hokmah,* or "Wisdom" in the book, as well as the Old Testament. This poem has nothing to do with what comes after in chapter 29, nor with one came before it in chapter 28.

There is also a problem in the third round of speeches between Job and his first three friends. There are speeches from Eliphaz and Bildad in the third round, as well as responses from Job but none from Zophar. Bildad's third speech is a mere six verses of chapter 25, and Job's response to Bildad is six chapters long, 26 to 31.

The opening verses of chapter 32 introduce a fourth, younger friend of Job. He is angry with Job and the other three friends and then proceeds to make some theological remarks, unlike the other friends. The fourth friend is named Elihu, and he speaks from chapter 32 until the end of chapter 37.

One curious fact about the introduction to this fourth friend, Elihu, is that it is written in prose, like the prologue and epilogue. This has led some interpreters of the book to conclude that Elihu was added to the original text at a later date.

These chapters are followed in the Book of Job by two monumental speeches by God Himself. The first of these is chapters 38 and 39, where God speaks of His control of the universe and provides a litany of animals He has created.[145]

This is followed by a description of two great beasts created by God, Behemoth and Leviathan, in chapters 40 and 41. The former is the greatest of land animals, the latter the greatest of the sea. There is much disagreement about the meaning of these great beasts that we will discuss later in this chapter.[146]

The final chapter of the Book of Job has two parts, the first of which includes 42:1–6, where Job responds to God's two speeches and perhaps apologizes for calling God's goodness into question. The key verses in this exchange are verses 5 and 6. In verses 7 to 17, the text reverts to prose, and it catalogs the restoration of Job's former life, except he gets everything back double.[147]

There also has been much disagreement about how to translate Job 42:5–6. Some say Job is giving up and recognizing the glory of God, while other scholars believe Job is as combative as he has been throughout most of the book.[148]

At the end of chapter 42, Job is blessed with ten children—seven sons and three daughters. It is not clear whether these are the same children in the prologue brought back to life by God or if they are a new set of children. At any rate, Job lives another 140 years, he sees his progeny to the fourth generation, and "He dies an old man and full of days."[149]

Several other aspects of the Biblical Book of Job must be understood in order more fully to understand the book and the people who wrote it. First, chapter 28 of the book is seen by most critics as a later addition to the book. This claim is made for a number of reasons, including the fact that the chapter has nothing to do with what comes before or after it.

Secondly, the Book of Job has far more Aramaic, Syriac and Arabic words or what is sometimes called "Aramaisms" than nearly any other book of the Bible. Thirdly, the Book of Job contains more *hapax legomena* or words that appear once and only once, than nearly any other book of the Bible, as well. Fourthly, beginning in chapter 38:39 until 39:25, the writer(s) of the Book of Job provide a litany of animals, beginning with the lion, raven and mountain goat, and ending with Behemoth and Leviathan. One important question about this list of animals is why and how they are in the order in which they appear in the book.

It is our view that the order of the animals mentioned in God's first and second speeches in the Book of Job go from the most domesticated to the least domesticated, ending in the beasts, Behemoth and Leviathan that humans may not control but the Almighty God does control.

The Book of Job has a unique vocabulary, far different in many ways than any other book of the Bible. The Book of Job, for example, has four different Hebrew nouns for "lion." Five separate words for "dark" and "darkness." Six different Hebrew terms to designate a "trap." The Book of Job also has four words to stand for "curse." Additionally, the writer(s) know the language of the ancient Jewish law courts, the vocabulary of the mining of precious metals (see 28:1–10), as well as the practices of hunting (see 16:12ff).

The Book of Job also contains five different terms for "plan," "counsel," "design" and "purpose." These are *esah* (10:13), *makashabah* (5:12 and 21:27), *zimmah* (17:11 and 31:11), *metzimah* (21:27 and 42:2), and *asah* (42:2).

The Book of Job also has a number of mythological creatures, including the Canaanite god *Reshaph* at Job 5:7. *Rahab*, a Kaos monster in the ancient Near East at Job 36:12–13. The mythological bird called *Chol* at 29:18 that some believe is the Phoenix. *Zaphon*, the mountain on which the Great Baal dwells. And, of course, Behemoth and Leviathan, the two great beasts, one on the land, and the other on the sea.

The Book of Job also bestows the daughters of Job—Jemima, Kezia, and Keren Happoch—rights that were not ordinarily given to women in the ancient Near East as well as Israel. These rights are expressed in the epilogue at 42:16–17.

The idea of the Book of Deeds can also be found in four separate passages of the Book of Job at 14:5 and 13, 18:17, 19:23–24, and 24:20. Interestingly enough, this same theme appears in the *Qur'an* at Surah 17:14, 45:29, and 69:19 to 24–32.

Many visions and dreams appear in the Book of Job. Some of these can be found in Eliphaz's first speech at 4:13–16, a vision that came to Zophar at 20:8, and a vision that appears in chapter 33:15–18.

The term, "Godless" also appears in the Book of Job many times, including 8:13, 13:16, 15:34, 17:8, 20:5, 27:8, 34:30 and 36:13, among other verses. In most of these, the writer contrasts the Godless with those who follow Yahweh.

Finally, there are a plethora of words that stand for God than in any other book of the Bible. These include *El, Elohim, Yahweh, Eloah, Shaddai* or the "Almighty," and *Asah* or "Maker" that is used ten times in the Book of Job.

From the introductory material we have supplied so far, it should be clear that the main characters in the Book of Job are God, the Satan, Job, Eliphaz, Bildad, Zophar and Elihu. Each of these characters has peculiar views about the issues of theodicy and the problem of evil, as we shall see in this chapter. Many of these answers and responses are the ones that have been introduced in the opening chapter of this study of evil and suffering in the Bible.

This brings us to an analysis of the deontological, or backward-looking answers and responses to why the patriarch Job suffers in the book. This will be followed by a third section on the chapter on teleological or forward-looking responses to the meaning and theological importance of Job's suffering.

Deontological Responses to Job's Suffering

The deontological, or backward-looking answers and responses to the evil and suffering brought on the patriarch Job are Retributive Justice, both Individual and Collective; the Influences of Demonic Forces View; Original Sin Theory; and the Two *Yetzerim* Theory, or the Free Will Defense.

The Retributive Justice Theory may be seen in a variety of passages, including 1:1 and 5; 4:7, 8:4; and 42:16–17, among many others. Some of these are Individual Retribution, and some are Collective. In Chapter One, we learned that Job is *tam va yashar*, or blameless and upright. And yet, he has visited upon him the most evil and suffering-filled circumstances. This is clearly not the way that Retributive Justice is supposed to work.

At 1:5 of the Book of Job, we are told by the omniscient narrator that:

> Job arises early in the morning to offer burnt offerings according to the number of all of his children, for Job said, "It may be that my sons have sinned and cursed God in their hearts."

Here Job suggests that the reason he is suffering may be because his sons have committed great sins, and the sacrifices are merely to compensate for those sins—a version of the Collective Retributive Justice Theory. In fact, by the time we arrive at 8:4, Job's second friend Bildad relates:

> If your children have sinned against him, he has
> delivered them into the power of his transgressions.

It should be clear that Bildad's suggestion is out of bounds, for Job already has taken care of the possible sins of his sons back at 1:5. By the time we get to the end of the book when Job receives everything back double, the notion of Individual Retribution ultimately appears to be at work. In the end, Job sees four generations of his progeny, something not seen very often in the ancient Near East.[150] In fact, Job ultimately is compensated double at the end of the book, where even Job's farm animals are doubled in number.

Eliphaz, in his first speech at 4:7, also refers to Individual Retributive Justice when he asks Job:

> Think now, who that was innocent ever perished?
> Or where were the innocent cut off?

At 8:3, Bildad asks:

> Does God pervert justice?
> Or does the Almighty pervert the right?

Zophar, the third friend, tells us at 11:20:

> But the eyes of the wicked will fail, and all way of escaping
>   shall be lost to them
> And their hope is to breathe their last.

For the most part, the major point of view of Job's first three friends, Eliphaz, Bildad and Zophar, is that of Retributive Justice, either the individual form or the collective variety, as in 8:4, where Bildad suggests it was Job's sons who caused his suffering. Interestingly enough, however, Bildad does not say they sinned, he says they *'im*, or "if" they may have sinned in their hearts, perhaps another example of the use of the Two *Yatzerim* Theory.

Job at 13:24 asks God why he hides His face and "counts him as an enemy," a clear reference to his blamelessness and uprightness. Again, at 16:6 Job asserts, "If I speak, my pain is not assuaged. And if I forbear, how much of it leaves me?" At 21:7, Job more explicitly raises the issue of theodicy when he asks, "Why do the wicked live, reach old age, grow mighty in power?" Again, at 21:17, Job asks about the wicked:

> How often is it that the lamp of the wicked is put out. That their calamity comes upon them. That God distributes pain in His anger?

At 24:24–25, Job again raises the issue of innocent suffering. The Man From Uz relates:

> They are exalted a little while, and then are gone.
> They wither and fade like the mallow.
> They are cut off like the heads of grain.
> If this is not so, who will prove me a liar
> And show that there is nothing in what I say?

Thus, the narrator of Job seems to endorse the Retributive Justice Theory with respect to Job. In chapter 31, at verses 3 and 4, Job again raises the issue of theodicy when he asks, "Does not calamity befall the unrighteous and disaster the workers of iniquity? Does He not see my ways and count my steps? Job then goes on to ask:

> If I have walked with falsehood and my foot has hastened
>   to deceit,
> Then let me be weighed in a just balance, and let God
>   know my integrity.

Even at times, the fourth friend Elihu appears to endorse the Retributive Justice Theory, such as at 35:7–8. In this text, Elihu says:

> If you are righteous, what do you give to Him or what
> does He receive from your hands? Your wickedness

concerns a man like yourself and your righteousness a
son of man.

One important aspect of the speeches of Job's fourth friend,
Elihu is that, at least theologically, his views are very distinct from the
Retributive Justice Theory of the other three friends, Eliphaz, Bildad
and Zophar, we have indicated earlier. At 36:15, Elihu endorses the
Moral Qualities Perspective. He does the same at 36:10 and 37:13,
where he tells us:

Whether for correction or for his land,
Or for his love, He causes it to happen.

And at the very end of his speeches, Elihu, at 37:14–20, in his
vocabulary and in his theology, looks very much like the Lord's opening
speech from the whirlwind at the beginning of chapter 38. Thus, Elihu
may be seen as endorsing the Divine Plan Theory, as well.

From all of these passages, we have established that many of the
characters in the Book of Job resort to the Retributive Justice Theory,
in both the Individual and the Collective forms, including Eliphaz,
Bildad, Zophar, Elihu, and of course, Job himself.

It should be clear that the Influences of Demonic Forces Theory
is most easily detected at 1:6–12 and 2:1–6, the two scenes in heaven
where the figure Satan appears. A number of Judeo-Christian thinkers
over the centuries have interpreted the beasts Behemoth and Leviathan
to be understood as Demonic creatures, and they are often depicted that
way in Medieval, Christian iconography. Indeed, Leviathan's mouth
often has been shown as the Mouth of Hell.

Four separate passages in the Book of Job have been pointed to
that ostensibly suggest the Original Sin Theory. These come at 5:7,
14:1–4, 15:14 and 25:4. The latter of these asks the question:

How then can man be righteous before God?
How can he who is born of a woman be clean?

At 5:7, the narrator tells us, "But man is born to trouble, as surely
as sparks fly upward." At the beginning of chapter 14, the narrator

again tells us, "Man that is born of a woman is of few days, and full of trouble." Many Christian interpreters, like Gregory the Great, for example, believe that the "trouble" here refers to Original Sin.

The passage in the Book of Job, at 15:14, again suggests the possibility of a belief in the Original Sin Theory. The text in question asks:

> What is man that he can be clean?
> Or he that is born of a woman that he may be righteous?

It is very clear that Job appears to be exercising his Free Will throughout the Book of Job. More directly, however, at 15:25, we see a direct reference to the Two *Yetzerim* Theory we have introduced back in the first chapter. This verse tells us:

> They conceive mischief and bring forth evil.
> And their hearts prepare deceit.

This is most likely a reference to the use of some sinners of their *yetzer ha ra*, or "evil imagination" or "evil inclination," and that it resides in the *leb*, or "heart," along with the *yetzer tov*, or "good inclination" or "imagination." In fact, there is a variety of words in the Book of Job that designate "imagine," and "imagination." In addition to the word *yetzer*, the book also employs *chashab*, or "imagine," at 6:26; *chamal* at 21:27, that also means "imagine," and the little-used *sheriroth* that usually designates "imagination" elsewhere in the Hebrew Bible, or Old Testament.

The writer(s) of the Book of Job also employ(s) a variety of words to stand for the "will." Among these are *midbar* at Job 1:19 and 38:26, *arbah* used at 12:24 and 39:6, *tsiya* at 30:3, and the classical, Hebrew word *chaphsha*, which stands for "free" at Job 3:19 and 39:5. The conclusion of all of this, of course, is that the writer(s) of Job seem to have endorsed what we have labeled the Free Will Defense back in Chapter One.

At three separate places in the Book of Job, we can find the use of the word *leb*, or "heart." The first of these comes at 11:3, where the noun is used as a synonym for the "self" or one's "life." The other two uses of *Leb* come in the Elihu speeches at 33:3 and 36:13. In both of these, the word is employed in the context that one's heart is the place where one's moral attributes are to be found.

In the former passage, the one at 33:3, Elihu quotes Job as saying, "In the uprightness of my heart…" In the latter verse, the one at 36:13, Elihu speaks of "the Godless in heart," suggesting there is no moral good to be found there.

This brings us to an analysis of the Teleological Responses that may be found in the Book of Job, the subject matter of the next section of this chapter. Several other passages in the book also seem to suggest that Job possessed Free Will.

Teleological Responses in the Book of Job

The teleological or forward-looking answers and responses to the issues of theodicy and the problem of evil are those that depend on consequences in the future rather than moral principles that look to the past. Among these teleological responses in the Book of Job, there are four to be found. These are the Contrast View, the Test Perspective, the Moral Qualities Theory and the Divine Plan Theory.

Each of these four answers or responses are employed in the Biblical Book of Job. The Contrast View can be seen in many places in the book, but we will point to four of them to show the theory is used in Job. These come at 17:12, 18:5 and 18, 24:13–14, and 30:26, in the final speech of Job's. At Job 17:12, the writer tells us: "They make night into day. The light, they say, is near to the darkness." At 18:5, the writer of the Book of Job again seems to adopt something close to the Contrast View when he writes:

> Yes, the light of the wicked is put out.
> And the flame of his fire does not shine.

At the very next verse, 18:6, the text tells us, "The light is dark in his tent, and his lamp above him is put out." A few verses later, at 18:18, the writer of Job reveals, "He is thrust from light into darkness and then driven out of the world." Many of these passages that use the Contrast View employ the theory in the context of the light being good, while the darkness stands for evil, such as at 24:13–14:

> There are those who rebel against the light
> who are not acquainted with its ways,
> and do not stay in its path.
> The murderer rises in the dark
> that he may kill the poor and the needy.
> And in the night, he moves as a thief.

Other verses in Job that imply the Contrast View also employ the images of light and darkness, and still present a stark contrast between good and evil, such as at 30:26, "But when I looked for good, evil came, and when I waited for light, darkness came."

The theory we have called the "Moral Qualities" View also can be seen in many passages in the Book of Job. We will look at four of these to establish the claim. Remember the Moral Qualities Theory says that certain moral qualities in human beings only can be developed in the presence of evil and suffering, often brought by the Divine.

At the Book of Job's 5:17–18, for example, the writer relates:

> Behold, happy is the man who God reproves;
> Therefore, despise not the chastening of the Almighty.
> For He wounds, but He binds up.
> He smites, but His hands heal.

The verbs "reproves" and "to chasten" are indications that these are attributed to God, so that those he reproves and chastens might become better morally. The same view may be seen at Job 22:29–30, where the writer tells us:

> For God abases the proud,
> but he saves the lowly.
> He delivers the innocent man;
> You will be delivered through the cleanliness of your
> hands.

The uses of the verb "abases," as well as the two employments of the verb, "to deliver," also suggest uses of the Moral Qualities View. We find another example of the Moral Qualities Theory at Job 36:10, where the text reveals about God, "He opens their ears to instruction and commands that they return from iniquity." Perhaps the best example of the Moral Qualities Theory in the Book of Job can be found at 36:15, just a few verses later in the book.

Indeed, at Job 36:15, the writer of Job tells us:

> He delivers the afflicted by their affliction,
> and opens their ears by adversity.

In this verse, we are told that God "delivers" His followers from affliction by using "adversity," a clear application of the Moral Qualities Approach. Even the fourth friend of Job, the young Elihu, appears to endorse the Moral Qualities View at Job 37:13, where the text relates:

> Whether for correction, or for his land,
> or for love, he causes it to happen.

The use of the word "correction" again implies that the writer of Job is employing the Moral Qualities Approach. We will move next to the writer of Job's uses of the Test Theory in relation to evil and suffering in the Old Testament, or Hebrew Bible.

It should be clear that the dialogue between Yahweh and the Satan in the first two chapters of the Book of Job may be interpreted as an example of the Test Theory. This theory also can be seen at passages like 7:18, where the text asks, "Dost thou [God] visit him every morning, and test him every moment."

At 23:10 of the Book of Job, the writer again employs the verb "to test" or "to try" when he tells us:

> But He knows the way that I take,
> When he has tried me. I shall come forth as gold.

This verse may be interpreted as an example of the Test View, or the Moral Qualities Perspective, for God's "trying" of humans has them come out as "gold." The same classical Hebrew verb *bachan*, "to test" or "to investigate," is also used by the writer of Job at 34:36 in the Elihu speeches, that tells us, "Would that Job was tried [past tense of *bachan*] to the end, because he answers like wicked men." The term *bachan* comes from an early Semitic root BCHN, that is rarely employed in the

Old Testament, or Hebrew Bible, though it can be found at Zechariah 13:9. The Revised Standard Version translates as:

> And I will put this third into the fire,
> And refine them as one refines silver,
> And test them as gold is tested.

In this verse, the writer makes a connection between the testing of human character and the refining of gold. Thus, the verse from Zechariah is like Job 23:10, for both passages make the same exact connection. This brings us to the final teleological or forward-looking theory that is used throughout the Book of Job, what we have labeled the Divine Plan Theory back in the opening chapter of this study of evil and suffering in the Bible.

More than any other theory of the meaning of evil and suffering in the Bible, and particularly in the Book of Job, the Divine Plan Theory is often advocated. We see this theory at Job 10:13, 11:7–9, 28:21, 36:22 and 26–29, 37:23–24, as well as many other passages in the book. In the first of these passages, the narrator of Job reveals:

> Yet these things hast Thou hid in thy heart
> I know that this was Thy purpose.

The final word from this verse is the classical Hebrew *esah*, which means "purpose" or "plan." The word is employed throughout the Old Testament, or Hebrew Bible, as well as the Book of Job such as at 5:3, where it is translated as "scheme" by the Revised Standard Version at 10:3, where it is rendered "designs" in the RSV; chapter 12:13, where I is translated as "counsel" in the RSV; 18:7 in which the RSV renders it "schemes;" *esah* is translated as "counsel" again at 21:16, as well as at 22:18.

A number of other classical Hebrew terms are also employed in the Book of Job to imply a "plan" or a "purpose." The word *chashab*, for example, is used in a variety of ways, including "count," "to think," " to imagine," and even "to esteem." *Chashab* means "counts" at 19:11 and 15, as well as at 18:3, 33:10 and 41:27.

At the Book of Job's 17:11 and 31:11, the writer employs another noun that means "plan" or "purpose." The word is *zimmah*.

At Job 17:11, the writer speaks of what the Revised Standard Version renders as:

> My days are past, my plans are broken off,
> the desires of my heart

Here the word *zimmah* is used in the female, plural form. Another classical Hebrew noun, which is not used in the Book of Job, is the word *Chephets*, which is also at times translated as "plan" often in relationship to God, such as at Ecclesia 3:1 and 17, 8:6, and Isaiah 1:11. Another word that is rendered "devices" at Job 5:12 is the term *makashabah*, used at 21:27 as well, where it is rendered as "thoughts" in the RSV. Thus, from this discussion, it should become clear that there are a variety of classical Hebrew words that mean "plan" or "purpose," and many of these refer to God, or are connected to His knowledge.

Many of the passages in the Book of Job that argue for the Divine Plan Theory are introduced in the context of discussions of the attributes of Yahweh, or God. Consider, for example, the question of Job 36:22, "Behold, God is exalted in His power, who is a teacher like him?" A few verses later, at Job 36:26–29, we see the Divine Plan Theory suggested in the context of Yahweh's Power and Knowledge. This text tells us this:

> Behold, God is great, and we know Him not;
> The number of His years are unsearchable.
> For He draws up the drops of water,
> And He distills His mist in rain.
> which the skies pour down
> and drop upon many abundantly.
> Can anyone understand the spreading of the clouds
> The thunderings of His pavilions?

At the end of the Elihu speeches, at 37:23–24, the fourth friend of the patriarch Job also appears to endorse the Divine Plan Theory by speaking of the attributes of God. These verses tell us:

> The Almighty—we cannot find Him.
> He is great in power and in justice.

And abundant righteousness He will not violate.
Therefore, people fear Him. He does not regard any who
    are wise
In their own conceit.

Clearly, the best example of the Divine Plan Theory is revealed in the first speech of Yahweh, at Job 38:4–7, where God asks:

Where were you when I laid the foundations of the Earth?
Tell me if you have understanding.
Who determined its measurements—surely, you know!
Or who stretched the line upon it?
On what were its bases sunk?
Or who laid its cornerstone
when the morning stars sang together
and all the Sons of God shouted for joy?

At the Book of Job's 28:23-24, what is sometimes called the "Wisdom chapter," the writer, speaking in the context of Abaddon the Underworld, relates, "God understands the way to it, and He knows its place, for He looks to the ends of the Earth, and He sees everything under the Heavens. At the Book of Job's 11:7 to 9, the writer of Job again asks in the context of the understanding of God, if humans can:

Find out the deep things of God?
Can you find out the limit of the Almighty?
It is higher than the Heavens—what can you do?
Deeper than Sheol—what can you know?
Its measure is longer than the Earth
And broader than the Sea.[151]

At Job 20:3, we see the employment of another classical Hebrew word for "plan" or "understanding." This text tells us, "I hear censure which insults me, and out of my understanding [asah] a spirit answers me." The classical Hebrew term asah is also employed in a variety of ways.

Many of the passages we have seen here point to the Divine Plan Theory, as we have suggested earlier in this chapter, often come in the context of what Yahweh knows and can do. A final verse in which the Divine Plan is called to mind in the Book of Job comes in a comment made by Job at 42:2–3. The RSV translates the line this way:

> I know that You can do all things
> And that no purpose of Yours can be thwarted
> Who is it that hides counsel without knowledge?

The word for "purpose" (*asah*) in the above quotation also sometimes means "to build" or "to make" something such as an Ark or a Universe. It is often used with the word *bara* that is a synonym. In Job, it is employed at 21:21, where the RSV renders it "has done." And at 27:18, where it is translated as "builds," in addition to 20:3 and 42:2 discussed in the above verses.

Thus, from all of these analyses, we may conclude that the writer(s) of the Biblical Book of Job regularly employed all of the following theories as answers or responses to the meaning or the purpose of the evil and suffering brought to the patriarch Job:

- The Free Will Defense
- Original Sin Theory
- The Influences of Demonic Forces View
- Retributive Justice Theory (both Individual and Collective)
- The Contrast Theory
- The Test Perspective
- The Moral Qualities Approach
- The Divine Plan Theory

In addition to these eight theories, the Book of Job also endorses one other traditional theory that might be called the "Hiddenness of God." Sometimes the same view is referred to as God "hiding His face," such as at Jeremiah 33:5, Isaiah 8:17 and 45:15. The writer(s) of the Book of Job also use(s) this theme on a number of occasions. These come at Job 13:24, 34:29, and in two sections of chapter 23, at verses 1–4 and 8–10.

In the first of these passages, Job simply asks:

> Why do You hide Your face
> and count me as Your enemy?

In the Elihu speeches, at 34:29, the fourth friend of Job says this about God, "When He is quiet, who can condemn? When He hides His face, who can behold Him, whether it be a nation or a man?" At Job 23:1–4 and 8–10, Job again laments the absence of God in his life. At verses 1–4, he says:

> Today, my complaint is bitter.
> His hand is heavy in spite of my groaning.
> O that I knew where I might find Him
> That He might come even to His seat.
> I would lay my case before Him
> And fill my mouth with arguments.

A few verses later in chapter 23, at verses 8 to 10, Job again laments the lack of communication between himself and Yahweh, his God. Job tells us about his life:

> Behold, I go forward but He is not there,
> And forwards and backwards, but I cannot perceive him.
> On the left, I seek Him out, but I cannot behold Him.
> I turn to the right, but I cannot see Him.
> But He knows the way that I take,
> Where He has tried me, I shall come forth as gold.

Among the ancient Jews "backwards" and "forwards" were East and West. The North is to the left, and the South to the right. Thus, verse 8 may begin with the word "West." And backwards and forwards may be rendered East and West. Thus, the word "left" could also be "North."

In this passage, the writer of the Book of Job combines the Hidden God Theory, in verses 8 and 9, with the mention of "test" or "try" in the

10 verse. Thus, another example of the Test View in the Book of Job. The Hebrew word for "tried" at Job 23:10 is *nasah*. It is also employed at Job 4:2. There the line may be rendered, "If one attempts a word with you," or "If one were to try you…"

The author(s) of the Book of Job at 15:10 also refer(s) to the idea of hiddenness when the text says, "The wicked man travels with pain in all of his days, and the number of his years is hidden to his oppressors." This may be an example of the Hidden God Theory, combined with the idea of the Book of Deeds. That is, only God knows the "number of years" of all human beings.

Thus, in our analysis, we may add the Hidden God Theory to the answers and responses to the issues of evil and suffering that may be found in the Book of Job. In chapter 3 of his book, at 3:16, Job speaks of his "hidden and untimely birth" and hoping that "it had not been, as infants who had never seen the light." Thus, we may add the Hidden God Theory to the answers and responses to be found in regard to the questions of theodicy and the problem of evil in the Book of Job.

One might say that for the character of Job, there is no light at the end of the tunnel. He laments the hiddenness of God. He reminds himself that although he does not see Him, he knows that God watches his every move. He may not see God, but God sees Him. Job knows that God is present, even in His hiddenness. Job seems determined to come out of his test clean and as pure as gold. Job is determined not to lose sight of the awareness of Yahweh's Power, Knowledge and Goodness.

The verb *bachan*, or "to test," is used three times in the Book of Job. These come at 25:10, as well as 34:3 and 34:36. The latter two of these examples are in the Elihu speeches. At 34:36, the fourth friend says, "Would that Job were tried to the end because he answers like wicked men." Thus, there are a variety of examples of the Test Perspective in the Book of Job.

In the process of the book, Job weeps, complains, cries out and reflects on his past glory. But he never loses sight of who his God is. He is the Almighty who can do all things, according to His will and wisdom. He knows that God has a plan for all of His creatures, and He providentially brings all of those plans to fruition. In this sense, the

Hidden God Theory in the Book of Job may be nothing more than what we have called the Divine Plan Theory.

In a variety of other passages in the Book of Job, the hero of the book protests against his friends, as well as the calamities that have befallen him. Many of these passages are the subject matter of the next section of this chapter.

Job's Denials and Protests

One final perspective on the issues of evil and suffering within the Book of Job is the patriarch's many denials that he has sinned and protests against his friends and against Yahweh, his God. Consider, for example, Job 6:28–30, where the patriarch says to God:

> But now be pleased to look at me,
> for I will not lie to your face.
> Turn, I pray, let no wrong be done.
> Turn now, my vindication is at stake.
> Is there any wrong on my tongue?
> Cannot my taste discern calamity?

Clearly, the answer to Job's question should be in the negative. In the next chapter, at 7:20, Job again refers to his possible sins. Again, he addresses God when he says, "If I have sinned, what did I do to you. O watcher of humanity. Why have You made me your target?" Job begins this remark with 'im, or "if," an indication that it is possible that Job sinned. At 9:15, however, the conditional is gone when Job remarks:

> Although I am innocent, I cannot answer Him.
> I must appeal for mercy to my Accuser.

A few verses later, at 9:21–22, Job again asserts his innocence when he says, "I am blameless. I do not know myself. I loathe my life. It is all one. Therefore, I say He destroys both the blameless and the wicked alike." Here the Man From Uz appears to lament over the fates of the innocent and the wicked and how they are often the same.

In the very next chapter, at 10:6–7, Job again asserts his innocence when he again comments to God:

> That You seek out my iniquity and search for my sin, al-
> though You know that
> I am not guilty.

A few verses later, at 10:14–16, Job is back to using the conditional three times when he remarks to Yahweh: "If I have sinned, You watch me and do not acquit me of my iniquity. If I am wicked, then woe to me. If I am righteous, then I cannot lift up my head." At chapter 12:4, Job again points out that he is *tam va yashar*, that is, "blameless and upright," when he exclaims:

> I am a laughingstock to my friends. I, who called upon God
> and He answered
> me, a just and blameless man, I am a laughingstock.

In the next chapter at 13:15, 23 and 26, Job again attempts to establish his moral innocence when he says:

> See, He will kill me, and I have no hope,
> But I will defend my ways to His face.
> How many are my iniquities and my sins.
> Make me know my transgressions and my sins.
> And at verse 26, Job asks God:
> For you write bitter things against me, and make me reap
> the iniquities of
> my youth.

By the time we get to chapter 16, verse 17, Job again asserts his moral innocence when he says, "Although there is no violence in my hands and my prayer is always pure." At 17:9, Job again raises the issue about why the innocent suffer and the guilty do not when he says, "Yet the righteous hold to their ways, while those with clean hands grow stronger and stronger."

At chapter 19:6, Job returns to his own situation when he tells us, "Know then that God has put me in the wrong and has closed His net around me." Job remains with the same theme in chapter 23, at verse 7:

> There an upright person could reason with Him,
> And I would be acquitted by my Judge forever.

The Man From Uz reasserts his moral innocence a few verses later at verses 11 and 12 when Job says:

> My feet have held fast to His ways. I have kept His ways
>   and I have not turned aside.
> I have not departed from the commandment from His lips.
> I have treasured in my bosom the words of His mouth.

In the very next chapter, at 24:25, Job again speaks of his righteousness, when he says, "If it is not so [that he is innocent], who will prove me a liar? Who will show that there is nothing in what I say?" He expresses his innocence again at 27:4 and 6, as well, when Job relates:

> My lips will not speak falsehood
> And my tongue will not utter deceit.

And at 27:6, the patriarch Job says:

> I hold fast to my righteousness and will not let it go.
> May heart does not reproach me for any of my days.

In his very last speech in chapter 31, at verses 3 and 4, Job one final time raises the question of the suffering of the innocent in general and his case in particular. Job simply asks about the nature of reality on the earth:

> Does not calamity befall the unrighteous
> And disaster the workers of iniquity?
> Does He not see my ways,
> And number all of my steps?

These many comments of Job about what he says about his innocence, as well as those about why the righteous in general often suffer, all seem to imply the following conclusions. First, Job believes he has done nothing morally wrong. Second, the world does not work according to the ways one might suppose. That is, that often the good suffer, while the wicked appear to be rewarded. Third, Job sometimes begins his remarks about his moral behavior with the conditional *'im*, or "if," suggesting the slightest possibility that he may have sinned.

In fact, in one other passage of the Book of Job, the hero suggests the possibility that he is now being punished for sins committed earlier in his life. This verse comes at 13:26, where Job relates in speaking again to Yahweh, his God:

> For You write bitter things against me,
> and make me reap the iniquities of my youth.

Job may be speaking of himself again at 20:11 when he says of the wicked, "Their bodies were once filled with youth," another occasion when he may be admitting a dalliance in his youth. Thus, we may conclude from these two passages that although Job, for the most part, protests his innocence, he leaves open the possibility that he may have committed sins in his youth.

One other way we can see Job's claim that he is innocent is in the many employments of the word *Naqiy*, or "innocent," in the Book of Job. The words appear eight times in the book. Of those, Job is the speaker seven times, and in the eighth, Elihu, Job's fourth friend, quotes Job directly that he is innocent.[152]

Finally, one way to interpret the various views of Job's suffering in his book is to look at how many verses are assigned to the various characters in the book. The predominant number of verses in the Book of Job are spoken by Job, God, and the fourth friend, the young Elihu. Indeed, the following conclusions might be made about this phenomenon. First, that Job's view is predominantly one that favors what we have called the "Silence of God" Perspective.

In responding to the retributive justice views of Eliphaz, Bildad and Zophar, Job reasons this way, "I am not wicked, yet I am suffering; therefore, God is silent and indifferent to me." Secondly, the predominant views of God and Elihu in the book are mostly the teleological perspectives. That is the Test View, the Moral Qualities Perspective and Divine Plan Theory. Third, we may conclude that the writer(s) of the Book of Job was/were against the Retributive Justice View while favoring the Divine Plan Theory.

This brings us to the major conclusions we have made in this fifth chapter. The subject matter of Chapter Six of this study is the places in the other books of the *Kethuvim*, or "Writings," where the issues of theodicy and the problem of evil are discussed at some length.

Conclusions

We began Chapter Five with a brief introduction to the Biblical Book of Job. In that introduction, we have pointed out that in Job, a more thorough and extensive treatment of evil and suffering may be found than in any other book of the Old Testament, or the Hebrew Bible. We also have pointed out in that introduction that the Book of Job consists of two major parts, a prose prologue and epilogue, and a poetic dialogue between the patriarch and his friends. Indeed, in the introductory section, we have maintained that the prose portion is older than the poetic part.

Along the way, in the introductory portion of the chapter of the Book of Job, we have shown that the book contains far more Aramasms and hapax Legomena than most other Biblical books, as well as a much different classical Hebrew vocabulary. Finally, we also maintained that the character of the Job of the prologue, who appears to be a Patient Job, is far different from the character of Job to be found in the poetry, where the patriarch appears as an angry or iconoclastic Job.[153]

In the second section of Chapter Five, we began by reminding the reader of the four major deontological, or backward-looking answers or responses to the issues of evil and suffering, Namely, the Free Will Defense, Original Sin Theory, the Retributive Justice View, both Individual and Collective, and the Influences of Demonic Forces Theory.

Indeed, in this second section of Chapter Five, we provided a catalog of places in the Book of Job where these five deontological answers or responses might be found. In fact, as we have shown, each of the four has regularly been employed by the writer(s) of the Man from Uz and his book.[154]

The third section of this chapter primarily has been devoted to the places in the Book of Job, where the teleological answers or responses to the issues of theodicy and the problem of evil may be found.

More specifically, in this third section, we identified and discussed the places in the Book of Job where the following theories have been employed: the Contrast View, the Test Theory, the Moral Qualities Approach, and perhaps most importantly, what we have labeled the Divine Plan Point of View in the opening chapter of this study of evil and suffering in the Bible.

After enumerating and discussing the many places where the forward-looking or teleological answers and responses to the origins of Job's evil and suffering, we turned our attention to the fourth section of Chapter Five in the many places in the Book of Job where the patriarch appears to deny that he has sinned and that Retributive Justice does not apply in his case, or where he protests to his friends, and to Yahweh his God, about the conditions of his life.

Indeed, in this final section, we have arrived and expressed four major conclusions about Job's denials and protests. First, he believes he has done nothing morally wrong. Second, that Job believes the world does not work according to the way it should, the good should be rewarded, and the wicked should be punished. Third, we have shown that Job sometimes begins his remarks about his evil and suffering with the Hebrew conditional *'im*, or "if," suggesting the slightest possibility that he may have sinned to deserve his lot. In fact, in chapter 31 of the Book of Job, the patriarch's final speech, he employs the word *'im*, or "if" seventeen times, and in many other places in the book, as well. The examples in chapter 31 come at verses 5, 7–9, 13, 16, 19–21, 24–26, 29, 31 and 33.

We have shown that in several places of his book, the patriarch Job seems to imply that he may have committed sins that occasioned his current conditions when the patriarch was in his youth, such as at Job 13:26, as well as at other places in the book.[155]

Finally, we have shown that one way to evaluate the theological points of view in regard to Job's suffering is to carefully look at how many verses in the book are dedicated to the various characters. Indeed, we have shown that more space in the book is assigned to Job, Elihu and God than to the other characters. One way to interpret this fact is to say that the theological points of view of these three characters are far more important than those of the others in the book.

To that end, we have shown that the teleological responses of these three characters are far more important than the Retributive Justice understanding of Eliphaz, Bildad and Zophar, as well as the views of the Satan in the book.

The subject of Chapter Six of this study shall be the examination of places in other books of the *Kethuvim*, or the "Writings," like Psalms, Proverbs and Ecclesiastes, where the issues of theodicy and the problem of evil have arisen, and have been discussed. Then we shall turn our attention to evil and suffering in the *Kethuvim,* the third portion of the Hebrew Bible or Old Testament.[156]

Chapter Six:
Evil and Suffering in the *Kethuvim*—Psalms, Proverbs, Ecclesiastes and the Book of Daniel

The Wisdom books of the Hebrew Bible are a construct through inference by scholarship and do not figure intrinsically in the constellation of the traditional canon.

—Robert Alter, *Wisdom Books*

The present Hebrew name of the Book of Psalms is *Tehillim*, or "Praises." But in the actual superscriptions of the Psalms, the word *tehillah* is only applied to one psalm, Psalm 145.

— William Smith, *Dictionary of the Bible*

There is no place in the Old Testament where the concept of actions with built-in consequences is so obviously at work as in the case of the Psalms. This is true of many different sections of the Psalms, but particularly in the individual laments.

—James Crenshaw, *Theodicy in the Old Testament*

Introduction

The purpose of this sixth chapter is to make some observations about what the other books of the *Kethuvim*, or Writings, in the Old Testament or Hebrew Bible have to say about evil and suffering. More specifically, we will examine evil and suffering in the Psalms, in Proverbs and Ecclesiastes, as well as in the Book of Daniel, one of the final books of the Hebrew Canon, usually dated to the mid-second century BCE.[157]

Before we get to our analyses of each of the above-mentioned books, however, we first will make some introductory comments on each of these four books, starting with the Psalms, then Proverbs, *Qoheleth*, or Ecclesiastes, ending with the ideas of evil and suffering to be found in the Book of Daniel. We move first, then, to this introductory section of Chapter Six.

Introduction to the Psalms

Until the Enlightenment in the Early Modern Period of the seventeenth and eighteenth centuries, the author of the Psalms was thought to have been King David, who lived around 1,000 BCE. Since the advent of modern Biblical scholarship, in the nineteenth century to the present, however, very few scholars still hold this point of view.

What most scholars of the Psalms now believe is that they were composed by many writers over time, beginning around the time of David on down to the early sixth century BCE. Indeed, most contemporary Biblical interpreters understand that many pairs of hands and minds went into the making of the book that the Hebrews called the *Tehillim*, or "The Praises."[158]

The Book of Psalms contains 150 of these poems or praises. They range in size from being very small, Psalm 117 only has two verses, to 176 verses that can be found in Psalm 119. The earliest texts of the Psalms attribute the work to David. At Psalm 72:20, the Hebrew text tells us that, "David's Psalms are ended." Later on, however, at Psalms 86, 101, 103, and 108 are also attributed to King David. This suggests that there may have been two separate collections of David's Psalms, but they were combined when the smaller was added to the greater.

There are many doublets or duplicates elsewhere in the Psalms, or elsewhere in the Hebrew Bible. Psalm 14 and 53 are nearly identical. Psalm 105:1–15 is very similar to First Chronicles 16:8–22. Many psalms were not included in the book, such as Moses' song of deliverance of Exodus 15:1–18, or Deborah's song of praise in Judges, chapter 5, for example.

Many contemporary scholars divide the Book of Psalms into five parts. These may be summarized this way:

- Part I: Psalm 1–41
- Part II: Psalm 42–72
- Part III: Psalm 73–89
- Part IV: Psalm 90–106
- Part V: Psalm 107–150[159]

Parts I, II and IV are believed to be before the Babylonian Exile. Part III, during the Exile, and Part V is believed to be post-Exilic. In Part I, all but 1, 2, 10, and 33, are attributed to David. Yahweh is used as the name for God 273 times, while Elohim is employed fifteen times.[160] In Part II, the name Elohim is used 164 times, and Yahweh is employed thirty times. In Part III, Yahweh is employed forty-four times and Elohim forty-three times.

In Part IV of the Psalms, Yahweh is used 104 times, and Elohim only has seven instances of God's name. And in Part V, Yahweh is the favored name for God, at 236 times, and Elohim is employed seven times. Psalm 14 and 53 are identical except for the name of God: Yahweh for 14, Elohim for Psalm 53.[161] At Psalm 103, Yahweh is both "Savior" and "Redeemer." At Psalm 104:2–7, Elohim is both "Creator" and "Sustainer."

There are many musical terms used in the superscriptions to describe different types of Psalms. A *shir* is a song of many kinds. *Maski* is used to designate a "special skill" in song. The meaning of a *mitchtam* is not clear, but the word is used six times. The word *palal*, which means "prayer," is used in the superscriptions of Psalms 17, 86, 90, 102, and 142, and maybe Psalm 122:6–9, as well.

The classical Hebrew term, *Shiggzion*, or "lament," is employed throughout the Psalms. This word is used to describe Psalms 6, 7, 38, 51, 59, among many others in the collection of 150.[162] There are also a number of musical terms employed in the Psalms that designate instruments or voices. A *mechiloth*, for example, is a wind instrument. A *Gittith* is a harp in the Psalms, and an *alamoth* is a word that designates a soprano's voice. It is employed four times in the Psalms.[163] A *Neginoth*, a word employed six times in the Psalms, is a "string instrument."[164] And *Sheminth* is used twice in the Psalms. It most likely means an "octave" or an "eighth," for a male voice, as at First Chronicles 15:21.

This brings us to the many places in the Psalms where the issues of the phenomena of evil and suffering may be found in the book. Before we get to that material, however, we will first point to five separate themes, besides answers and responses to evil and suffering, that also contribute to what the Psalms have to say about evil and suffering. We will list them here, and then speak of them one at a time. These five themes are:

- God's Relationship to evil.
- The Book of Deeds.
- The Hidden God Theme.
- Psalms of Lament.
- Justice in evil and suffering.

We will deal with these five themes in the Psalms in reverse order. In several places in the Psalms, the writer(s) speak(s) simply about justice and the distribution of evil and suffering in the lives of people. Psalm 49:10, 73:2–3 and 11–13, and 82:2–5, are three representative examples. In the first of these, the writer says:

> Yea, he shall see that even the wise die
> and the fool and the stupid alike must perish,
> and leave their wealth to others.

The Psalmist wonders why the good and the wise sometimes suffer while the wicked prospers. At Psalm 73:2–3 and 11–13, he wonders about the same issue. The Psalmist relates:

> But as for me, my feet had almost stumbled
> My steps had well-near slipped, for I was envious
> of the arrogant, when I saw the prosperity
> of the wicked.

Also:

> And they say, "How can God know? Is there knowledge in
>   the Most High?"
> Behold these are the wicked, always at ease, and they
>   increase in their riches.

Already, we have spoken of our second theme, the Lament Psalm, that generally may be described as prayers in which the writer laments of God not keeping His side of the Covenantal Relationship. Thus, we see Psalms of Lament at 6, 38, 48, 51, 59, and 88, among many others Consider, for example, Psalm 88:3–5, that reveals:

> For my soul is full of troubles and my life draws near Sheol.
> I am reckoned among those who go down to the Pit,
> like a man who has no strength and one who is forsaken among the dead
> like the slain that lie in the grave, like those who are re-membered no more
> for they are cut off from Thy hand.

The beginning of Psalm 6:1–2 is also the beginning of a Psalm of Lament:

> O Lord, rebuke me not in Thy anger
> Nor chasten me in Thy wrath
> Be gracious to me, O Lord, for I am languishing;
> O Lord, heal me, for my bones are troubled.
> My soul also is sorely troubled.

The theme of the Hidden God, which we have introduced earlier in this study, also can be seen in the Psalms at places like 10:1, 22:1–2 and 38:21. Psalm 10 begins with this question, "Why do you stand afar off, O Lord? Why do you hide yourself in times of trouble?" The opening of Psalm 22 has a similar question, "My God, my God, why have you forsaken me? Why are you so far from helping me from the words of my groaning? O my God, I cry, but you do not answer; and by night but find no rest."

At Psalm 38:21, we see another Song of Lament, where the Psalmist says:

> Do not forsaken me, O Lord!
> My God be not far from me.

The Book of Psalms also contains many examples of the theme of what might be called the "Book of Deeds," which says that God writes down the futures of peoples' lives that must be played out as written. Psalm 56:8 is a good example of that theme:

> Thou has kept count of my tossings.
> Now put my tears in a bottle.
> Are they not in Your book?

Finally, many places in the Book of Psalms explicitly refers to God's relationship to evil, such as at 5:4–6, where it is revealed:

> For You are not a God who delights in wickedness.
> evil may not sojourn with You.
> The boastful may not stand before Your eyes,
> for You hate the evildoers.
> You destroy those who speak lies.
> The Lord abhors bloodthirsty and deceitful people.

In many verses of the Book of Psalms, the Psalmist explicitly tells us that God does not do evil. He does not delight in those who do evil. And He hates all those who are bloodthirsty and deceitful. This brings us to a discussion of the many answers and responses to evil and suffering to be found in the Book of Psalms, the topic of the next section of this sixth chapter.

Responses to evil and suffering in the Psalms

Next to the Book of Job, and perhaps the Proverbs, the Book of Psalms has a wider and deeper understanding of evil and suffering than of any other book of the Bible. Indeed, in the course of the 150 Psalms recorded in the Hebrew Bible, or Old Testament, there is a large variety of answers and responses to be found in the book.

The Psalmist, for example, often endorses both the Individual and the Collective forms of the Retributive Justice Theory. The former may be seen at 37:12 and 29:11, for examples, while the Collective form may be detected at 48:19 that tells us:

He will go to the generations of his fathers
Who will never again see the light.

At Psalm 73:15, the text speaks of, "If I had said I will speak thus, then I would have been untrue to the generations of Your children." Collective Retribution also may be seen at Psalm 112:1–2, as well as a variety of other passages in the book. Individual Retributive Justice Theory may be found at 37:25, 59:12, 45:7, 136:1, 118:1, 73:27, and at many other places in the Book of Psalms.

In one verse of the Psalms, many critics have detected a belief in the Original Sin Theory. It comes at Psalm 51:5 that relates:

Behold, I was brought forth in iniquity
And in sin did my mother conceive me.

Another verse of the Psalms, at 109:6, the Psalmist uses the word *Satan* to designate an "Accuser." Many Christian exegetes have pointed to this verse as an application of the Influence of Demonic Forces Theory. A third verse in the Psalms also has been pointed to as a proof text for the Original Sin Theory. This one comes at Psalm 58:3. Saint Augustine and others, lie Gregory the Great and Thomas Aquinas, find Original Sin in these verses:

The wicked go astray from the womb.
They err from their birth speaking lies.

The Free Will Defense also is advocated by the Psalmist both as indications of choice or as using the Two *Yetzerim* Theory. Psalm 37:4 and 119:108 are examples of the former, and 56:5; 51:17, 72:13, and 73:1, as examples of the latter view.

The writers of the Psalms also regularly employed the two classical Hebrew words for "test" or "try." These are *bachan* and *tsaraph*. Psalm 12:6 uses *tsaraph*, 105:19 and 139:23 employ *bachan*, and 17:3 and 66:10 use both words. Other places in the Psalms where the Test View is assented include 26:2 and 7:9.

Psalm 26:2 relates:

> Prove me O lord, and try me,
> test my heart and my mind.

At 7:9, the Psalmist says to God:

> O let the evil of the wicked come to an end, but establish
>   your righteousness.
> You Who tries the minds and hearts.

On rare occasions, the Psalmist appears to endorse the Contrast View, such as at 17:12, and a variety of other passages in the book. The Book of Psalms regularly mentions what can only be construed as the Divine Plan Theory. The Psalmist, for example, uses future tense verbs at 57:7–10, to speak of a time when the writer will be beyond his present suffering. At Psalm 39:4, the writer asks God to, "Let me know my end, and what is the measure of his days," an obvious reference to the Divine Plan Theory.

At Psalm 33:11, the writer makes another possible reference to the Divine Plan Theory. The verse begins, "The counsel of the Lord stands forever," suggesting that God's plan is an ongoing one. The word for "counsel" here is *etsah* that we saw many times in the Book of Job.

The writers of the Psalms also regularly refer to the chastening of God, His correction, or what we have called the Moral Qualities Theory. At 22:8, 38:1 and 39:11 this theory can be seen. The last of these three tells us, "When You do chasten me with rebukes for my sin." The Psalmist at 22:8 speaks of God "delivering" the writer. And Psalm 38:1 begins with the words:

> O Lord, rebuke me not in Your anger
> Nor chasten me in Your wrath.

The opening of Psalm 6 also employs the verbs "chasten" and "rebuke," or *yasar* and *gaar*. The former is also employed at 2:10, 16:7, 38:1 and 39:11, while the latter is used at 9:5, 68:39, 106:9 and 119:21. And all of these appear to be references to what we have labeled the Moral Qualities Theory.

Finally, of all of the books of the *Kethuvim*, or Writings, the Hidden God Theory may be found more frequently than in any other book. The idea may be found dozens of times in the Psalms, but we will offer three examples. The first of these comes at 13:1, where the Psalmist asks, "How long, oh Lord, will you forget me forever? How long will you hide your face from me?"

A few chapters before this passage, we find the Psalmist at 10:11 again says, "God has forgotten. He has hidden his face. I will never see it again." At Psalm 143:7, the Psalmist again addresses the god Yahweh when he writes:

> Answer me quickly, oh Lord, my spirit fails. Do not hide
>   your face from me,
> or I will become like those who go down into the pit.

One curious fact about uses of the Hidden God Theory in the *Kethuvim* is that they almost entirely come in the context of the Psalmist being in the state of experiencing distress or suffering This is not only true of the Psalms but of other books of the Writings, as well.

This brings us to some introductory comments on the Book of Proverbs, followed by a discussion of the places in that book where the issues of theodicy and the problem of evil are mentioned or discussed.

Introduction to the Book of Proverbs

Like the Book of Psalms, the Book of Proverbs traditionally has been attributed in the Judeo-Christian tradition to a Hebrew king. In this case to King Solomon, King David's son. The Book of Proverbs is mostly made up of pithy sayings or Proverbs. The Hebrew word for these pithy sayings is *mashal*, and the plural is *mashalim*. The verbal form of this word is employed at Psalm 143:7, where it refers to a comparison of two things.

The word *mashal* is used in a variety of ways in the Hebrew Bible, or Old Testament. It may refer to a popular pithy statement, such as at Ezekiel 18:2 or Jeremiah 31:29. The word is also sometimes used to designate a significant, personal experience, as at First Samuel 24:13. The same word is also employed to convey a piece of moral instruction, particularly in what is called the "Wisdom Books" of the sacred text.[165]

In classical Hebrew, the word *mashal* is used to express an allegory or a riddle, as, for example, at Ezekiel 17:2. The same word sometimes stands for a short, didactic poem or essay, such as at Proverbs 1:10 to 19 or 31:10–31. Because of the broad use of the term, Crenshaw is probably correct when he says that the best rendering of the classical Hebrew words *mashal* and *mashalim*, are "saying" and "sayings."[166]

These pithy sayings in ancient Hebrew often come in four separate types. These are called:

- Antithetical Sayings
- Synonymous Sayings
- Synthetic Sayings
- Numerical Sayings[167]

In the first variety of proverbs, the two parts of the text say contradictory things. In the second type, the two parts convey the same idea in both parts. In the Synthetic Sayings, the second line extends what the first line already has said. In the final variety, the numerical Sayings numbers are used to create a poetic structure.[168]

Writers of these ancient Sayings often employed a number of themes and verbal clues in the creating of these sayings. Certain ideas are frequently present in texts that use these sayings. Among these ideas are the following:

- The notion of *Hokmah*, or Wisdom.
- The idea of the Fear of the Lord.
- The ideas of Good and evil.
- The notion of Moral Teachings.
- The idea of Divine Guidance.[169]

Most modern scholars divide the Book of Proverbs into three separate parts. These may be summarized this way:

- Part One: Prologue on Wise Living (chapters 1–9)
- Part Two: Principles for Wise Living (10:1 to 31:9)
- Part Three: Personifications of Wise Living (31:10–31)[170]

The first part mentioned above is mostly the instruction of the young by the old and wise. The first nine chapters are primarily about young believers and how they should be trained in the Wisdom traditions. The second part is about wise sayings for everybody who follows the Lord. These chapters are full of references to wisdom, the fear of the Lord, and the idea that before honor first comes humility. The third part of the Book of Proverbs introduces several personifications, including the referring to wisdom in the feminine form, or with the pronouns she and her.[171] There are other personifications in the Book of Proverbs, as we shall see in this section of this sixth chapter.

The expression the "Fear of the Lord" is mentioned fifty-two times in the Book of Proverbs. It is a complex expression encompassing many aspects of an absolute dependency of humans to the Will of God, submission to His wishes and a turning away from evil. The idea of the Fear of the Lord, we learn from Proverbs 1:7, is the beginning of *binah*, or knowledge.[172]

The Fear of the Lord requires understanding (Prov. 2:5). It involves making choices (Prov. 1:29). It demands absolute obedience, as well as a departure from evil (Prov. 3:7). The result of following these precepts is to live a prolonged life (Prov. 10:27).[173]

The Fear of the Lord may be seen in many places in the Book of Proverbs. Among these are the following passages:

1:17	10:27	16:6	24:21
3:7	14:26	20:2	
8:13	14:27	22:4	
9:10	15:33	23:27[174]	

The Book of Proverbs also contains a large number of mentions of the idea of "Wisdom," as well as many references to the phenomenon of death. The word *ma'veth*, or death, occurs twenty times in the Book of Proverbs. Many of these come in the context of punishment for evildoers. Among these are 2:18; 5:5; 7:27; 8:36; 10:2; 11:4, 7 and 19; 12:28; 13:14; 14:12, 17 and 32; 16:14 and 25; 18:21; 21:6; 24:11; and 26:18.

The word *hokmah*, or wisdom, can be found thirty-eight times in the Book of Proverbs. Many of these occur in the book in the context of the believer acquiring wisdom, such as at 1:2 and 7; 2:2, 6 and 10; 3:13 and 19; 4:5, 12 and 21; 5:1; 7:4; 8:1, 11 and 22; 9:10; 10:13, 23 and 31; 11:2; 13:10; 14:6, 8 and 33; 15:33; 16:16; 17:16 and 24; 18:4; 21:30; 23:23; 24:4 and 14; 28:26; 29:3 and 15; 30:3; and 31:26.[175]

The word *hokmah,* and its verbal forms, are predicated of craftsmen (Exodus 31:3 and 35:31). Also, of skilled persons, such as at Jeremiah 9:17 and 10:9. There appears to have been a Wisdom class in ancient Israel. They were called the *Hokahim*, such as at Jeremiah 18:8 and Ezekiel 7:26, for example.[176] This brings us to the places in the Book of Proverbs, where observations about the phenomena of evil and suffering can be found.

Evil and Suffering in the Book of Proverbs

Like the Books of Job and the Psalms, a variety of answers and responses to evil and suffering may be found in the Book of Proverbs. Both forms of Retributive Justice can be found there, as can the Influences of Demonic Forces Theory, the Free Will Response and the Two *Yetzerim* Theory, Original Sin Theory, as well as the Contrast View, the Test and Moral Qualities Theories, as well as the Divine Plan Point of View.

Individual Retribution is mentioned in at least twenty places in the Book of Proverbs. We will look at three examples to prove the point. At 10:27, for example, the writer of Proverbs relates:

> The fear of the Lord prolongs life,
> But the years of the wicked shall be short.

At Proverbs 16:5, we are told:
> Everyone who is arrogant is an abomination to the Lord.
> Be assured, he will not go unpunished.

A few verses later, at 16:17, we see another example of Retributive Justice:

> The highways of the upright turn aside from evil.
> He who guards his ways, preserved his life.

Three verses later, at Proverbs 16:20, the writer observes, "He who gives heed to the word will prosper, and happy is he who turns to the Lord." At 14:22 of Proverbs, the writer asks the question, "Do they not err who devises evil? While those who are good exhibit loyalty and faithfulness."

Collective Retributive Justice may be seen in the Book of Proverbs at 12:7, 17:13 and at 28:17. In the former, the writer tells us, "The wicked are overthrown and are no more, but the house of the righteous shall stand." At Proverbs 17:13, the text relates, "If a man returns evil for good, then evil will not part from his house." And at Proverbs 28:17, the writer relates:

> If a man is burdened with the blood of another.
> Let him be a fugitive until death. Let no one help him.

At Proverbs 16:28, a number of Christian exegetes, like Thomas Aquinas and John Calvin, for example, have found the influence of perverse men or demons. The text in question tells us:

> A perverse man spreads strife,
> And a whisperer separates close friends.

For both Aquinas and Calvin, the "whispering" refers to the whispering of Satan to get human beings to do evil acts.[177] In fact, in classical Arabic, word *was was*, or "whispering," is only predicated of *Shaytan wa Iblis*, or "Satan" and "Demons."[178]

Some Christian exegetes also suggest that Proverbs 13:17, 18:8 and 30:19 are also related to Satan and his minions. The first of these uses the term "bad messenger who plunges men into trouble." The writer of Proverbs 18:8 again speaks of the "words of a whisperer," which is interpreted by many to be a reference to Satan. And the Proverbs at 30:19 speaks of, "the way of a serpent on a rock," and this too has been seen by many Christian interpreters to be a reference to the Demonic.

There is also a pair of verses in chapter 20 of Proverbs in which many interpreters find the advocacy of the Original Sin Theory. These come at Proverbs 20:9 and 30. The former verse asks this question, "Who can say 'I have made my heart clean? I am pure from my sin.'"

Augustine of Hippo uses this verse as a proof text for the Original
Sin Theory.[179] Augustine also has the same understanding of Proverbs
20:30. The text refers to:

> Blows that would cleanse away evil
> And strokes that make clean the innermost parts.

Both Augustine of Hippo and Gregory the Great of Rome
understand this verse in the Book of Proverbs to be a reference to the
phenomenon of original sin, as well as its eradication by the sacrament
of baptism in the early Christian churches.

The Free Will Defense and the Two *Yetzerim* Theory may be at
the heart of the explanations of Proverbs 6:12–15, 18 and 20, as well as
7:25, among many other passages of the book. At 6:14, the text refers
to a "perverted heart that devises evil." A few verses later, at 6:18, the
writer of Proverbs mentions, "a heart that devises wicked plans," an
obvious reference to the *yetzer ha ra*. Proverbs 6:20–21 provides some
advice for the young:

> Keep your father's commandments
> And forsake not your mother's teaching
> Bind them upon your heart always,
> and tie them around your neck.

In the following chapter, at Proverbs 7:25, the writer again
provides some advice about Free Will. He relates, "Let not your heart
turn away from her ways, do not stray into her paths." This verse
refers to the following of the way of a prostitute. The text advises
the hearer to follow his *yetzer tov,* or "good imagination" or "good
inclination," in a moral sense. References to the Two *Yetzerim* Theory
also can be detected at Proverbs 4:4, 5:12, 6:14, 7:25 and 12:20 that
tells us that:

> Deceit is in the hearts of those who devise evil
> But those who plan good have joy.

In addition to the uses of the Two *Yetzerim* Theory to indicate the
Free Will Defense, the Book of Proverbs provides a number of other

passages that seem to indicate a belief in Free Will. Among these are 1:29, 3:31, 14:22, and 16:1 and 9. Proverbs 1:29 speaks of not "choosing the fear of the Lord," an indication that the writer believes men are free. At Proverbs 3:31, the reader is given some advice about how to use his or her freedom. The text relates:

> Do not envy a man of violence
> And do not choose any of his ways.

At Proverbs 16:9, the text relates:
> A man's mind plans his ways
> But the Lord directs his steps.

Again, this seems to indicate that in the Book of Proverbs, a man's mind is allowed to choose between or among the alternatives that are offered to him. Thus, another indication of the belief in the Free Will Defense. Ultimately, however, as this passage suggests, it is God who determines the steps in life taken by all individuals.

There are also many places in the Book of Proverbs where the text advocates the teleological, or forward-looking responses to the phenomena of evil and suffering. The notion of "chastening," or the Moral Qualities Theory, may be seen at Proverbs 3:11, 16:22 and 19:18, for example. In the former verse, a young man again is given some advice, "My son, do not despise the Lord's discipline or be weary of His reproof, for the Lord reproves him whom He loves as a father the son in whom he delights."

At Proverbs 16:22, the text relates, "Wisdom is a fountain of life to him who has it, but folly is the chastisement of fools." These three verses in chapters 3, 16 and 19, all employ the verb *yacar*, "to chasen," or its derivative, *musawr*, that is most often translated as "chastening."[180]

The Book of Proverbs advocates the Contrast View in several places. The clearest of these is 17:13, where the writer tells us, "If a man returns evil for good, then evil will not depart from his house." This verse uses the word *'ra*, or "evil," twice.

By far, the most references to evil and suffering in the Book of Proverbs come in the context of a belief in the Divine Plan Theory. This view is employed in dozens of places in the book, but we will point to five examples to establish the view in Proverbs. The first of these passages comes at Proverbs 3:5–6, where the text relates:

> Trust in the Lord with all your heart
> and do not rely on your own insight.
> In all of your ways, acknowledge Him,
> And He will make straight your paths.

The writer makes the Divine Plan Theory more explicit at Proverbs 16:4 that tells us, "The Lord has made everything for its purpose, even the wicked for the day of trouble." A few verses later, at 16:9, the writer again endorses the Divine Plan Theory when he observes:

> A man's mind plans his ways,
> But the Lord directs his steps.

And at Proverbs 23:18, the writer again appears to endorse something close to what we have labeled the Divine Plan Theory, when he relates, "Surely, there is a future, and your hope will not be cut off." The only point of view that could explain the meaning of this verse is that God knows how the future will come about, and it will turn out for the Good.

Finally, the Book of Proverbs rarely employs the Hidden God Theory, but it may be found at 2:3–4 and 25:2. In the former, the text speaks of a "search for hidden treasures," of which God only knows. At Proverbs 25:2, the author tells us, "It is the glory of God to conceal things," and that appears to include Himself, as well.

This brings us to an introductory section of this sixth chapter on the Book of Ecclesiastes, followed by an analysis of what that book has to say about the issues of theodicy and the problem of evil.

Introductory Remarks on Ecclesiastes

The Book of Ecclesiastes, or *Qoheleth* in classical Hebrew, is another of the Wisdom books of the Hebrew Bible or Old Testament. The book stands between the Song of Songs and Lamentations, and with them, it belongs to what is called the *Megillot* of five scrolls that are read at various Jewish festivals of the religious calendar.[181]

The common Christian name for the book follows the Greek Septuagint translation that places Ecclesiastes between Proverbs and the Song of Solomon. This makes it consistent with the traditional view that King Solomon wrote Qoheleth, along with Proverbs and the Song of Solomon.[182]

The book reflects the idea of one who questions the traditional doctrine of Retributive Justice. The author's observations on life convinced him that, "The race is not to the swift, nor battle to the strong, nor bread to the wise, nor riches to the intelligent, nor favor to the men of skill, but time and chance happen to them all."[183]

The author of Ecclesiastes suggests that man's fate does not depend on righteousness or wicked conduct, but rather it is an inscrutable mystery that remains hidden in God's Plan alone.[184] All attempts to penetrate this mystery and thereby gain the wisdom necessary to secure one's fate are merely exercises in "vanity" or futility. In the face of such uncertainty, the writer of Ecclesiastes advises us to enjoy the good things that God has given us, while one has them to enjoy.

The writer of Ecclesiastes has a peculiar, Hebrew vocabulary of words and expressions, including the word *hebel*, or "vanity," mentioned earlier. Other words and expressions found in Qoheleth are "striving after wind," "under the Sun," the "fear of God or the Lord," and various words for "curse" and "vow." The word *hebel*, or "vanity," appears at Ecclesiastes 1:2 and 14; 2:19 and 22; 3:19; 4:7 and 16; 6:2, 4, 9 and 11; 7:6; 11:8 and 10; and twice at 12:8. It usually means "futility" in Ecclesiastes, but it also means "vapor" and a number of other things in Ecclesiastes and the rest of the Old Testament.[185]

The expression, "striving after wind," is another way in Ecclesiastes to express futility or meaninglessness. It can be found at Ecclesiastes 1:14 and 17; 2:11, 17, 19 and 26; and 4:5. The expression, "under the sun," is used to express anything that happens on earth in the Book of Ecclesiastes. This phrase is employed twenty-nine times in Ecclesiastes. In all of these, it implies activity of earth, as opposed to the events in Heaven.[186]

Like the other Wisdom books, expressions the "fear of God" and "fear of the Lord" also appear many times in Ecclesiastes, including at 3:14, 5:7, 7:18, 8:5, and 12 and 12:13. These expressions play the same roles as they do in Job, Psalms and Proverbs.[187]

The writer of Ecclesiastes employs two different words for a "vow" or an "oath." These classical Hebrew terms come from the same Semitic root NDR. These words are *nadar* and *neder*. They are used together, and separately, at Ecclesiastes 5:4, 5:4, again, and at 5:5, among other places in the book.[188]

Finally, there are several words in *Qoheleth* that designate "curse." Among these are *sheb'uah* at Ecclesiastes 8:2 and 9:2 and *maroyth* employed at 7:26. Like the other Wisdom books, the writer of Ecclesiastes often spoke of the fate of those who do not keep an oath or promise to Yahweh.

This brings us to the many places in the Book of Ecclesiastes, where the issues of evil and suffering are discussed. As we have mentioned earlier, the writer of *Qoheleth* has serious reservations about what we have labeled the Retributive Justice Theory. This can be seen by looking at 2:12–14; 3:16–21; 7:15; 8:14 and 9:1–3, for good examples. In the first of these, the writer tells us, "The wise man has his eyes in his head, but the fool walks in darkness; and yet, I perceive that one fate comes to them all." At 3:19, the writer of *Qoheleth* tells us that, "The fate of the sons of man and of the beast is the same."

At Ecclesiastes 7:15, the writer expresses the problem of innocent suffering in a very clear way:

> There is a righteous man who perishes in his righteous-
> ness. And there is a
> wicked man who prolongs his life in his evil activity.

The preacher of Ecclesiastes makes the same point at 8:14, when he observes, "There is a vanity which takes place on Earth that there are righteous men to whom it happens according to the deeds of the wicked, and there are wicked men to whom it happens according to the deeds of the righteous."

At the beginning of chapter 9 of Ecclesiastes, at verses 2 and 3, the writer of the book observes:

> Since one fate comes to all, to the righteous and the
> wicked, to those who are good and those who are evil,

to the clean and the unclean, to those who sacrifice and those who don't. As is the good man so is the sinner. And he who swears is the same as one who shuns an oath. This is an evil in all that is under the son—that one fate comes to all.

Although the preacher is skeptical of the Retribution Theory, nevertheless, he seems to imply that theory on several occasions. He also seems to endorse the Contrast View, the Influence of Demonic Forces Theory, possibly the Original Sin Perspective, the Test View, the Free Will Defense, using the Two *Yetzerim* Approach, as well as the Divine Plan Theory.

At 2:26, the preacher tells us:

To the man who pleases him God gives wisdom and knowledge, and joy, but to the sinner he gives the work of gathering and heaping, only to give God one who pleases him.

In the very last verse of the Book of Ecclesiastes, the writer again seems to support the Retributive Justice Theory when he writes, "For God will bring every deed into judgment, with every secret thing— whether good or evil." At Ecclesiastes 7:29, we find an example of the Free Will Defense, when the preacher writes, "See this alone, I found that God made human beings straight forward, but they have devised many schemes." This devising, of course, could only come about by the exercising of Free Will.

The writer of Ecclesiastes also appears to assent to the Test View at 2:1, 3:18 and 7:23. In each of these, he employs the verb "to test" or "to try." In the former verse, the writer speaks of "making a test of pleasure." At Ecclesiastes 3:18, the preacher speaks, "God testing humans to show that they are but beasts." And at 7:23, the writer relates that "All of this I have tested by wisdom."

In at least two places, and perhaps more, the preacher refers to what we have called the Contrast View. These come at 2:13 and 3:16. The former tells us, "Then I saw that wisdom excels folly, as light excels darkness." At 3:16, the preacher relates:

> Moreover, I saw under the sun that in the place of
> justice, there was even wickedness, and in the place of
> righteousness, there was even wickedness.

Both at Ecclesiastes 9:3 and at 10:2, the writer of the book uses the Two *Yetzerim* Theory. In the former, the writer tells us that the hearts of human beings are "full of evil." And in the latter, "A wise man's heart inclines him toward the right, but a fool's heart toward the left." The ancient Jews, like those in Medieval Europe, saw the left as evil, while the right inclines one toward the Good. In fact, the Medieval Latin word for the Left was *Sinestre*, or "Sinister."[189] This may have something to do with the good thief to Jesus' right at the Crucifixion and the bad thief to the left.

The preacher of Ecclesiastes may assert a belief in the Influence of Demonic Forces Theory in three separate verses. The first of these comes at 10:8, which relates, "He who digs a pit will fall into it, and a serpent will bite him who breaks through a wall." The second passage comes three verses later, at 10:11 that relates:

> If a serpent bites before it is charmed, then there is no
> advantage to the charmer.

Many Christian interpreters of the Book of Ecclesiastes understand 3:17 and 10:8 as references to both good and bad angels when the text reports:

> I said in my heart, God will judge the righteous and the
> wicked, for He has appointed a time for every matter,
> as well as every work.

Among the Christian thinkers who believe that this verse is about the good and the bad angels is Thomas Aquinas in his *Summa Theologica*.[190] Thomas Aquinas also thought that the Original Sin Theory was at the heart of the explanation of Ecclesiastes 7:20. This verse reveals:

> Surely, there is not a righteous man on Earth who does
> the good and who never sins.

The same interpretation of Ecclesiastes also can be seen in Gregory the Great's *Moralia in Job*.[191] Finally, many interpreters of the Book of *Qoheleth* have found the Divine Plan Theory as an explanation for evil and suffering. The poem at 3:1–9, for example, speaks of a "time" for various phenomena in life as if these "times" are only known to God. The preacher makes a similar observation at Ecclesiastes 3:17 when he writes:

> I said in my heart that God will judge the righteous
> and the wicked, for He has appointed a time for every
> matter, and for every work.

In summary, then, we have maintained that the preacher of *Qoheleth* has asserted, or assented to, the following answers or responses to the issues of evil and suffering: Retributive Justice Theory, the Free Will Defense, Original Sin Theory, the Influences of Demonic Forces View, the Test Perspective, the Contrast View, and the Divine Plan Perspective.

The author of *Qoheleth*, or Ecclesiastes, also endorses the Hidden God Theory at three places. These come at 3:11, 8:17 and 12:14. In the first of these, the text relates:

> He has made everything beautiful in its own time. He
> also has put eternity into men's minds, yet they cannot
> find out what God has done from the beginning until
> the end.

The preacher of Ecclesiastes continues the same theme at 8:17, where he says, "Then I saw the work of God that man cannot find out, the work that is done under the sun." And at 12:14, the preacher brings the Hidden God Theory together with Divine Plan Perspective, when he relates:

> For God will bring every deed into judgment, with every
> secret thing, whether good of evil.

This brings us to the final two sections of this sixth chapter—an introduction to the Book of Daniel, and the issues of theodicy and the problem of evil in the Book of Daniel in the Hebrew Bible, or Old Testament. The conclusions to Chapter Six will follow these sections.

The subject matter of Chapter Seven of this study shall be the many places in what is sometimes called the "Intertestamental Period," where discussions and perspectives on evil and suffering may be found.

Introduction to the Book of Daniel

The Book of Daniel is the final text we will analyze of those among the *Kethuvim*, or "Writings." In the Christian canon, however, the Book of Daniel is numbered among the *Nabiim*, or Prophets. The first half of the Book of Daniel, chapters one to six, contains narratives written in the third person about the experiences of Daniel and his friends under King Nebuchadrezzar II, Darius the First, and King Cyrus the Second.[192]

The second half of the Book of Daniel is mostly written in the first person. It contains reports of three of Daniel's "visions," as well as the account of one of his dreams. The second half of the book also names Daniel as the author who, according to chapter one, was exiled during the Babylonian captivity.

Most modern scholars date the Book of Daniel to the second century BCE. The overall message of the book is clear: In the same way that the God of Israel saved Daniel and his friends from their enemies, so He will also save and restore all of Israel in his present oppression.

Another interesting feature of the Book of Daniel is that the book is written in classical Hebrew in chapters one and eight to twelve, while chapters two to seven are written in the Aramaic language. The Aramaic portions of Daniel are constructed in a chiastic form that might be described as "A, B, C, B, A."[193] Most scholars describe the contents of the Book of Daniel this way:

- Chapter One: Introduction in Babylon
- Chapter Two: Nebuchadnezzar's Dream of Four Kingdoms
- Chapter Three: The Fiery Furnace
- Chapter Four: The Madness of Nebuchadnezzar
- Chapter Five: Belshazzar's Feast
- Chapter Six: Daniel in the Lion's Den
- Chapter Seven: Vision of the Beasts from the Sea

- Chapter Eight: Vision of the Ram and the Goat
- Chapter Nine: Vision of the Seventy Weeks
- Chapter Ten to Twelve: Vision of Kings of the North and South[194]

One other feature of significance about the Book of Daniel is that in the Greek version, the Septuagint Bible, the text of Daniel is much longer than the Hebrew/Aramaic text. This is due to the additions of three supplemental narratives that remain in the Roman Catholic and Orthodox Bibles but were rejected by the Protestant churches beginning in the sixteenth century. This was mostly because these three stories do not appear in the Hebrew Canon.[195]

The names of these additional narratives are The Prayer of Azariah and the Song of the Three Holy Children (placed after Daniel 3:23). The story of Susanna and the Elders (placed before chapter 1 in some Greek texts and after chapter 12 in others). The Story of Bel and the Dragon (placed at the close of the book in the Septuagint).[196]

It is most likely the case that the Book of Daniel originated as a collection of Aramaic tales with later classical Hebrew revelations and editing of the text. The book is preserved in the twelfth chapter Masoretic text, as well as in two longer Greek Septuagint versions. The final version of the Hebrew-Aramaic text is most likely dated sometime around 100 BCE.[197] This brings us to the final section of Chapter Six— an analysis of the issues of evil and suffering in the Book of Daniel.

Evil and Suffering in the Book of Daniel

The variety of answers and responses to the issues of theodicy and the problem of evil in the Book of Daniel is not nearly as large as the other books of the writings that we have examined. For the most part, the major theological responses in Daniel are examples of the Retributive Justice Theory, Collective Retribution, the Contrast Perspective, and Divine Plan Theory, including indications of that view using future tense verbs, particularly in chapters 11 and 12.

The Book of Daniel is filled with examples of the Individual Retributive Justice, such as at 3:6, 11, 15, 24, and 30; 6:23–28; and

12:1–3 and 13. In the first of these, the text relates, "Whoever does not fall down and worship the king shall be cast into a fiery furnace." A similar verse may be found at 3:11, where it tells us, "Whoever does not fall down and worship the golden image shall be cast into a burning, fiery furnace." Similar verses also may be found at 3:15, 24 and 30.

At the end of chapter 6, Daniel triumphantly emerges from the lion's den, mostly because he "trusted in his God." As a result, King Darius orders his people to fear "before the God of Daniel." This also may be interpreted as the Individual Retributive Justice Theory. Occasionally, the Book of Daniel appears to assent to the Collective Retributive Justice Theory, as well. Consider, for example, 9:16:

> O Lord, according to all of Your righteous acts, let Your anger and Your wrath turn away from the city of Jerusalem, Your holy will because for our sins and the iniquities of our fathers, Jerusalem and Your people have become a byword among all who are around us.

In a few examples in the Book of Daniel, the Contrast View may be detected, such as at 2:21–22 that relates to God:

> He changes times and seasons.
> He removes kings and sets up kings.
> He gives wisdom to the wise,
> and knowledge to those who have understanding.
> He reveals deep and mysterious things.
> He knows what is in the darkness
> And the light dwells within Him.

Like many of the other books of the *Kethuvim* that we have examined in this study, the Divine Plan Theory is the foundation of the views on evil and suffering to be found in the Book of Daniel. At chapter 4:26, for example, the text tells us, "Your kingdom shall be sure for you from the time that you know that Heaven rules." A few verses later, at 4:34, the writer of Daniel relates:

> I blessed the Most High, and praised and honored him who lives forever, for His dominion is an everlasting

dominion, and His kingdom endures from generation
to generation.

In several verses of chapters 11 and 12 of the Book of Daniel, the
writer employs future tense verbs to indicate the Divine Plan Theory,
such as at 11:2, 3, 5, 7, 9, 11–13, and 29–33. There is no place in the
Old Testament, or Hebrew Bible, however, that is more explicit about
Yahweh's final dispositions of human life on Earth than Daniel 12:1–3
and 13. At 12:2, the writer of Daniel exclaims:

And many of those who sleep in the dust of the Earth
shall awake, some to everlasting life, and some to
everlasting contempt. And those who are wise shall
shine like the brightness of the firmament.

The final fulfillment of Yahweh's Plan in the Book of Daniel is
the belief that at the end of time, the righteous shall be rewarded and
the wicked shall be punished. Indeed, at the final verse of the Book of
Daniel, at 12:13, the holy text reiterates:

But go your way until the end comes, and you shall rest,
and you shall stand in your allotted place at the end of
the days.

The Hidden God theme does not explicitly appear in the Book of
Daniel, but two verses of the book suggest the theory. These come at
2:22 and 2:28. In the former, the text says of God, "He reveals deep
and mysterious things. He knows what is in the darkness and the light
dwells with Him." A few verses later, at Daniel 2:28, the writer again
refers to "mysteries" that he has made known to King Nebuchadnezzar
now, and to everyone in the "latter days."

This brings us to the major conclusions of this chapter. The
subject matter of Chapter Seven of this study is the phenomena of evil
and suffering in the Intertestamental Period, which is the period from
roughly 150 BCE until 50 CE.

Conclusions

We have begun this sixth chapter with an introduction to the Book of Psalms by arguing against the traditional ascription of the book to King David around 1000 BCE. Instead, we have suggested that the book evolved over time until sometime around the fifth century BCE. We also have indicated in the opening section of Chapter Six that five major themes appear throughout the Book of Psalms. These theological themes were: God's Relation to evil; the Book of Deeds; the Hidden God Theory; Psalms of Lament; and Justice, evil, and suffering in the book.

This material was followed by a discussion of the places in the Psalms where answers and responses to evil and suffering may be found in the book. In that second section, we have shown that the writers of the Book of Psalms have asserted to, or have endorsed both forms of the Retributive Justice Theory, the Original Sin Perspective, the Influences of Demonic Forces Theory, the Test View, the Contrast View, and the Divine Plan Theory.

An introduction to the Book of Proverbs was the next section of Chapter Six, followed by the answers and responses to evil and suffering that may be found in the Book of Proverbs. In that section we pointed out uses of the writers of Proverbs of both forms of Retribution; the Demonic Influences Theory; the Original Perspective; the Free Will Defense, including uses of the Two *Yetzerim* Theory; as well as the Contrast View; the Test Perspective; and the Moral Qualities Approach.

These sections of Chapter Six were followed by an introduction to the Book of Ecclesiastes, as well as a separate section on the answers and responses to evil and suffering that may be found in that book. In the summary of those sections of Chapter Six, we maintained that the writers of the Book of Ecclesiastes have assented to theRetributive Justice Theory, the Free Will Defense, Original Sin Theory, the Contrast View, the Influences of Demonic Forces Perspective, and the Divine Plan Theory.

In the final two sections of Chapter Six, we supplied an introduction to the Book of Daniel, followed by a summary of the places in the book where answers and responses to the issues of theodicy and the problem of evil may be found.

More specifically, we have shown at the end of the chapter that the writer of the Book of Daniel has employed both forms of the

Retributive Justice Theory, the Contrast Perspective and, above all, to an assenting to the Divine Plan Point of View, particularly with respect to resurrection of the body in chapter 12 of that work, in regards to the end of time, or the resurrection of the dead.

We shall now turn to Chapter Seven, the subject matter of which shall be evil and suffering to be found in the Intertestamental Period. That is, the time between the close of the Old Testament and the beginning of the New Testament. So next, we turn to answers and responses in the Intertestamental Period to the issues of theodicy and the problem of evil.

Chapter Seven:
Evil and Suffering in the Intertestamental Period

The period between the Old Testament and the New
Testament is one of the most overlooked eras of Biblical
history. During that era, Aristotle developed his system
of thought and logic that are still with us today.

—R. C. Sproul, "The Intertestamental Period"

During the four-hundred-year intertestamental period,
God's people experienced significant challenges and
spiritual declension. The four-hundred-year period was
characterized by six historical eras: the Persian Era; the
Greek Era; the Egyptian Era; the Syrian Era; the Maccabean Era; and the Roman Era.

—D. W. Ekstrand, "The Intertestamental Period"

The "Four Hundred Years of Silence," of the intertestamental period were broken by the greatest story ever
told—the Gospel of Jesus Christ.

—Raymond Surburg, *Introduction to the Intertestamental Period*

Introduction

The main purpose of this chapter is to explore the many places in the
period known as the Intertestamental Period, from the Book of Malachi,
around 400 BCE, until the time of John the Baptist in the early first
century CE. The "Intertestamental Period" is a Protestant term for

that period of time. Whereas, Catholics and the Orthodox Christian Churches refer to the period as the "Deuterocanonical Period."[198]

We will begin Chapter Seven with a summary of many of the texts that are believed to have been written in the Intertestamental Period. In that opening section of this chapter, we will mention approximately two dozen works believed to have come from this period.

In a second and central section of Chapter Seven, we shall enumerate several theological ideas that, for the most part, are not found in the Old Testament, but are found in the New Testament. This raises the question of where these ideas have originated and how they were borrowed or incorporated into Judaism and Early Christianity in the Intertestamental Period.

Among these ideas, as we shall see in the second section of this seventh chapter, are:

- Satan as a Demonic Force
- Original Sin
- The Fallen Angels Story
- Resurrection of the Body
- Immortality of the Soul
- The Final Judgment
- Many other ideas

Although many of these ideas sporadically may be found in the Hebrew Bible, they are abundantly present in the New Testament.

This brings us to a description of many of the books constructed during the Intertestamental Period, and when these books were written. Many of these books, as we shall see, have a number of answers and theological responses to the issues of Theodicy and the problem of evil.

Intertestamental Books

Among the ancient works that have been associated with the Intertestamental Period are the following: the *Book of Enoch*, written sometime between 300 and 100 BCE; the *Book of the Watchers,* written around 300 BCE; The *Epistle of Enoch*, constructed around 170 to 150 BCE; *Ecclesiasticus*, also known as *Sirach*, written between 200 and 170 BCE; the *Book of Tobit*, usually dated between 350 and 250 BCE; and the Books of *First and Second Maccabees*, constructed between 175 and 150 BCE.

Other books generally associated with the Intertestamental Period are the *Book of Wisdom*, from the mid-second century BCE; *First and Second Esdras,* most likely from the first century CE; The *Gospel of Bartholomew*, a first-century CE Gnostic text; and the *Testament of Job*, a first-century BCE or first-century CE work. The *Ascension of Isaiah* is another first-century CE text as well as the *Apocalypse of Baruch*, which was originally written in Syriac and is quoted by Origen, a church father in the third century CE.[199] Also, the *Gospel of Thomas*, most likely a first century CE text, and many other ancient texts not mentioned here.[200]

The fourteen books of the Biblical Apocrypha are also considered texts from the Intertestamental Period, as are the texts known as the *Pseudepigrapha,* including the *Assumption of Moses*, the *Letter of Aristeas*, and the *Testament of the Twelve Patriarchs*, among many other works.

We also will comment in this chapter on a number of texts to be found among the Dead Sea Scrolls, another source of material in the Intertestamental Period. Indeed, many of the ideas that can be found in the Dead Sea materials are precursors to theological ideas that may be found in the New Testament, as we shall see.

All the texts we have mentioned in this section were written or developed in the period from the final book of the Old Testament, Malachi, around 400 BCE, to the development of the earliest portions of the New Testament in the early first century CE. Thus, each is an exemplary book of the Intertestamental Period.

There are two separate ways in which these books contribute to Biblical understandings of what the writers believed about the questions of theodicy and the problem of evil. The first of those ways is the many places where these intertestamental works employed many of the answers and responses to the phenomena of evil and suffering that we have seen throughout this study.

Indeed, many of these intertestamental works assent to both the deontological, or backward-looking responses, as well as the teleological, or the forward-looking, theological answers and responses we have introduced back in Chapter One of this study. In the next section, we will look at some of these examples.

The second way that works in the Intertestamental Period have contributed to the history of theological views about evil and suffering is the many places where we can see the early development of ideas that appear in the New Testament, but, for the most part, are not to be found in the Old Testament.

As we have indicated earlier in this chapter, among those Biblical theological ideas were the following:

- Satan as a Demonic Force
- Original Sin
- The Fallen Angels Story
- Resurrection of the Body
- Immortality of the Soul
- The Final Judgment at the End of Time

All of these ideas, as we shall see in this chapter, may be found in the Intertestamental Period. Before we get to that material, however, we will first examine how the intertestamental books have used, or assented to, many of the theological answers and responses to evil and suffering we have seen throughout this study.

Answers and Responses to Evil and Suffering in the Intertestamental Period

Among the intertestamental books is a work called "The Gospel of Thomas," also known as the "Coptic Gospel of Thomas." It was discovered near Nag Hammadi in Egypt in December of 1945, among a group of other works known as the Nag Hammadi Library.[201] Scholars have proposed dates for the Gospel of Thomas from as early as 60 CE to as late as 140 CE.[202]

The Gospel of Thomas is important for our purposes because It seems to employ at least three of our answers and responses to evil and suffering in the "114 Sayings of Jesus." In this sense, the work is more like a compendium of quotations from Jesus than it is a biography, like the four canonical Gospels, Matthew, Mark, Luke and John.[203]

At saying 13, Jesus relates, "If I tell you one of the sayings He has spoken to me, you will pick up rocks and stone me, and fire will come from the rocks and devour you."[204] This saying, which appears to be an example of the Retributive Justice Theory, also adds at saying 14:

> After all, what goes into your mouth will not defile you.
> But what comes out of your mouth will.[205]

Again, the author of the Gospel of Thomas seems to suggest, in a retributive way, that one is not what he eats. Rather, he should be understood in terms of what comes out of his mouth, an example of the Retributive Justice Theory.[206] At Saying 18, Jesus relates something that reminds us of the Divine Plan Theory, when he observes:

> Have you found the beginning, then, that you are looking for the end? You see the end will be where the beginning is. Congratulations to the one who stands at the beginning—that one will know the end and will not taste death.[207]

In this saying, it is clear that Jesus knows the beginning, as well as the end of things, and the relationship between the two, as well as how things will turn out for the good in the end. At Saying 24, Jesus' remark reminds us of the Contrast View, when he says:

> Anyone here with two ears had better listen. There is light within a person of light, and it shines on the whole world. If it does not shine, then it is dark, and the person is not a person of the light.[208]

Here, the writer of the Gospel of Thomas uses the ancient Persian contrast in which light is a symbol of the good, and darkness a symbol of evil. In addition to the writer of the Gospel of Thomas assenting to the Retributive Justice Theory, the Divine Plan View, and the

Contrast Perspective, on at least two occasions, he also speaks of the Two *Yetzerim* Theory, at Sayings 28 and 69. In the first of these, Jesus proclaims:

> My soul ached for the children of humanity, because
> they are blind in their hearts and they do not see, for
> they came into the world empty, and they also seek to
> depart from the world empty, as well.[209]

The idea of being "blind in their hearts" may well be a reference to the Two *Yetzerim* Theory, for the heart, or *leb*, in first-century Judaism, was believed to be the center for the self, as well as one's moral decisions.[210] At Saying 69 in the Gospel of Thomas, the writer again comments in a way that suggests the same first-century idea, when Jesus remarks:

> Congratulations to those who have been persecuted in
> their hearts. They are the ones who have truly come to
> know the Father.[211]

In this saying from the Gospel of Thomas, it may be seen as a combining of the *yetzerim* theory with the Moral Qualities or the Test View, for the heart has been "persecuted," presumably to make him, or her, better morally.

Many of the other books of the Intertestamental Period also have remarked on the issues of evil and suffering. Adolf Neubauer, an editor of *The Book of Tobit*, for example, gives this summary of the book:

> Theodicy, the vindication of God's justice, is the book's
> central motif. Tobit, the story's protagonist, is by every
> account a pious and upright Israelite who does not
> deserve the intense suffering he experiences.[212]

Indeed, Neubauer goes on to discuss a number of central affinities to the Biblical Book of Job, including the righteousness of the heroes and their lack of confidence in physicians to alleviate their troubles.[213] The *Testament of Job* is an anonymous text purported to be the final testament of the Hebrew patriarch Job. Most authorities date the *Testament of Job* between 200 and 170 BCE. The book includes Job's combat with Satan, his debates with his friends, who are kings in the testament, and the book ends in a Retributive Justice twist when Job dies peacefully and full of grace.

Thus, the *Testament of Job* endorses the Influences of Demonic Forces Theory, the Test Perspective, Retributive Justice Theory, and perhaps the Divine Plan Point of View, for everything works out for the good at the end of the book.[214]

The Book of Sirach, or *Ecclesiasticus*, mentions the figure of Job. Indeed, the book places a premium on the patriarch's patience. The writer of *Sirach*, at 49:9, relates "Job who held fast to all the ways of justice."[215] The Book of Sirach also mentions the Two *Yetzerim* Theory at 17:16, where it speaks of the heart (Free Will Defense). It speaks of God creating human beings with the "power of choice" at 15:24 (Free Will Theory); he speaks of the "Testing" of human beings at 27:5 (the Test View); and the writer of Sirach appears to endorse the Divine Plan Theory when the text relates:

> God gave human beings a set number of days, as well
> as a fixed time.[216]

This may be an example of the Old Testament idea of the Book of Deeds, in which it was thought that God has written down in a book all that will happen in the lives of humans from the beginning of time. If this is true, the writer ties this idea here to the Divine Plan Theory.

The *Book of Jubilees*, a second-century BCE work completed between 135 and 105 BCE, makes a number of references to evil and suffering in the text, including extensive comments on the *Akedah* narrative, the Sacrifice of Isaac story of Genesis 22. It also treats the fallen angels' story as the first use of the Free Will Defense in the Judeo-Christian Tradition.[217] Thus, we have seen that there are a variety of views in the intertestamental books, where the writers of these books appear to endorse many of the traditional answers and responses we have seen throughout this study.

The two best places in intertestamental literature to see references to the Fallen Angels narrative are Jubilees 10 and First Enoch 10:11–13. The same narrative also appears in two of the Dead Sea Scrolls, at

1QM 13:11–12 and 1QS 3:21–24. In these stories, God creates the evil, demonic angels to rule the realm of evil, until the eschatological times when the evil forces will be destroyed.

Another theological theme in all of these works, as well as in the New Testament, is the idea that there will be realms of Light and Darkness that will be restricted to a certain period. At 1QS 2:19, the text refers to, "The days of Belial's dominion." At First Enoch 16:1, as well, we find a similar term to describe the realm of evil. The *Damascus Document*, also found among the Dead Sea Scrolls, relates that "During those years, Belial will be sent against Israel."[218]

This notion that there will be epochs of evil and good may be another example of how Zoroastrianism, which had a deterministic view of time, can be seen in the texts from Qumran, at places like the *Damascus Document* and 1QpHab 7:13–14.[219] We will say more about these epochs of good and evil in the next section.

This brings us to the central section of this chapter, an analysis of the many places in the intertestamental books where ideas found in the New Testament are not found in the Old Testament, while at the same time, they may be found in the intertestamental literature.

Intertestamental Influences on the New Testament

The purpose of this central section of Chapter Seven is to show that the Intertestamental Period literature had a major influence on theological principles that appear in the New Testament, while not, generally speaking, being ideas promulgated in the Old Testament. In this section, we will speak of six of these ideas, and point out where they can be found in the intertestamental texts.

The first of these ideas is the notion that Satan is to be conceived as a Demonic figure. This idea can often be seen in the books between the testaments, such as at Sirach 15:11–17, 21:27, and 27:5–6. The Book of Jubilees 17:18 also has the same idea, as do the sixth and eleventh chapters of the *Ascension of Isaiah*. At the Book of Jubilees 17:18, the demonic figure's name is Mastema. He is called to entice the patriarch Abraham to kill his son, Isaac, principally by the act of whispering. Thus, Jubilees combines here the Influences of Demonic Forces Theory with the Test Perspective.

It is difficult to find the idea of Original Sin in the Old Testament, but it may be seen in three places of the intertestamental literature. These come at Tobit 12:9, in the Wisdom of Solomon, at 2:24 and 8:19–20, as well as at Sirach 12:4–7. At the Wisdom of Solomon 2:24, the writer of the text tells us:

> Nevertheless, through envy of the Devil, death came
> into the world, and those who hold to his side will find
> it. For all shall die for all suffer from sin.

Three passages in Second Esdras also advance the idea of Original Sin. These come at 3:21–22, 4:30 and 7:118. In the first of these, the text relates:

> For the first Adam, burdened with an evil heart,
> transgressed and was overcome, as were all who were
> descendants from him. Thus, the disease became
> permanent. The Law was in the hearts of the people,
> along with the evil root, but what was good departed,
> and the evil remained.

At Second Esdras 4:30, the book again reveals, "For a grain of evil again was sown in Adam's heart from the beginning, and how much ungodliness has it produced, and will produce until the time of threshing comes." The "time of threshing," of course, is the resurrection of the dead at the end of time.

At 7:118 of Second Esdras, we see another nod in the direction of the Original Sin Theory. The text tells us:

> O Adam, what have you done? For though it was you
> who sinned, the fall was not yours alone, but ours as
> well who are your descendants.

Scholar Geza Vermes, in his book, *Christian Beginnings from Nazareth to Nicea*, suggests that the idea of "ancestral fault" may have arisen with Classical Greek culture. He quotes Greek critic, Celsus, who attributes this ancestral fault to a priest of Apollo or Zeus. Vermes quotes Celsus as saying, "The mills of the gods grind slowly, even to their children, and their children's children, and to those born after them."[220] Thus, the idea of ancestral fault, and therefore Original Sin may be a Greek influence on the New Testament.

Japanese scholar F. Onayemi holds the same view in his essay, "Sin, punishment, and Forgiveness in Ancient Greek Religion," published in the *Journal of Philosophy and Culture*.[221] Onayemi refers to ancestral sin as *progonikon hamartema*, and he suggests the idea may have arisen related to the idea of *Hubris*, which may have been believed to be inherited in ancient Greek religion.[222]

The third chapter of the *Book of Tobit*, verses 8 and 17, speaks of a demon known as Asmodeus. This same figure can be seen throughout the book, such as a narrative in which Asmodeus kills the nine successive husbands of a woman named Sarah on their wedding nights. Asmodeus is called the "Demon of Demons" in some ancient Jewish texts.

The narrative known as the Fallen Angels story is not featured in the Old Testament, but versions of the narrative can be seen in the Book of Watchers in chapter 6, in chapter 18 of Enoch, and chapters 4 and 5 of *Jubilees*. In the Book of Watchers, the Fallen Angels story is told at chapter 6, verses 1–7. In the *Book of Jubilees*, the same tale is told at 4:15 and 5:1.

In *Second Enoch*, the story of the Fallen Angels narrative can be found when Enoch travels to the Fifth Heaven, where we are told that some of the angels "rebelled against their Maker."

The idea of Resurrection of the Body can be seen in the Old Testament at the Book of Daniel 12:1–3, but the idea first appears among the texts of the Intertestamental Period, such as in the "Gospel of Bartholomew," in Second Maccabees, the *Testament of Job*, the *Ascension of Isaiah*, the *Apocalypse of Baruch*, and the Books of Enoch.

The best examples in these books come at 36:11 of the *Apocalypse of Baruch* and the Book of Enoch that divides Sheol into four compartments while awaiting the Resurrection of the Dead at the End of Time. At the *Apocalypse of Baruch's* 36:11, the narrator speaks to the evil occupants of Sheol, awaiting the resurrection. It tells us:

> And now reclining in anguish and rest in torment until
> your last time has come, In which you will come again,
> and then be tormented even more.

The Book of Enoch divides Sheol into four compartments, while the residents await the Resurrection of the Dead. This text tells us about these four compartments: Faithful Saints (they will be resurrected and rewarded), The Moderately Good (they await their reward), The Moderately Wicked (they will be punished at the resurrection of the Dead), and The Faithless Wicked (they do not warrant resurrection).[223]

This view of the writer of Enoch is far more sophisticated than anything that may be found in the Old Testament. While at the same time, it is comparable to ideas about the Resurrection of the Body in the New Testament. Similarly, there is very little to be found in the Old Testament about the *nefesh* and *ruah*, or "soul" and "spirit," nor about the possibility of Immortality of the Soul.

Among the books of the Intertestamental Period, however, immortality is often featured there in such works as *Second Esdras*, the *Wisdom of Solomon*, the *Testament of Job*, as well as the *Book of Tobit*. At *Second Esdras* 2:45, for example, speaks of those "who have put away their mortal clothing, and then put on their immortal clothing."

There are portions of the *Testament of Job* that also suggest a belief in the book of both Immortality of the Soul and Resurrection of the Body. At 39:5 of the *Testament*, Job's wife asks some soldiers to pick through the ruins of their house to find the bodies of their dead children. But Job 39:9 says the search would be fruitless for the children, "Already have been taken up into the Heavens by their Creator." This would appear to be a belief in the immortality of the soul or eternal life.

In *Wisdom of Solomon* 2:21–24, the writer again relates, "For God created men to be immortal and also to be the image of His own eternality." Thus, it is clear that a number of writers of books from the Intertestamental Period appear to have advocated beliefs in both the Resurrection of the Body, as well as in Immortality of the Soul, or Eternal Life.

The theological idea of a Final Judgment at the End of Time is an idea that may be found many times in the New Testament. It is difficult, however, to find that idea in the Old Testament, except in the narrative in the Book of Daniel 12:1–3. Nevertheless, the idea of a Final Judgment may be found in the intertestamental literature at *Second Maccabees* chapter 2:45ff and in chapter four of the *Apocalypse of Bruch*.

The text in *Maccabees* tells us:

> For if it were not explained that those who were fallen would rise again, then it would have been superfluous to pray for the dead. But if we were looking for a love for those who have fallen asleep, it has a long and pious thought. Therefore, he made atonement for his sin, so that at the resurrection he will be delivered from his sin.

The scene of the Final Judgment can also be seen in chapter 5, verses 1 to 6 of the *Apocalypse of Baruch*. The text relates:

> Yahweh said, "My name and My splendor shall last for all eternity. And My judgment shall assent its right in its own time."

In the first Book of Enoch, an account of the Final Judgment may be found at 54:7. This account is interesting because, a little later in the text at 56:5–8, it gives an account of the judgment of Azaz'el, the Demon in the Books of Enoch, who rules the other Demons. Thus, among these books of the Intertestamental Period, we have seen various names to stand for the Demonic, including Satan, Mastema, Asmodeus and Azaz'el.

Earlier in this chapter, we mentioned the idea that in intertestamental literature, there was a belief that there will be epochs of evil and the good in human history, an idea first seen in Persian Zoroastrianism. At the Dead Sea Scroll text, 1QS 2:19, it speaks of the "Days of Belial's dominion." This idea will be discussed later in this seventh chapter. The same view can be seen in the Book of Revelation.

Another Intertestamental Period idea that is difficult to find in the Old Testament but proliferated in the Intertestamental Period is the New Testament idea of the Holy Spirit. This idea or theme may be found at First Maccabees 4:46, 9:27 and 14:41. In the first of these, the text tells us, "And put the stones in a suitable place on the temple hill, where they were to be kept until the Holy Spirit appears to decide what to do with them."

At First Maccabees 9:27, the author reveals:

It was a time of great trouble for Israel, worse than anything that had happened to Them since the time of when the Holy Spirit ceased to appear to them.

In the third passage from First Maccabees, the one at 14:41, the text tells us:

The Jews and their priests have resolved that Simon should be their leader and High Priest forever, until the trustworthy Holy Spirit should arise and should have control over them.

As we have indicated earlier in this chapter, First Maccabees was written by a Jewish scholar in Hebrew, most likely in the latter half of the second century BCE. It is clear that this anonymous author at that time had a burgeoning perspective of what will become the idea of the Holy Spirit in the New Testament texts.

This brings us to a section in Chapter Seven in which we speak of the cultures who had ruled the Jews in the Intertestamental Period, and how those cultures may have influenced these theological ideas we have explored in this present section.

Cultural Influences on Intertestamental Literature

In the four-hundred-year period of the Intertestamental Era, six different cultures had significant influences on the Jewish and early Christian faiths. These six cultures were the following, along with the dates of their influences:

- The Persian Influence (397 to 336 BCE)
- The Greek Era (336 to 323 BCE)
- The Egyptian Influence (323 to 198 BCE)
- The Syrian Era (198 to 165 BCE)
- The Maccabean Period (165 to 163 BCE)
- The Roman Influence (63 to 4 BCE)[224]

Each of these six cultures added much to the development of the Judeo-Christian religion during the Intertestamental Period. The Persian religion, now called Zoroastrianism, had a dualistic metaphysics of a good god and a bad god.[225] The Persians also believed in the resurrection of the body and immortality of the soul, as well as a belief in angels and other spirts that could influence the activity of human beings.[226]

The advocates of Zoroastrianism also believed in a Final Judgment to take place at the end of time. They also had a priestly class that included a High Priest who had some measure of civil authority. It should be clear that many of these ideas appear to have been adopted in the Intertestamental Period, and they also show up in the New Testament.[227]

For about two hundred years after the time of the Prophet Nehemiah, the Persians controlled Judah, but the Jews, as we have indicated earlier, were allowed to carry on their religious observances, and the Persians did not interfere. During this time, Judah was ruled by a High Priest and his followers who were responsible for the Jewish government.

In 333 BCE, the Persian Army stationed in Macedonia was defeated by Alexander the Great. Alexander permitted the Jews to observe their laws and even granted them an exemption from a tribute, or tax, during their Sabbath years. When Alexander built the city of Alexandria, he encouraged the Jews to move there, and he gave them some of the same privileges that he afforded to Greek subjects of his realm.

This Greek conquest prepared the way for the translation of the Hebrew Bible into Greek called the Septuagint that was completed around 250 BCE. Alexander also built a great library in Alexander, as well as one of the seven wonders of the world, the lighthouse on the Alexandrian coast.

The major contributions of the Greek influence were the following: the translation of the Hebrew Bible into Greek, the Septuagint version; and the development of Greek philosophy, principally through the adoption of Plato and Aristotle in places in the Intertestamental Period. In fact, many of the earliest Church fathers adopted the ideas of these two philosophers. During the Greek period, divisions grew within

Judaism. Some stayed in their ancestral home, and others did not. Some adopted Hellenistic culture and language, while others clung to the Hebrew ways of doing things.

A third contribution of the Greeks to the Intertestamental Period is the Greek language that became the major tongue throughout the Mediterranean. In fact, by the time of Christ, many Jews in the ancient Near East were bi-lingual. Indeed, the New Testament was written in the Koine Greek language.[228]

When Alexander the Great died in 323 BCE, his empire was divided into four parts, the Ptolemies, the Lysimacheans, the Cassanderites and the Selenusians. The followers of Ptolemy ruled northern Egypt, as well as Israel. The Jews were treated favorably by Ptolemy, and they transported some of their "mystery religions" to Palestine. The influences of these mystery cults can be seen in certain elements in the Intertestamental Period, as well as the New Testament.[229]

The Greek Septuagint translation of the Hebrew Bible was also completed in Alexandria, Egypt, a scholarly center of the ancient world in the third and second century BCE. Under the rule of Antiochus the Third, the Jews came under the rule of Syria. They allowed the Jews to maintain their local rulers, as well as their system of priests, with the High Priest at the head.[230]

By 168 BCE, however, Antiochus was intent on destroying the Jewish faith in Israel. He outlawed circumcision, the observance of the Sabbath, and the celebration of Jewish feast days. He also obliterated every copy of the Hebrew that he could find.[231] By the Maccabean Period, the Jews began to revolt, first led by an elderly, Jewish priest named Matthaeus.

One of the major developments in this period was the formation of political parties in Palestine. These included the Pharisees or Separatists, the Sadducees, the Zealots, and the Essenes. The former group was the most conservative. They believed in a strict following of the Hebrew scriptures. They recognized no king of the Jews unless he was from the lineage of King David. [232]

Those who opposed the Pharisees and supported the Hasmoneans were called the Sadducees. They adopted their name from a Hebrew word that means "Righteousness." The Sadducees were much less strict about following the Law of Moses.[233]

The Zealots were revolutionaries. They were intent on expelling Greco-Roman involvement in Israel. They often attacked Roman garrisons and were much like what we now call "modern terrorism."[234] The Zealots were also against the rule of the Herodians, the ruling political figures of the day.

The Essenes were the community that developed the Dead Sea Scrolls that began to be discovered in the mid-twentieth century in a number of caves in the area. The Essenes were a highly religious cult that felt the need to withdraw from normal human and Jewish society. They practiced a monastic life and a mystical form of Judaism, perhaps borrowed from the mystery cults of the Greco-Roman world or from the Egyptians.[235]

One way to see the tensions among these groups in first-century Palestine is to examine Acts of the Apostles 23:6–9, where the Sadducees and the Pharisees fight over their respective interpretations of Jewish law.

The word *Saddoukaois*, or "Sadducees," appears fourteen times in the New Testament. The koine Greek noun *Pharisious*, or "Pharisees," is employed eight times in the New Testament. These sects first began to form during the Greek period of the intertestamental era.

The independence from the Jewish Revolt ended in 63 BCE when a Roman general named Pompey conquered Syria and entered the land of Israel. Perhaps the major contribution of the Romans in the Intertestamental Period was its system of roads that suddenly made it much easier to travel from place to place in the Roman Empire and beyond.[236]

This brings us to a summary of the major contributions that each of these six cultures that ruled the Jews added to the Intertestamental Period. From Persia came the Zoroastrian faith and many of its dualistic metaphysical beliefs, including a Final Judgment and a belief in the Demonic, among many other ideas.

They also believed in a form of determinism that there will be successive epochs, where the world will be ruled by the evil god and the good deity, in succeeding periods in a repeatable and a deterministic fashion.

The Greek contributions to the Intertestamental Period, as we have shown, included the phenomenon of Greek philosophy, the development of the Greek language in Palestine, and the Greek translation of the Hebrew Bible, or the Septuagint. In fact, as we have shown, the Septuagint was actually completed in the Egyptian period in the scholarly city of Alexandria.

The formation of political parties in Israel during the Maccabean and Roman periods was one of the major contributions in the Intertestamental Period. As we have seen, these four parties had very specific political points of view regarding the Romans.

In 37 BCE, the Roman Senate appointed Herod the Great to be "King of all of Palestine." Until his death in 4 BCE, Herod maintained his power by cooperating with whatever Roman figure was in power at the time. Herod was king when Jesus was born. It was Herod who killed boy babies in Bethlehem (see, Matthew 2:16–18). Herod also carried out great building projects. He enlarged, for example, the temple in Jerusalem. Additional improvements in the structure continued until 64 CE, or so says the Gospel of John at 2:20.[237]

Herod's kingdom was divided among his three sons. Archelaus was given half of the kingdoms of Judaea, Samaria and Idumea. His poor management skills led to his ouster in 6 CE. He was succeeded by a number of governors that included Pontius Pilate, who ruled from 26 to 36 CE. Pilate was governor during the final years of Jesus' life.

The other two sons of Herod, Philip and Herod Antipas, both ruled a "fourth of a kingdom." Philip's lands were northeast of Galilee. Antipas asked Emperor Gaius to give him the title of King, the same title afforded to his brother, Agrippa.[238]

Two other Roman governors from the same period were Felix, who ruled from 52 to 60 CE, and Festus, whose reign lasted from 60 to 62. Saint Paul was held prisoner by these two, and it was Festus who sent Paul to Rome for trial.[239]

It is estimated that four million Jews lived in the Roman Empire during New Testament times. Only about 700,000 of these people lived in Palestine. There were more Jews in Alexandria at the time than in the city of Jerusalem.

The Jews revolted against the Romans in 66 CE. Before the overthrow of the city and the destruction of the temple in 70 CE, Jerusalem Christians fled, many to the Decapolis city of Pella. Later, early Christian activity in the first century was limited but seems to have continued in Galilee.

The Roman victory over this Jewish revolt brought the Intertestamental Period to its end. A new era of Jewish history followed, which is called Rabbinic Judaism. It began around the year 90 CE, still under Roman rule. From the second century on, Jerusalem was now a gentile city, and Christianity was largely a gentile movement.

Latin was the official language of the Roman Empire, but it was mainly used in the West. In the East, the lingua franca was Greek. In addition to Greek, the Jews of the day spoke Hebrew and Aramaic. In this sense, it is most likely the case that Jesus was trilingual.

At any rate, the most important influences of the Romans on the Jews were their language and their system of roads that made it much easier to travel from place to place in the empire.

This brings us to one final section of this seventh chapter in which we will show some of the places in the New Testament, where these ideas from the Intertestamental Period may be detected.

Intertestamental Ideas in New Testament

Many of the ideas that developed in the Intertestamental Period were adopted in the New Testament times. Ideas that we have seen developed about the Demonic in the period may be seen throughout the New Testament, including the adoption of the name "Satan" to designate the Demonic.

The Persian dualism also may have contributed to the early development of the Demonic in Christianity. This is also true for the Persian ideas of a Final Judgment that many scholars believe came from the Persian Period, in the first half of the fourth century BCE.[240]

The idea of a belief in Free Will in the Greek Period was more fully developed in the early Christian Church in places like Galatians 5:13, the Gospel of John 18:36 and 5:16, and Matthew 15:19 that uses the idea of the Two *Yetzerim* Theory.

Even as a Christian, Paul readily identifies himself as "a Pharisee and the son of a Pharisee," at Acts 23:6.

The Gospel of Luke 2:1 speaks of the census commanded by Julius Caesar during the Roman Era of the Intertestamental Period. The *Wisdom of Solomon* contains a number of passages that Saint Paul seems to have adopted in the Book of Romans. Romans 1:20 is connected to Wisdom 13:5–8, for example; Romans 1:21 to Wisdom 13:1; 1:22 to Wisdom 12:24; Romans 1:26–31 may have been borrowed from Wisdom 14:24–27.

There are also striking similarities between Wisdom 12:12, 15:17 and 12:20 and the Book of Romans 9:20–23. Other similarities in the *Wisdom of Solomon* may be found in the Gospel of John, Hebrews, James, Ephesians, and the Books of the Corinthians. The Apocryphal tale named "Bel and the Dragon," may have been the model for the idea of the Dragon at Revelation 12:1–3 and 9, and 20:2.

The narrative of the "Bel and The Dragon" is a text that is incorporated into the Book of Daniel during the Intertestamental Period. The tale survives in a single Septuagint manuscript. The story may originally have developed during the Persian Period during the time of Cyrus the Great. There are striking parallels between the "Bel and the Dragon" and Revelation 12:1–3.

First and Second *Maccabees*, particularly at II *Maccabees* 7:11ff and 7:36, with their emphasis on life after death for the righteous, may have been a source for the Gospel of Luke's term "Resurrection of the Just" at 14:14. The New Testament Book of Jude also appears to have adopted several theological ideas from other books of the Pseudepigrapha.

Saint Paul also seems to have quoted directly from *The Sentence of the Syriac Meander* in his speech to the Athenians. Paul also turned to apocryphal writings at Romans 3:2, Galatians 3:24 and 4:4–5, and Philemon 4:8. In each of these instances, Paul appears to be using an idea from the Intertestamental Period, from 400 BCE to his own time in the first century CE.

The idea of the soul at Second Timothy 3:16, with its notion of to "breathe in," is another idea that the New Testament writers adopted from the Intertestamental Period. In fact, in general, New Testament ideas about Immortality of the Soul, as well as Resurrection of the Body, may first have been seen in the *Testament of Job*, the Books of Enoch, and the *Apocalypse of Baruch,* and many other intertestamental texts.

The notion of "Men of God who speak as they are moved by the Holy Spirit," at Second Peter 1:21, is another idea that can first be found in the *Wisdom of Solomon* and the *Gospel of Thomas*, among other places. Even the finds of many of the works of the Dead Sea Scrolls, other texts of the Intertestamental Period, we find similarities between the *Book of Jubilees*, chapter 10 and 1QM 13:11–12, between Persian Dualism of good and evil and 1QS 3:15 to 4:26.

In the Persian *Gathas*, humanity and the Supreme God had to choose between two Great Spirits, one of whom is Holy and the other of which is a Destroyer.[241] A text among the Dead Sea Scrolls, 4QAmram, features the appearance of the "Prince of Darkness," a term similar to others found at Acts 28:18, Matthew 6:23, Colossians 1:13, and the Gospel of John 8:12 and 14:30. In Persian Zoroastrianism, the good god, Ahura Mazda, and the evil deity, Angra Mainya, were symbolized by Light and Darkness.[242]

This idea of the Prince of Darkness can also be seen in First Enoch 8:1, where his name is *Azazael*, the leader of the Watchers. First Enoch tells us that Azazael taught some woman alchemy. In one of the texts from the Dead Sea Scrolls, 1QH 13:26–29, this same woman is called the "Women of Wickedness," who is numbered among the "people of Belial." The name Belial, of course, is one of the demonic names for Satan at Second Corinthians 6:15, which is also found in the intertestamental texts.

Among the books of the Intertestamental Period, the name "Belial" was used to designate the demonic in the *Testimony of Levi*, in *Jubilees*, in the *Ascension of Isaiah*, as well as in the *Syballine Oracle* that may have been as early as the fifth century BCE. Among the Dead Sea Scrolls, the *War Scroll* (11Qm 1:1–14) contains an eschatological battle between the Sons of Light, led by Michael the Archangel and Belial, the leader of the Sons of Darkness. In this conflagration, Belial and his followers defeat the traditional opponents of Israel, Edom, Ammon, Moab and the Philistines.

This text also features a version of the world being controlled in successive epochs by Light and Darkness, or God and the Devil, that is suggested at First Corinthians 15:24 and other places in the New Testament.

In the same Dead Sea text, it refers to Belial's followers "plotting evil in their hearts," and that they possess "lying tongues," like those of a viper. The expression "lying tongue" is employed at James 3:6.

The idea of there being separate epochs of rule on Earth by evil and the good—an idea that can be found in Zoroastrianism, as well as a few of the Dead Sea Scrolls texts, was adopted by the writer of the Book of Revelation in chapter 20, where the writer speaks of two "thousand-year epochs" to be ruled by the Devil/Belial and the God of Israel. [243]

In many of the intertestamental works, the demonic figures are compared to the behavior of vipers or asps. This also has been a tradition in the Old Testament at places like Psalm 58:4 and 91:13, as well as Isaiah 11:8. The New Testament word for viper is *elhidna*. It is employed at Acts of the Apostles 23:1–3, where the viper is associated with being a murderer.

The Fallen Angels narrative existed in two of the Dead Sea Scrolls, at 1QM 13:11–12 and 1QS 3:21–24, in the intertestamental literature. And it can be seen at Second Peter 2:4, in the New Testament, as well as Jude 6 and the Book of Revelation 12:7–9. Similarly, the idea of a Final Judgment can be seen in two of the Dead Sea Scrolls, as well, at 4Q369 and 4Q462. In the New Testament, of course, the Final Judgment may be seen at the Gospel of John 5:29 and 16:8, as well as Acts 24:25, Matthew 12:42, and Revelation 20:11–13.

Many passages from the Intertestamental Period assent to the idea of the Demonic being associated with vipers, asps and serpents. And the same idea may be found at Matthew 3:7, 12:34, 23:33 and the Gospel of Luke 3:7. The Greek words *esh* and *ophis*, or "asp" and "serpent," are used in the Book of Enoch (10:11–13) and in some of the Dead Sea Scrolls, such as 1QH 12:12–18, and these same terms appear in Romans 3:13 and Revelation 12:9, 14, 15, and 19.

The Demonic is associated with lying in many of the works of the Intertestamental Era. And the same idea may be seen in the New Testament at the Gospel of John 8:44, Second Corinthians 11:3, and the Book of Revelation 20:3, among many other passages.

The notion of the *yetzer ha ra*, or the "evil imagination," or "evil inclination," is also an idea that came be found sporadically in the Old Testament and in a number of places in the Intertestamental Period. This reference comes in the third-century BCE Book of Judith in which the heroine speaks of her evil "thoughts."[244] The idea of the two inclinations, one to good and one to evil, also can be seen in several of the Dead Sea Scrolls.

Saint Paul adapted the idea of the Two Yetzerim Theory in Romans 7:7–10 and 10:4–8. It also can be seen in the Gospel of Matthew 5:27–28, as well as Luke 6:45, Hebrews 2:9–10, Mark 7:21–22, Romans 6:12, the Gospel of Matthew 24:48–49, and Second Timothy 4:5. In most of these, the texts speak of decision making being "in the heart."[245]

Finally, another idea that we see in the Intertestamental Period but very rarely in the Old Testament is the notion of the Messiah. This idea can be seen in the *Testament of the Twelve Patriarchs*, in the *Testament of Reuben* (2:26–30), and in the *Testament of Simeon* (3:5–11). The idea of the Messiah, or *Messiach* in classical Hebrew, is only used two times in the Old Testament. These come in the Book of Daniel 9:25–26.

The notion of a Messiah, or "anointed one," to come also can be found in the Book of Jubilees 31:13–17 and 18–20, as well as the *Wisdom of* Sirach, chapter 36:1–17, and a Qumran text called the *Patriarchal Blessings*, which is designated as 4QPBless 3. This text gives us the line "until the coming of the Righteous Messiah."

In the Zoroastrian faith, there is also a figure, the Son of Zoroaster, who will take on a Messiah-like role at the Resurrection of the Dead at the End of Time. This Persian source also may be the origin of the idea in the New Testament.

The idea of the Messiah, of course, became a central belief in the Early Church, and we see it mentioned in a variety of passages in the New Testament, such as at John 1:10–12, Luke 2:25 to 38, and Matthew 16:13–17, for some examples. The first of these tells us that most people did not accept Jesus as the Messiah.

In the second passage, the one from the Gospel of Luke, both Simeon and Anna, by the power of the Holy Spirit, recognized that the baby Jesus was the Messiah. At the Gospel of Matthew 16:13–17, by the spirit of revelation, Peter knew that Jesus was the Messiah.

Another idea that often occurs in the Intertestamental Period and infrequently in the Old Testament is the notion of the "Kingdom of God." We also find a plethora of mentions of the Kingdom of God in the New Testament, such as at the Gospel of Matthew 5:20, 7:21, and 10:5–15, as well as 12:28, 13:11 and 25:31 and 34.

The two best places in the literature of the Intertestamental Period to find the idea of the Kingdom of God are at First Enoch 54:3–6 and the Book of Jubilees 23:29. In the former passage, Satan is depicted as the ruler of a kingdom of evil that will be replaced by the Kingdom of God. The Book of Jubilees, at 23:29, also suggests a golden age to come in which God Himself will usher in His Kingdom and reversing the Age of Satan.

In this view, ultimately good will triumph, healing will occur, and the Demonic will be defeated, much like the successive ages of rule by the evil god and the good deity in the Zoroastrian faith.[246]

The idea of the Kingdom of God, of course, regularly can be found in the New Testament in verses such as the Gospel of Matthew 4:17, 6:10, 11:12, 12:28, 18:1–5, 25:34, and 26:20 as well as Mark 1:15, and the Book of Revelation 20:1–6.

In an earlier section of this chapter, we have shown that the Jewish author of the book called *First Maccabees*, in at least three separate passages, introduces the idea of a Holy Spirit who one day will assist in the ruling of the Land of Israel. Thus, we may add the theme of the Holy Spirit to our list as well.

Another idea that appears in the Old Testament, although infrequently, is what we have called the Test Theory back in Chapter One. This theory can be found in *Sirach* 2:1, 6 and 7, as well as 6:7, 27:5 and 7, and 36:1. The word that the author of Sirach uses in these instances is the masculine, Greek noun *pirasmos* that is related to "testing" and "temptation." The same word, of course, is regularly employed by the writers of the New Testament, as we shall see in a later chapter.

The Book of Sirach, also called *Ecclesiasticus*, was part of the Wisdom Literature of the Septuagint version of the Hebrew Bible. The book, which was one of the texts of the Intertestamental Period, was not included in the Hebrew Canon. Most scholars date Sirach to the first century BCE.

Thus, we may conclude for the analysis of this section that several ideas from the Intertestamental Period, from 400 BCE until the time of John the Baptist, can also be discovered in the pages of the New Testament. Among these ideas are theological beliefs about Dualism, Determinism, Original Sin, the Fallen Angels story, the Demonic, Resurrection of the Body, Immortality of the Soul, the Coming of the Messiah and a Final Judgment at the End of Time.

Among the other ideas from the Intertestamental Period that seem to have influenced the development of the New Testament are the idea of certain moral virtues, like patience and fortitude, that are necessary to living a religious life; that the Demonic has been embodied in several forms over the period, some of which found their way into the New Testament; that the Qumran community borrowed the Deterministic view of time in Zoroastrianism; that the images of Light and Darkness have stood for good and evil in many cultures that held sway over the Jews and early Christians; that there will be epochs of evil and good on Earth; that Satan will be identified with lying; that in the Intertestamental Period the Jews waited for the appearance of the Messiah, and many other ideas.

In some texts from the Intertestamental Period, the Messiah was believed to be a "Warrior" Messiah, with full military dress and mindset. This idea does appear in a few passages in the Hebrew Bible, or Old Testament, but it can more easily be found in the *Psalms of Solomon, First Enoch, Fourth Esdras,* and *Second Baruch.*

The notion of a Warrior Messiah can be seen in at least five of the Dead Sea Scroll texts. These come in the *Rule Scroll*, the *War Scroll,* or 1QM, the *Rule of War*, designated as 4Q235, the *Messianic Apocalypse* (4Q521), and the *Son of God* text, designated as 4Q246. All of these Qumran texts speak of the Messiah to be as a military warrior.

The idea of a Warrior Messiah may be found in a number of verses in the Gospels, as well as the Letters of Paul. These include Matthew 12:22–29, Mark 3:20–30, Luke 11:14–22, the Gospel of John 6:16–21, as well as Romans 16:20, Ephesians 6:10–17, Colossians 2:14–15, and the Book of Revelation 12:13, 19:11–21 and 17:14.

In addition to all of the examples given above where texts from the Intertestamental Period and the Dead Sea Scrolls show great similarity to places in the New Testament, there are also many instances in which the language of the Dead Sea Scrolls is often quite like the language of the Greek Gospels. One illustrative example will make the point.

In a text designated as 4Q521 and named the "Messianic Apocalypse" dated around 150 years before the Gospels, the text speaks "healing the eyes" so the blind might see. In the Gospel of Luke 7:21–22, an almost identical phrase appears, where it speaks of Jesus "healing the wounded" so that the blind can see. Many additional examples from the Dead Sea Scrolls also may be pointed to, where there may have been an influence on the Gospel narratives.[247]

There are also several references to the idea of the Holy Spirit to be found among the texts of the Intertestamental Period. The expression "Holy Spirit" is used, for example, at First Maccabees 4:46, 9:27 and 14:41. Zechariah was visited by a spirit being who may have been an angel or the Holy Spirit. This text may have been the precursor of the Gospel of Luke 1:5–13.

This brings us to the major conclusions we have made in Chapter Seven. Beginning in Chapter Eight, we turn our attention to the phenomena of evil and suffering in the New Testament. Chapter Eight deals with the Synoptic Gospels; Chapter Nine with the Gospel of John; Chapter Ten with the letters of Paul; and Chapter Eleven is a conclusive chapter of what has come before it in this study of evil and suffering in the Bible.

Conclusions to Chapter Seven

We began Chapter Seven with a catalog of texts associated with what has come to be called the Intertestamental Period, the period in history between the end of the Old Testament, around 400 BCE, until the emergence of John the Baptist in the early first century CE.

After the enumeration of about two dozen books from the Intertestamental Period in the second section of Chapter Seven, we introduced and discussed several places in these works where their writers appear to have mentioned or endorsed many of the theological answers and responses to evil and suffering that we have seen throughout this study.

In this material, we have seen endorsements of the Retributive Justice Theory, the Divine Plan View, the Contrast Perspective, the Two

Yetzerim Theory, and thus the Free Will Defense, the Moral Qualities Theory, Original Sin Theory, and the Influences of Demonic Forces Perspective.

This material was followed in Chapter Seven with a section on many of the ways in which the Intertestamental Period appears to have influenced the New Testament. More specifically, we have shown that in the period between the testaments, the idea that Satan is a Demonic Force, the Fallen Angels Narrative, the ideas of Resurrection of the Body and Immortality of the Soul, the idea of the Messiah, and the notion of a Final Judgment, all can be seen in the Intertestamental Period, as well as later in the New Testament.

In the third section of this chapter, we described and discussed many of the cultural influences on the New Testament that can be seen from the Intertestamental Period. In that section, we outlined theological influences from Persia, Greece, Egypt, Syria, in the Maccabean Period, and from Rome. Each of these cultures, as we have shown, provided an important cultural influence on the Judeo-Christian religion in Biblical times.

In the final section of Chapter Seven, we introduced and discussed numerous theological ideas and principles that earlier can be detected in the books and texts from the Intertestamental Period. Among these ideas were beliefs in survival after death, the Cosmic Dualism of the Persians in the New Testament, the idea of the Prince of Darkness, the Fallen Angels Narrative, and many other theological ideas and principles.

Along the way in Chapter Seven, we explored many of the texts of the Dead Sea Scroll—another source in the Intertestamental Period— where many theological and philosophical ideas can be detected, such as the Persian notion of Determinism and its belief of successive Cosmic Epochs, where the good god and the evil deity alternate periods of earthly control.

The bottom line for this chapter should be clear: Many of the principal theological ideas in the New Testament that often were not found in the Old Testament first can be detected in the time known as the Intertestamental Period, that began around 400 BCE and continued to the early first century CE with the coming of John the Baptist.

Beginning in Chapter Eight, the focus of this study shifts from the Old Testament to the New Testament. In Chapters Eight, Nine and Ten, the major task is to examine how the Synoptic Gospels (ch. 8), the Gospel of John (ch. 9), and the Letters of Paul (ch. 10), have dealt with the issues of theodicy and the problem of evil.

This brings us to Chapter Eight, where we will examine the many places in the Synoptic Gospels—Matthew, Mark and Luke—where the writers of these texts have made important observations about the notions of evil and suffering. Then we turn to the Synoptics.

Chapter Eight:
Evil and Suffering in the Synoptic Gospels

The question of the relationship between the Gospels is often discussed but not easily answered. This is especially true when attention is focused on the Gospels of Matthew, Mark, and Luke, designated as Synoptic Gospels.

—Daniel Akin, "The Synoptic problem"

An overmastering sense of human ills can be taken as the world's invitation to deny her Maker, or it may be taken as God's invitation to succor His world. Which is it to be?

—Austin Farrer, *Love Almighty and Ills Unlimited*

The earliest followers of Jesus and the literature they produced were thoroughly Jewish in nature. As a result, the more one knows about Judaism during the time of Christian origins, the stronger basis we have for understanding the New Testament.

—James VanderKam, "Christianity and Judaism"

Introduction

The tasks of this chapter are three-fold. First, to make some observations about terms in the New Testament that designate "evil" and the "demonic." Secondly, to speak of what has come to be called the "Synoptic Problem," that is, why are Mark, Matthew and Luke so similar while the Gospel of John seems very different from the other three canonical Gospels?

Our final task will be to explore the many places in the Synoptic Gospels where questions about evil and suffering, or the issues of theodicy and the problem of evil, may be found in the Gospels of Mark, Matthew and the Gospel of Luke. We move in the next section of Chapter Eight to the Koine Greek language and words related to bad, evil, Satan, demons, etc.

Words for Evil and Suffering in the New Testament

Greek words for evil and suffering in the New Testament, for the most part, are related to four collections of words. The first of these is the word *phaoulus*, which means "foul" or "wicked." It is used at John 3:20 and 5:29, as well as Tutus 2:18 and the letter of James 3:10.[248] The second collection of Greek terms related to evil are those words associated with the term *ponos*, meaning "anguish" or "pain." Words in the New Testament connected to this root word are *ponero*, *poneros* poneron, *poneria*, *ponepateos* and *ponerou*.[249]

The words *ponero* and *poneros* are generally translated as an "evil man" and "evil One." The genitive case, *ponerou* is also rendered as "evil One." The *pomeron* are "evil men," and *peneros*, when used as a singular, masculine is often translated as "the Devil," but also can be the "evil One."

The Greek word *poneros*, "evil" or "wicked," is an adjective sometimes used as a noun. *Poneros* is used seventy-six times in the New Testament. In First John 3, John tells us that people who sin are children of the Devil. In verse 12, he goes on to say that Cain was from the evil One, or *Poneros*, because "he murdered his brother." In First John 5:18, the noun *poneros* is masculine, so it means a male "evil One."

The word *kakos* in Koine Greek is at the center of a third collection of bad and evil words in the New Testament. Words connected to this root, such as *kakopoleo*, often designate "harm" and "evil."[250] *Kakos* can be seen at Mark 3:4 and 7:21, as well as Matthew 28:48. *Kakos* is also used by Paul at Romans 14:20, where in the Revised Standard Version, it is rendered as "wrong."

The final Koine Greek cluster of words related to evil and suffering are terms connected to the word *anomos*, like *anomia*, for example.

The word *nomos* usually means "law," thus *anomos* or *anomia* means "lawlessness" or "without law." Words connected to this root in the New Testament may be found at First Timothy 1:9 and Second Timothy 3:13. [251] In the former, *anomia* is used to designate "Lawlessness." In the latter, at Second Timothy 3:13, it is usually translated as "wicked."

In addition to the Koine Greek terms mentioned in the above analysis, there are also many Greek words associated with the Devil, Satan and the Demonic in the New Testament. First, there are words associated with *Daimon* that usually gets rendered as "Demon." This cluster includes the Greek terms *Daimonion, Diabolos, damonion* and *damonizomai*. And all of these words mean "devil" or "demon."

These Koine Greek words also are sometimes rendered as "devil" or "evil spirit." Some of these may be found at Matthew 7:22, 10:8, 11:18, 12:27–28, 12:43, Mark 7:9, 16:17, Luke 11:18–20, and Luke 13:32, as well as the Gospel of John 8:49. At Luke 13:32, for example, we find the casting out of "demons," while at John 8:49, the singular "demon" is employed.

Luke 11:13–23 introduces a new term to stand for the Devil, the word *Beelzebub*. The same noun is used at Matthew 10:25, 12:24 and 27, and Mark 3:22. Thus, all of the Synoptics agree that the word *Beelzebub* is another noun employed to designate the Devil or Satan. In one Synoptic passage, the one in Mark, the scribes speak of Jesus, who is "possessed by Beelzebub," and that "He cast out demons by the ruler of the demons."[252]

It is most likely that Beelzebub is the title of a foreign deity to whom some of the ancient Jews ascribe the sovereignty of evil. The correct reading of the name is probably *Beelzebul*, and not *Beelzebub*. Some say the word means "Lord of the House," while others that it means "Lord of the Flies." And thus, would be a Greek onamonapia.[253]

There are also two noun forms associated with *ponos*. These are *poneros* and *ponerou*, which both designate an "evil One" frequently in the New Testament.[254] There are also two noun forms associated with the word *kakos*. These are *katalaleo* and *kathaplezo*, which most often designate the "evil One."[255]

The word *diablos* in New Testament Greek is most often translated as "Devil." It appears in places like First John 3:8, where the word *diabolos* is employed three times, and the Gospel of Matthew 13:37–39, where it is used along with *poneros,* or "evil One." *Diabolos* is also employed at Matthew 13:3 and 25:41, as well as Luke 8:12, and the Gospel of John 8:44.

Finally, the word *Satanas*, or "Satan," is employed dozens of times in the New Testament texts. In the Hebrew Bible, or the Old Testament, *ha Satan* means an "adversary" and is so used at First Samuel 29:4, Second Samuel 19:22, First Kings 5:4 and 11:14, and Numbers 22:22 and 32, as well as Job 1–2.[256]

In the Old Testament, as in the Book of Job, for example, the figure of *Satan* appears with the definite article *ha*, or "the Satan." In First Chronicles 21:1, the word Satan appears without the *ha*, suggesting it may be a proper name at that point.

The figure of Satan or the Devil in the New Testament goes by a variety of names, including the "Father of Lies" at the Gospel of Matthew 9:34, the "Murderer from the beginning" at the Gospel of John 8:44, and the evil One at First John 5:18. Satan is also called "the Deceiver" at Revelation 12:9, the "Schemer" at Ephesians 6:11, the "Ruler of Demons" at Matthew 12:24, the "Power of Darkness" at Luke 22:53 and Colossians 1:13, and the "Tempter" in the Gospel of Matthew 4:3.

As we have shown in the Intertestamental Period, the influence of Persian Dualism on the ancient Jews, and the conflict between Ahura Mazda and Angra Mainya, the evil god, may have been the source of the idea of Satan as a demonic figure in the New Testament. *Satanas*, or "Satan," in the New Testament, is called a "spirit" at Ephesians 2:2. He is called the "Ruler of Demons." in Matthew 12:24–26, and at Matthew 25:41, we learn that Satan has angels subject to him, perhaps a reference to the Fallen Angels narrative.

In several places in the New Testament, it is suggested that *Satanas* has the power to "tempt" or "to incite" human beings. This can be seen in the Gospel of Luke 4:56 and the Epistle of James 1:2–4, where the word "temptation" is associated with the figure. Many verses say that Satan has particular influence over the "hearts" of men, suggesting the Two *Yetzerim* Perspective.

The word *Satanas*, or Satan, is used three times in Matthew at 4:10, 12:26 and 16:23; five in Mark at 1:13, 3:23, 3:26, 4:15 and 8:33;

five in the Gospel of Luke at 10:18, 11:18, 13:16, 22:3 and 22:31; and only a single time in the Gospel of John at 13:27.

In still other passages of the New Testament, the text speaks of human beings being "possessed" by Satans or Demons. This idea of demonic possession in the New Testament is another idea that may first have been developed in the Intertestamental literature. Episodes of, or reference to, demonic possession may be seen in the New Testament at Mark 1:27, 5:15, and 9:26 and 17; Acts 8:7; Matthew 4:24; and the Gospel of John 7:21, 8:48 and at 10:1.

In the New Testament, those who are possessed are sometimes called "Demoniacs." Often the sign that they are possessed is sickness, dumbness or blindness, epilepsy or signs of insanity, such as at Matthew 9:32 and 12:22, for examples. Also see Mark 5:1–5, as well as Matthew 8:28. As we shall see in the next chapter, it is a curious fact that the Gospel of John makes no reference to demonic possession. He also uses the word "Satan" only two times at 8:44 and 13:27.

At several places in the New Testament, it suggests that Jesus had the power to heal the demoniacs, such as at the Gospel of Mark 9:14–29, Luke 8:2 and the Gospel of Matthew 10:28. The power of the Demons is also said to be limited, as is implied by Matthew 12:28–29 and the Gospel of John 12:31. Ultimately, however, Satan and his minions were defeated by the death and resurrection of Jesus Christ, as Hebrews 2:14 and Acts of the Apostles 10:38 seem to imply.

At times, the New Testament indicates that these demons are possessed with superhuman knowledge, often a superpower of evil, such as Mark 1:24 and 5:7 Matthew 8:29, Luke 4:41, for examples. Also, there is an example of demons possessing the bodies of a herd of swine in the Gospel of Mark 5:10–14.

Thus, the world of the Gospels was a world full of demons and other kinds of spirits. These spirits appear to have power and knowledge that goes well beyond the normal knowledge and power of human beings. We also have indicated that much of these demonic ideas in the New Testament may have come from foreign sources, like Persia, for example, during the Intertestamental Period.

The koine Greek vocabulary of the Synoptics Gospels does not include many of the words for "test" or "trial." For example, the words *peira* and *dokime*, which both mean "trial" or "test," are used seven times in the New Testament, but not in the Synoptic Gospels. Another word that generally means "patience" in the New Testament is *mikrothomia*. It is employed fourteen times in the New Testament but not in Matthew, Mark and Luke.

A word for "patience" that does appear in the New Testament is *hupomone*. It can be found at Luke 8:15 and 21:19, as well as at Matthew 18:26 and 29. In addition to "patience," this word also is sometimes used to designate "endurance" or "fortitude." Thus, these examples may be versions of the Moral Qualities Theory.

Another New Testament term related to evil is the word *katalaleo*. It means to "speak evil of someone" or "slander." This word is employed in First Peter 3:16 and twice in the letter of James 4:11. The word *katalaleo*, however, does not appear in the Gospels, nor in the Letters of Paul.

Another Koine Greek word that is used to designate "temptation" is *pirasmos* and is employed nine times in the Synoptics and six times in Paul and Acts, but this word cannot be found in the Gospel of John. In the expression at Matthew 6:13, "Lead us not into temptation," the word for "temptation" is *piasmos*. Another Koine word for "temptation" is *ekpidrazo*, which is used in Matthew, Mark and Luke, but it cannot be found in the Gospel of John.

This brings us to the second section of Chapter Eight, where we introduce the phenomenon known as the "Synoptic Problem." That is, why are Matthew, Mark and Luke so similar, while the Gospel of John is radically different from the other three?

The Synoptic Problem

The first three books of the New Testament—Matthew, Mark and Luke—are commonly known as the Synoptic Gospels. This word synoptic comes from "syn" and "optic," or "seeing together," meaning they see things the same way. In fact, the similarities among the Synoptic Gospels are very many, while they are quite different from the Gospel of John. One reason that this is the case is that there are many episodes that only appear in John's Gospel.

Among these events that are peculiar to the Gospel of John are:

- The Raising of Lazarus (John 11)
- The "I am the good shepherd" speech (John 10)
- The Judgment of the Word (John 12)
- The Nicodemus Narrative (John 3)
- The Intercessory Prayer (John 17)
- The Discourse on Death (John 8)
- The Promise of the Paraclete (John 14)
- Disciples taking offense at Jesus (John 6)
- The journey to Jerusalem in secret (John 7)
- The woman caught in adultery (John 7)
- The Man Born Blind (John 9)

There are also many stories that appear in the Synoptics but cannot be found in the Gospel of John. Among these episodes are the following:

- Discourse on divorce and celibacy
- Jesus blessing the children
- On Riches and Rewards
- The greatest commandment
- The Coming of the Son of Man
- The Parable of the fig tree
- The Betrayal by Judas
- Discourse on False Prophets
- The Parable on the Flood
- Preparation for the Passover[257]

Far more often than the differences between John and the Synoptics, however, are the many similarities to be found in all four Gospels. Among those many similarities are the following:

- Pilate is the Governor of Judea.

- Joseph is Jesus father and Mary his mother.

- Jesus has brothers.

- His country is called Israel and not Palestine.

- Jesus is called "Jesus of Nazareth."

- Jerusalem is called the "Holy City."

- All four Gospels speak of honoring the Father and the Son.

- Jesus refers to himself as the Son of Man.

- He accepts the title of Rabbi.

- He calls himself a Prophet.

- He accepts the title Lord.

- He calls his disciples.

- Peter is mentioned the most often.

- Thomas is named in all four.

- Jesus began his ministry in Galilee.

- Jesus ministers to Samaritans.

- The Jordan River is important in the life of Jesus.

- The Synagogue rejects his disciples.

- He washes the disciples' feet.

- He quotes the Torah.

- He quotes the Psalms.

- He feeds thousands of people.

- He raises the dead.

- Eternal Life is a theme.

- Jesus enjoys the company of wine drinkers.

- Humans have the capacity for evil.

- Satan is opposed to Jesus.

- He is popular with the masses.

- His opponents accuse him of demonic possession.
- Zechariah 9:9 is quoted by Jesus.
- Satan prompts or enters Judas.
- The disciples ask who Jesus' betrayer is.
- Judas leads an armed mob to arrest Jesus.
- Pilate asked Jesus if he is King of the Jews.
- He is crucified on a cross.
- Two other criminals are crucified along with him.
- A sign on the cross reads, "King of the Jews."
- He is resurrected from the dead.
- John is put in prison.
- Simon's brother is Andrew.
- Jesus chooses twelve men to be his followers.
- Jesus says the Synagogue will not accept his followers.
- He washes the disciples' feet.
- The disciples are called "witnesses."
- Jesus feds thousands of people.
- Jesus uses the word "amen."
- Satan opposes Jesus.
- Jesus is a Shepherd to his sheep.
- Jesus uses the verb "to sleep" to represent death.
- He refuses to perform miracles in all four accounts when his opponents asked him to do so.

These four Gospels are so similar because they all tell the same narrative. Jesus was the son of a carpenter. He had a public ministry for three years. He was eventually crucified in public on a cross, and, most importantly, he resurrected from the dead three days after his death.

Of the three Synoptic Gospels, Mark is the shortest of the three, yet large portions of it are also found in Matthew and Luke. There are also about two hundred verses shared by Matthew and Luke that are not to be found in Mark. These similarities include subject matter, exact wording, and even the order of events. There have been proposed several theories about the similarities among the Synoptic Gospels. There are also scholarly views that suggest that there is no "problem" in the "Synoptic Problem."[258]

We may divide these theories into the following scheme:

- The Traditional View
- The Two Gospel Hypothesis
- The Two Source Theory
- The Three Source Theory
- The Farrer Theory[259]

Theory number one suggests that Matthew was the first of the gospels, followed by Mark, and Luke, which relied on Matthew. This view was held by many of the prominent Early Church Fathers, such as Irenaeus, Origen and Augustine.[260] Later advocates of this theory include Hugo Grotius, H. G. Jameson, Basil Butler and John Wenham.[261]

The Two Gospel Hypothesis was devised by German scholar Jakob Griesbach (1745–1812). Like the traditional theory, Griesbach maintains the priority of Matthew. He also believed that Luke was the second Gospel and Mark was the third. In his view, Mark used Matthew and Luke as sources.[262]

The Two Source Theory has become the most predominant view in New Testament scholarship in the last fifty years. In this view, Mark is the first of the Gospels, and a second source known as "Q" is the other source in this view. The letter "Q" is short for the German word *Quelle*, which means "source" or "spring."[263] Proponents of the Two Source Theory suggest that the Q document was a collection of the sayings and acts of Jesus compiled by and circulated among first-century CE Christians. In this theory, Q is prior to all of the Gospels. Although it is an interesting theory, there is no tangible proof that the Q document ever existed.[264]

The Three Source Theory retains the priority of Mark and the existence of the Q document, but it also suggests that Matthew was a large influence on the Gospel of Luke. Thus, in the Three Source Theory, the order is Mark, Matthew and Luke. Most people in contemporary New Testament scholarship reject this theory because the idea of Luke depending on Matthew would seem to contradict the reason for the development and the positing of Q in the first place.[265]

The final theory listed above, the Farrer Theory, was named after Austin Farrer (1904–1968), an English philosopher and Biblical critic. Farrer gives priority to Mark, and Matthew was the second gospel to be added to the New Testament, followed by the Gospel of Luke. In this view, Matthew used Mark, while Luke used both Mark and Matthew.[266]

In Farrer's view, he believes he has eliminated the need for the Q source because there is no need, in his view, for an outside source. A number of subsequent New Testament scholars—mostly in Britain—have endorsed Farrer's Theory, such as J. H. Ropes, M. D. Goulder and Mark Goodacre.[267] This brings us to an analysis of the many places in the Synoptic Gospels where the issues of theodicy and the problem of evil may be detected in the Gospels of Matthew, Mark and Luke.

Evil and Suffering in the Synoptic Gospels

All three of the Synoptic Gospels often use the Influences of Demonic Forces Theory. Examples in Matthew can be seen as 4:8, 8:16–17, 12:43–45, 13:36–39 and 18:32. At Matthew 4:8, the text uses the word *Diablos* to stand for the Devil. The same term is employed in verse 11, as well.

At Matthew 8:16–17, the text speaks of "people who were possessed with demons, and "He cast out the spirits with a word and cured all who were sick." Matthew, at 12:43–45, speaks of what happens when an evil spirit leaves a body. He observes, "When an unclean spirit has gone out of a person, it wanders through waterless regions looking for a resting place, but it finds none." And at 13:38–39, Matthew uses both "evil One" and "Devil" to refer to the Demonic.

In the Gospel of Mark, we also find many references to the demonic, such as at 1:13–16, 5:1–13 and 9:14–20. In the first of these, the text relates:

> Just then there was in the Synagogue a man with an
> unclean spirit, and he cried out "What have you to do

with us, Jesus of Nazareth. Have you come to destroy us? I know who you are, the Holy One of God." But Jesus rebuked him, saying, "Be silent and come out of him."

At Mark 5:1–13, Jesus heals a Gerasene demoniac. And at Mark 9:14–29, Jesus heals "a boy with a spirit," suggesting he had been "possessed by a demon." The writer of the Gospel of Luke also is committed to the view of the Influences of Demonic Forces on human beings. This can be seen at Luke 4:5–7, 7:33 and 11:14–16, for three good examples. In the first of these, the *Diabolos*, or the Devil, entices Jesus to fall down and worship him. At Luke 7:33, we find the following:

For John the Baptist came, eating no bread and drinking no wine, and you say, "He has a demon;" the Son of Man comes eating and drinking, "Look a glutton and a drunkard, a friend of tax collectors and sinners."

At the Gospel of Luke's 11:22–26, the text speaks of an "unclean spirit" and makes references to seven other "unclean spirits." At Mark 3:26, we find a reference to Beelzebub, a first-century name for Satan. And at the Gospel of Luke 7:36–40, we find a narrative about a person being possessed by a "spirit."

At the Gospel of Luke's 7:33, the text tells us that some people in the first century saw John the Baptist, and then pronounced that, "He has a Demon." This is another indication that the Influences of Demonic Forces Theory can often be seen in the Gospels of Matthew, Mark and Luke. As we shall see in Chapter Nine, this is another big difference between the Gospel of John and the Synoptic Gospels.

The name *Beelzebub*, a synonym for the Devil in the Synoptics, appears at Mark 3:31, Luke 11:15 and 18 and 19, and the Gospel of Matthew 10:25 and 27, as well as 12:24. The name Beelzebub does not appear, however, in the Fourth Gospel, the Gospel of John.

The word *Satanas* or "Satan" is employed thirty-six times in the New Testament. Of those, fifteen are in the Synoptic Gospels. There are three in Matthew, six in the Gospel of Mark and seven instances in Luke. The word Satan can only be found in the Gospel of John at 13:27.

Satan appears by name in the Synoptics at Matthew 4:10, 12:26 and 16:23. In the Gospel of Mark at 1:13, 3:23 twice, 3:26, 4:15 and 8:33. The word *Satanas* may be found in the Gospel of Luke at 4:8, 10:18, 11:18, 13:16, 22:3, 22:3 again, and 22:31. Thus, Satan appears sixteen times in the Synoptic Gospels and only a single time in the Gospel of John at 13:27.

From all of this, then, we have established that all the writers of the Synoptic Gospels endorsed the idea of the Influences of Demonic Forces Theory on the lives of human beings. It is just as clear that Matthew, Mark and Luke assented to the use of the Retributive Justice Theory, as well.

At Matthew 15:17, for example, Jesus tells us, "Do you not see that whatever goes into the mouth and enters the stomach, then goes into the sewer?" The parable of the Sower and the Seeds may also be seen as an example of Retributive Justice, for one only receives good grain if the seed fell on good soil.

In the Gospel of Mark, at 2:1–12, Jesus heals a paralytic man. After he told him his "sins had been forgiven," the man picked up his mat and could walk. At the Gospel of Luke 6:43–45, Jesus speaks more specifically about the Retributive Justice Theory when he observes:

> No good tree bears bad fruit, nor again does a bad tree bear good fruit, for each tree is known by its own fruit. Figs are not gathered from thorns, nor are grapes picked a bramble bush. The good person out of the good treasure of the heart produces the good, and the evil person out of the evil treasure produces evil. For it is out of abundance of the heart that the mouth speaks.

Although this narrative is ostensibly an example of the Retributive Justice Theory, it may also be seen as an example of the Free Will Defense, with the mentions of the "heart" (*cardia*) producing both good and evil words and actions. In this sense, this passage from Luke 6 may be a use of the Two *Yetzerim* Theory, as well.

At the Gospel of Luke's 6:37–38, the writer tells us that "What one gives will also be given in return." And at Matthew 5:27–30, the text suggests that "if one's right hand has sinned, then cut it off and throw it into the fire," another clear indication of the Retributive Justice Theory in the Synoptic Gospels.

Another text that shows a clear reference to the Retributive Justice Theory in the Synoptic Gospels is Luke 13:1–5, in which a tower at a place called Siloam falls down, killing several people. Jesus asks those present, "Do you think these Galileans were worse sinners than all the other Galileans because they suffered in this way?" Then Jesus responds to this question this way:

> No, I tell you, unless you repent, you will all likewise perish or those eighteen on whom the tower of Siloam fell and killed them. Do you think that they were worse offenders than all the others who lived in Jerusalem? No, I tell you but unless you repent, you will all likewise perish.

In this passage, Jesus seems decidedly to be against the interpretation of the Retributive Justice Theory in regard to the eighteen people who died when the tower of Siloam collapsed to the earth. Jesus makes a similar conclusion in chapter nine of the Gospel of John when he is asked by one of his disciples whether a man born blind sinned or his parents did. In that case, as well, as we shall see in the next chapter, Jesus rejected the Retributive Justice Theory in favor of the Divine Plan View.

The idea of the Retributive Justice Theory also can be seen at the Gospel of Matthew's 12:33–36, where the writer speaks of the relationship of "good trees" to "good fruit." In fact, bad trees cannot produce good fruit, by extension, a narrative about good and bad people and their thoughts and actions. At verse 34, we see the question, "How can you speak good things when you are evil?"

This analogy to people is continued at verses 35 and 36 when Matthew says:

> The good person brings good things out of a good treasure; and the evil person brings evil things out of an evil treasure. I tell you on the day of judgment you will have to give an account of every careless word you utter, for by your words you will be justified, and by your words you also shall be condemned.

Clearly, this is another Synoptic passage where the writer combines the Retributive Justice Theory with future tense verbs and thus the Divine Plan Theory related to the Resurrection of the Dead at the End of Time.

The idea of the Test View is only used in rare instances in the Synoptic Gospels. One example comes at the Gospel of Matthew 6:12–13. In this passage, the writer of Matthew observes:

> And forgive us our debts, as we have forgiven our debtors. And do not bring us to the time of trial, but rescue us from the evil One.

The word for "trial" in this passage is the Greek term *pirasmos*. The word is used in the New Testament to designate "testing," "test" and "trial." It is employed in all the Synoptics, such as at Matthew 26:46, Mark 14:38, and the Gospel of Luke 4:14, 8:13, 11:4, 22:29 and 22:40.

In the opening of chapter 4 of the Gospel of Matthew, the writer combines the Influences of Demonic Forces Theory with the Test View when the text suggests, "When Jesus was lead by the Spirit into the wilderness to be tempted by the Devil, he fasted forty days and forty nights, and afterwards he was famished." The same text continues by saying, "And the Tempter came and said to him..." This is obviously another reference to the Test View, as well as the Demonic Forces Theory.

The same word may also be found at Matthew 26:21, Luke 22:28, Matthew 5:11, 37, 39, and 45, as well as 6:23, 7:11, 17, and 18, 9:4, and 12:34. It is also employed at the Gospel of Mark 14:38, which is usually rendered as "temptation."

Another word for "testing" is also used in the New Testament. The Koine word is *dokimion*. It is not used in the Synoptics, but it can be found at First Peter 1:7.

A host of other words in the Synoptic Gospels may be found that imply a "test" or "trial," as well as words for patience and forbearance. One of the latter is the Greek term *hupomene* that generally designates "patience" or "endurance" in the Synoptics. *Hupomene* can be seen at Luke 8:13 and 21:19. In the former, it means "endurance," and in the latter, it is closer to forbearance.

Thus, we may add the Moral Qualities Theory to the list of answers and responses to evil and suffering to be found in the Synoptic Gospels. At the Gospel of Luke 8:18, the test speaks of a "time of testing" in the context of the story of the Sower and the Seed. We will speak of other examples of the Test View in the Synoptics later in this chapter.

The Two *Yetzerim* Theory also can be detected in the Synoptic Gospels at the Gospel of Matthew 5:27–28, where we are told:

> You have heard that it was said, "You shall not commit adultery." But I say to you everyone who looks at a woman with lust has already committed adultery with her in his heart.

The Two *Yetzerim* Theory can also be seen at work in the Gospel of Mark 7:21–22. The writer of these verses relates, "For it is from within, from the heart, that evil intentions come. Fornication, theft, murder, adultery avarice, wickedness, deceit, licentiousness, envy, slander, pride and folly. All of these evil things come from within, and they defile a person."

Mark 8:17 and the Gospel of Luke 6:45 may also be seen as two good examples of the *Yetzerim* Theory. The former speaks of hearts being "hardened," and Luke 6:45 makes references to the *yetzer ha ra*, as well as the *yetzer tov*. The word *kardia* or "heart" appears fifty-eight times in the New Testament. About half of those are in the Synoptic Gospels. Many of these references indicate that the heart is the affective center of being, as well as the seat of moral decision-making.

This view was adopted by the writers of the New Testament and was adopted from similar ideas in the Old Testament. Among the New Testament passages where the use of the *Kardia* appears to be analogical to the Two *Yetzerim* Theory are:

- Gospel of Matthew 5:28, 9:4, 12:34, 13:15 and 15:19.
- Gospel of Mark 2:6, 7:21 and 11:33.

To cite one example, Luke 9:4 asks, "Are you thinking evil in your hearts?" Matthew 12:43 speaks of that "of which fills the heart." The Gospel of Matthew's 13:15 suggests that "one's understanding is done with the heart." And Matthew 15:19 is quite explicit about the relationship of the heart to evil. It tells us, "For out of the heart comes evil."

The use of the word *Kardia* to indicate the thoughts and feelings of the mind is employed forty-six times in the Synoptic Gospels, but a mere seven times in the Gospel of John. These come at John 12:40, 13:2, 14:1, 14:27, 16:6 and 16:22. We will say more about these passages in the next chapter on evil and suffering in the Fourth Gospel.

The same understanding of the Self to the *Kardia*, or heart can be seen in the Gospel of Mark, as well. At Mark 2:6, we are told that "one's reasoning occurs in the heart." A similar view can be seen at the Gospel of Mark's 7:21, where it speaks of what comes "out of the hearts of men." At Mark 11:23, we learn that even the process of doubting comes from the heart. It tells us, "And does not doubt in his heart, but believes."

This same position can be seen in the Gospel of Luke at 1:51, where the apostle speaks of having "scattered the proud in the imagination of their hearts." The Greek term for "imagination" in this verse is the word *Phantasia*, from which we get the English "fantasy" and many other words.

A similar view of the evil inclination or imagination theory at Luke 3:15 that tells us, "And as the people were in expectation, and all men mused in their hearts," is another indication that the organ for thought and moral decision making was believed to take place in the heart among first-century Christians.

At the Gospel of Luke 6:45, the follower of Jesus combines the *Yetzerim* Theory with the Influences of Demonic Forces View, when Luke writes, "The good man out of the good store of his heart gives good things, and the evil man [*poneros*], out of his evil store [*ponerou*], brings evil [*poneros*]. For out of the full store of the heart comes the words of the mouth."

This verse comes immediately after verses 43 and 44, where Luke relates the Retributive Justice View that good trees do not bear bad fruit and bad trees do not bear good fruit. Luke also tells us in these verses that "Men do not get figs from thorns, nor grapes from blackberry bushes."

In the Gospel of Matthew, however, at 5:38–39, we find a passage against the idea of the Retributive Justice Theory. In these verses, Matthew relates:

> You have knowledge that it was said, "An eye for an eye and a tooth for a tooth." But I say to you do not use force against an evil man [*ponero*]. But to him who gives you a blow on the right cheek, turn and let the left cheek be struck.

At this passage in the Gospel of Matthew, as well as in chapter nine of the Gospel of John, as we shall see in the next chapter when Jesus is asked whether a man born blind was responsible for his condition, or if his parents' sin was the cause of the calamity.

First-century Christians also employed two other words for the "mind." These are *logismos* and *dianoia*. Th former is used at Romans 2:15 and Second Corinthians 2:5, while the latter can be found at Matthew 22:37, Mark 12:30 and Luke 10:27. Thus, *dianoia* is used to express the "mind" in all three of the Synoptic Gospels.

It is of some interest that the word *Poneros*, or "evil One" or "evil Man," is employed thirty-six times in the Synoptic Gospels of Matthew, Mark and Luke, while it is only used three times in the Gospel of John. This is another big difference between the Synoptics and the Fourth Gospel, as we shall see in the next chapter.

The overall conclusion we clearly can make from these passages is that the authors of the Synoptic Gospels were all believers in the view that the *Kardia*, or the heart is the location of the Self, and it is there where one's moral decisions are made. In other words, the writers of Matthew, Mark and Luke's Gospels all appear to be proponents of what we have called the Two *Yetzerim* Theory back in Chapter One of this study.

In addition to the Two *Yetzerim* Theory, belief in the Free Will Defense also can be seen in a variety of Synoptic Gospels passages, where it appears that the writers believed in the idea of human free will. Matthew 23:37, for example, speaks of Jerusalem being a city "that kills its prophets," suggesting that this was done voluntarily. Similarly, Matthew 23:16 speaks of anyone who "swears by the sanctuary," another case where it seems to be intentional.

The word for "trial" in Matthew 6:12–13 is *pirasmos*. The same term is employed in a variety of places in the Synoptic Gospels, including Matthew 5:10–12 and 26:41; Mark 14:38; and the Gospel of Luke 4:13, 8:13, 11:4, 22:8, 22:28, and 22:40 and 46. At 5:11, the New Revised Standard Version renders the word *pirasmos* as "evil," rather than as a "test," or a "trial." In general, however, "test" or "trial" is the meaning of the term in the New Testament. Another Greek word, *peira*, from the same root, also means "test" or "trial." This noun may be found at the Letter to the Hebrews 11:29 and 11:30.

The Test View is sometimes employed in the Synoptic Gospels with the use of the Koine Greek verb *ekpiradzo*, which means "to try" or "to test." This verb is used at Luke 4:12 and 10:25, at Matthew 4:7 and 19:3, and in the Gospel of Mark 10:2. Luke 4:12 and Matthew 4:7 both speak of God being put to the test, rather than the other way around. Both of these texts relate, "Again, it is written, don't put your Lord your God to the test."

At Matthew 19:3, we are told that "Some Pharisees came to him [Jesus] and to put him to the test." The verse then continues with a discussion of the phenomenon of divorce for cause. The Gospel of Mark 10:2 has a version of the same story. It begins, "Some Pharisees came to Jesus and they put him to a test." A similar tale is told at Luke 10:25 that begins, "Just then a lawyer stood up to put Jesus to the test."

At the Gospel of Matthew's 6:13, the text makes another reference to, "And let us not be put to the test but keep us safe from the evil One [*Poenerou*]." This is clearly a combination of the Influences of Demonic Forces Theory with a mention of the Test Perspective.

There are also many passages in the Synoptic Gospels that appear to assent to what we have called the Divine Plan Perspective. Two representative examples from the Gospel of Luke can establish this point. These come at Luke 22:22 and 24:26–27. In the passage from chapter 24, the writer asks:

> Was it not necessary that the Messiah should suffer these things and then enter into his glory? Then the beginning with Moses and all the prophets, he interpreted to them the things about himself in all the scriptures.

These verses seem to suggest that many passages in the Old Testament were thought to be precursors to the life, death and resurrection of Jesus Christ as part of a Divine Plan that began long before first-century Christianity. Similarly, at the Gospel of Luke 22:22, the text makes a kind of pronouncement that smacks of Determinism, in this case, the Theological kind.

Verse 22 tells us, "For the Son of Man is going as it has been determined, but woe to the one by whom he shall be betrayed." The Koine Greek term for "determined' is *horidzo*. It generally means to "set a limit" in a geographical sense. The English word "horizon" comes from the same ancient Greek source, the word *horizo*. This word is only used once in the Synoptics, but Paul uses it at Romans 1:4 and Hebrews 4:7. The same word is also found many times in the Acts of the Apostles, such as at 2:23, 10:42, 11:29, 17:26 and 17:31, among other places.

The Gospel of Luke uses future tense verbs at 22:22, which may be another indication of the Divine Plan Theory in the Synoptic Gospels. Similarly, at Matthew 12:36, the text speaks of the Day of Judgment, in which some will find a "good resurrection," and others will find a "bad resurrection." Thus, Matthew 12:36 may be seen as a combining of the Retributive Justice Theory with the Divine Plan Perspective using future tense verbs. In this verse, the writer combines the Retributive Justice Theory with his belief in the Divine Plan Theory, in which, ultimately, each individual will be held morally accountable for his or her words and actions. In this case, this verse in Matthew may be an endorsement of the Free Will Defense combined with the Divine Plan Theory, in that people will be punished for the bad choices of words that they have voluntarily chosen.

The Contrast Theory is another view found in each of the Synoptic Gospels, as well as the Gospel of John, for that matter. As with what we have seen in earlier chapters in the Old Testament, the uses of the Contrast View among the Synoptics are mostly in the context of discussions of light and darkness, where light is something good, and darkness is associated with evil.

In that regard, Matthew 4:16 and 10:27; Mark 4:21–22; and the Gospel of Luke 1:79, 8:17 and 12:3, are all representative examples of the employment of the Contrast View, with respect to the issues of evil and suffering in the New Testament. At Matthew 4:16, Jesus remarks:

> The people who have sat in darkness now have seen a great light. And for those who sat in the region and the shadow of death, light has dawned.

Here Jesus associates light with the good and darkness with evil. At 10:27 of Matthew's Gospel, Jesus again uses the same metaphor. He relates:

> What I say to you in the dark, tell in the light. And what you hear in whispers, proclaim from the rooftops.

At Mark 4:21–22, the writer offers a short discourse from Jesus about a light under a basket. In these verses, Jesus asks:

> Is a lamp brought in to be put under a bushel basket, or under the bed, and not on the lampstand? For there is nothing hidden, except to be disclosed, nor is anything secret, except to come to the light.

Again, light is seen as good, while darkness is associate with evil. The final verse of the first chapter of the Gospel of Luke, at 1:79, Jesus gives some advice by using a familiar image:

> To give light to those who sit in darkness and in the shadow of death is to guide our feet in the way of peace.

The writer of the Gospel of Luke at 8:16–18 changes the metaphor of the light and the basket. For him, it is a "light under a jar." About it, the author related, "For nothing is hidden that will not be disclosed, nor is anything secret that will not become known or that will be shown in the light."

In the Gospel of Luke at 12:3, the writer gives a warning against hypocrisy by employing a familiar metaphor. Jesus relates in this discourse:

> Therefore, whatever you have said in the dark will be heard in the light, And what you have whispered behind closed doors will be proclaimed from the rooftops.

At the Gospel of Mark 4:22, we find another example of the Contrast View, when the disciple says:

> For there is nothing hidden except to be disclosed, nor
> is anything secret except that it comes to the light.

We find a similar view at the Gospel of Luke's 8:17, where he informs us, "For nothing is hidden that we have not disclosed, nor is anything secret that will not become known and comes to the light." The light in these examples, of course, is related to the good, while hiddenness and darkness are associated with evil.

We have done enough here to establish that the writers of the Synoptic Gospels often employ the theory we have labeled the Contrast View. As we shall see in Chapter Nine, however, this theory is used much more often in the Gospel of John than in Matthew, Mark and Luke.

So far in this chapter, we have shown that the writers of the Synoptic Gospels—Matthew, Mark and Luke—regularly assented to the following answers and responses to the issues of theodicy and the problem of evil:

- The Influences of Demonic Forces Theory
- The Retributive Justice Perspective
- The Test Theory
- The Two *Yetzerim* Point of View
- The Free Will Defense
- Divine Plan Theory
- The Contrast View

There are also several places in the Synoptic Gospels where what we have called the Moral View may be found. Among these are Luke 22, 28 and 40, Mathew 26:4, and Mark 14:38. In each of these verses, a follower of Jesus does something that he rewards with kind words, bringing out moral virtue with those words. In Mark's Gospel, for example, a woman washes Jesus' feet, and his response is gentle words followed by faith in his disciples. Thus, we may add the Moral Qualities Perspective to our list of answers and responses to be found in the Synoptic Gospels.

Finally, there are two places in the Synoptic Gospels that seem to be an application of the Hidden God Theory. The first of these comes at the Gospel of Luke 18:1 and the other at the Gospel of Matthew 5:3–4. In the former, the message seems to be, "Keep on praying in your faith to your great God, no matter how silent Heaven may seem. In the verses from Matthew's Gospel, at 5:3–4, the text suggests that there is no seeking of the face of God apart from "mourning" and being "poor in spirit." We cannot turn to God without prayer. Matthew suggests that though at times God may hide his face, one can still hear His voice in the Scriptures.

There is one other approach to the issues of evil and suffering to be found in the Synoptic Gospels. We shall call this view the "Practical Approach." This approach is the subject matter of the next section of this eighth chapter.

The Practical Approach to Evil and Suffering in the Synoptics

By the "practical approach," we mean the general point of view about evil and suffering that Jesus generally makes in the Gospels. This approach may be summed up, we believe, simply by saying that in the Gospels, Jesus responds to evil and suffering, for the most part, in very general, practical ways. Mostly, by responding to evil and suffering the best way that he practically could. That is to fight suffering whenever and wherever he finds it.

In many narratives of Jesus in the New Testament, when he deals with people who are suffering from evil, he most often responds by relieving that suffering the best way he can. He cures blindness by putting mud on a man's eyes, for example. And in so many other cases, he performs the most practical or morally acceptable response simply by listening to what people ask of him.

This Practical Approach may be seen in a number of ways in the New Testament, but nowhere is this view more clear than at three passages from the Synoptic Gospels, one each from Matthew, Mark and Luke. These come at Matthew 9:36, Mark 6:34 and the Gospel of Luke 13:34.

The verse from the Gospel of Matthew tells us this:

> When he saw the crowds, he had compassion for them because they were harassed and helpless, like sheep without a shepherd.

We see a similar passage in the Gospel of Mark 6:34 that reveals:

> As he went ashore, he saw a great crowd, and he had compassion for them, because they were like sheep without a shepherd; and he began to teach them many things.

In the Gospel of Luke, the writer changes the metaphor. He gives us this at 13:34:

> Jerusalem, Jerusalem, the city that kills its prophets and stones those who are sent to it. How often have I desired to gather your children together as a hen gathers her brood under her wings, and you were not willing. And I tell you, you will not see me until the time comes when you will say, "Blessed be the one who comes in the name of the Lord."

The writer of the Gospel of Luke changes the metaphor from a shepherd and his sheep to a hen and her chicks. In each of these three verses from the Synoptic Gospels, we are given examples of the practical approach we have been describing in this section of Chapter Eight. In each of these narratives, the writers begin by pointing out that Jesus had "compassion" for the crowd. The Greek word employed here is *splagchnizomai*.

In all three uses of this word "compassion," it is used in relation to one who has authority over some other creatures, a shepherd for his sheep, and a hen with her chicks, or Jesus for his followers. These relationships are also, Jesus argues, like a parent and child, or a God and His creatures. What Jesus may be telling us in these narratives is how to behave in the presence of those over whom we have some authority. And that this behavior is the same behavior that God shows to His followers.

The shepherd, the hen and the parent would not hesitate to act in a practical way for what their subordinates need—the sheep, the chicks or the children. Jesus may be instructing us on how to behave in these circumstances. We should exhibit both compassion and mercy.

A second word that is sometimes used to designate "compassion" or "Mercy" in the Gospels is the term *eleeo*. These words are used throughout the New Testament, but there is a preponderance of their use in the Synoptic Gospels. Just as important is who uses these words and in what context they are employed.

The word *splagchnizomai*, interesting enough, is only used in the Synoptic Gospels when Jesus has compassion for someone else. The only exception to this rule comes at the Gospel of Mark 1:41, where John the Baptist has compassion for sinners. At Matthew 9:36, 14:14, 15:32, 18:27, 20:34, and Mark 6:34, 8:2, and 9:22, Jesus has compassion or pity almost always for someone who is suffering.

This same conclusion can be made about the uses of the word *eleeo* in the Synoptic Gospels. Jesus shows "mercy" to two blind men, a demoniac, to the blind Bartimeus, to the rich man and Lazarus, to another demoniac, and to the blind man near Jericho. And in all of these cases, the two dominant words for describing how Jesus behaves are *splagchnizomai* and *Eleeo*, or "Compassion" and "Mercy."

A variety of other Koine Greek verbs also are used to describe the treatment of Jesus to those less fortunate than He. Among these words are *sumpathes*, from which come the English "sympathy." *Oketeiro* and *metriopathia* means one should have compassion for everyone.[268]

In short, what we mean by the Practical Approach to evil and suffering is that, at least in the Christian tradition, one should behave the way a shepherd behaves toward his sheep or a hen towards her chicks. Often the best way to respond to evil and suffering, at least according to Jesus, is by compassion, mercy and pity, in the most practical of ways.

If we are in important roles of authority, Jesus seems to relate, we always should act with compassion, mercy and pity in mind. In other words, we should follow the "Practical Approach" outlined by Jesus in the Gospels.

Finally, along the way in this eighth chapter, we have indicated a propensity among the writers of the Synoptic Gospels that they often combine two or more of the answers and responses we have introduced back in Chapter One. Indeed, we have seen the linking of the Demonic

Forces Theory with the Test Perspective, as well as Matthew combining the Retributive Justice Theory with the Divine Plan Point of View. We also have seen in the Gospel of Luke, a combination of the Two *Yetzerim* Theory with the Influences of Demonic Forces Theory.

This brings us to the major conclusions we have made in Chapter Eight. The subject matter of Chapter Nine, as we shall see, is the phenomena of evil and suffering in the Gospel of John, a document very different in theology and in tone from the Synoptic Gospels.

Conclusions

We began Chapter Eight with a summary of the Koine Greek vocabulary of words related to evil, suffering and the demonic, including many of the places in the Synoptic Gospels where these words are used. In this section, we have related that these words may be seen to cluster around four separate terms in the New Testament. These words are *roydezon*, *ponos*, *kakos* and *anomia*, or "Lawlessness."

In the same section of Chapter Eight, we introduced many of the Greek terms associated with the Devil and his minions in the New Testament. Among these terms we discussed were Satan, the Devil, Demons, the Prince of Darkness, and many others.

In the second section, we introduced what has come to be known as the Synoptic Problem. That is, why are the Synoptic Gospels— Matthew, Mark and Luke—so similar, while at the same time, the Gospel of John is very different? After introducing the nature of the problem, we went on to describe five separate theories and how the proponents of these theories have sought to answer the issue of the Synoptic Problem. Along the way in this second section of Chapter Eight, we also provided a catalog of the many similarities and the differences between the Synoptic Gospels and the Gospel of John.

In the third and fourth sections of this chapter, we explored the many answers and responses to the questions of theodicy and the problem of evil that may be found in Matthew, Mark and Luke. Indeed, in section three, we maintained that the writers of the Synoptics have consented to, or endorsed, seven separate theories regarding evil and suffering. These seven theories we have discovered in the Synoptics were Retributive Justice Theory; the Influences of Demonic Forces

View; the Free Will Defense, particularly with the Two *Yetzerim* Theory; the Test View; the Contrast Perspective; the moral Qualities Perspective; and the Divine Plan Theory.

In the fourth and final section of Chapter Eight, we introduced another approach to the issues of evil and suffering that we have called the "Practical Approach." In this view, we have argued, the best ways to respond to the issues of evil and suffering are to respond in ways that Jesus did—that is with compassion, pity, and mercy, in the most practical of ways.

In this fourth section, we made the claim that Jesus' behavior in the face of those around him who were suffering is the best approach to the issues of when evil and suffering arise in our lives, as well as those around us. Jesus did what he could to make the lame walk and the blind see. He fed the hungry, and he responded to the needy in whatever practical way he could ameliorate that suffering.

In the Synoptic Gospels, Jesus did not respond to evil and suffering with theology or religious dicta. He responded in ways that are most practical, and this may be the best way that any Christian should respond to the questions of theodicy and the problem of evil.

Along the way in Chapter Eight, we also have shown that the Koine Greek vocabularies of the writers of the Gospels of Matthew, Mark and Luke, often do not contain many of the terms for evil and suffering, as well as words for trial, test and patience that can be found in the Gospel of John, as well as the Epistles of Paul. We will say much more about these differences in Chapter Nine on the Gospel of John, as well as Chapter Ten on the Epistles of Paul and the Acts of the Apostles.

This brings us to Chapter Nine. The major task in this chapter, as we shall see, are the answers and responses to evil and suffering that may be found in the Fourth Gospel—the Gospel of John.

Chapter Nine:
Evil and Suffering in the Gospel of John Theodicy

This work [Gospel of John] is about when God is silent.
The silence of God, which in theology it is theodicy. Why
does God not immediately vindicate His children?

—Sir Robert Anderson, *The Silence of God*

John's account of the healing of the man born blind is
certainly a sign, for it points to Jesus the Healer of Light
of the World. At the same time, it contrasts physical
blindness that can be healed, with spiritual blindness
that cannot.

—Ralph F. Wilson, "Healing Blindness: John 9:1–41"

"A Religious classic can prove meaningful in every age.
They have an enduring power to open new horizons,
to stimulate thought, to expand the mind and heart,"
writes Pope Francis. One such religious classic is the
fourth Gospel, commonly known as the Gospel of John.

—Peter Edmunds, S. J., "Story, Theology, and Drama in
the Gospel of John"

Introduction

There are two main tasks to be explored in this ninth chapter of this study of evil and suffering in the Bible. The first of those is to give a very general introduction to the fourth Gospel, the Gospel of John, in the Christian Church, as well as how it is different as well as similar to the Synoptic Gospels.

The second, and central, task of this chapter is to explore the many ways that the writer of the Gospel of John answers or responds to the questions of theodicy and the problem of evil in his work. As we shall see in this chapter, the fourth Gospel gives a broader and deeper collection of answers and responses than any other parts of the New Testament, except for the Letters of Paul and the Acts of the Apostles. Indeed, the writer of the fourth Gospel appears to utilize nearly all of the theological answers and responses to the issues of evil and suffering we have seen throughout this study.

Introduction to the Gospel of John

The Gospels of Matthew, Mark, and Luke—the Synoptics—had been circulating for over thirty years when the apostle John wrote his account of the life, death and resurrection of Jesus Christ. Nevertheless, John had much to add to the record of Jesus' life and ministry. In fact, nearly ninety percent of the content of the fourth Gospel is not covered in the Synoptic texts.

It is only John's Gospel that discusses Jesus' pre-human existence in the prologue to his Gospel. In fact, the Gospel of John begins with the claim that Jesus is God, and it later includes testimony by John the Baptist and by Jesus himself that this claim is true.[269]

There are six miracles that only appear in the Gospel of John, including Jesus' first miracle of turning water into wine, and his final miracle, just after his resurrection when he made a huge catch of 153 fish after others had caught none at the same location.[270]

The apostle John is usually credited with the authorship of the fourth Gospel. The author must have been an eyewitness to the ministry of the life of Jesus (see 1:14, 19:35 and 21:24). Also, he must have had some familiarity with Palestine before the destruction of the Temple in 70 CE. And he would have had to have been familiar with the everyday Jewish life of the first century.

The Apostle John fits all of these criteria, but he is not the only individual who fits them. Early traditions in the Church also identify the author of the fourth Gospel to be the Apostle John. Irenaeus, a disciple of Polycarp, who, in turn, was an associate of John, asserts the identification of John as the author of the fourth Gospel. In the earliest extant manuscripts, the Gospel of John is associated with the apostle. One manuscript begins, "*Kata Ioannes*," or "According to John."[271]

The "Egerton Gospel," as it is known, is a collection of papyrus fragments of a previously unknown Gospel. It was discovered in Egypt in 1934 and sold to the British Museum in the same year. It was in print a year later in 1935. The fragments consist of four narratives that include the following:

- A controversy similar to John 5:39–47.

- A curing of a sinner, much like Matthew 8:4, Mark 1:40–45 and Luke 5:12–16.

- A controversy about paying tribute to the Roman Emperor like Matthew 22:15–22, Mark 12:13–17 and Luke 20:20–26.

- An incomplete account of a miracle on the Jordan River, much like the story of the Seeds and the Sower.[272]

There are both similarities and differences among the canonical Gospel and the Egerton Gospel. There are many disagreements among New Testament scholars and archeologists about the date of these fragments. Most date these in the second century CE, but a few scholars believe it came from the first century and may have used the Q Sources. Ronald Cameron, one of those scholars, suggests, "It was probably composed in the second half of the first century in Syria shortly before the Gospel of John was written."[273]

The text designated as P45 is one of three papyrus codices, the other two being P46 and P47, purchased by British mining engineer, A. Chester Beatty from an Egyptian dealer in the 1930s. These fragments are now housed the Chester Beatty Museum, Dublin, Ireland. P45 contains parts of all four canonical Gospels, as well as Acts of the Apostles.

Codex P46 contains several letters of Paul, including Romans, Hebrews, First and Second Corinthians, Galatians, Philippians, Colossians and Second Thessalonians. Codes 47 contains the oldest known text of the Book of Revelation.

The Gospel of John is generally considered to be the last written of the four canonical Gospels. There is no limit about how early the fourth gospel was written, but the author did not use Matthew, Mark and Luke to construct his work. In the nineteenth century, some scholars dated the book to the second century CE, but that view gradually has decreased since that time. When two manuscripts of John from the early second century CE were discovered, what is known as P46 and the Egerton Papyrus2, the majority of scholars now date the Gospel of John to the late first century CE, between 90 and 99.[274]

Where the Gospel of John was written has been a matter of some dispute from the second half of the twentieth century to the present time. The two possibilities that have gained the most acceptance are Syria and in Asia Minor. Syria has been suggested because of the possible connection to the "Odes of Solomon," and to Ignatius of Antioch, who, around 110 had some association with the Gospel.

The "Odes to Solomon" is a collection of forty-two odes, or poems, attributed to King Solomon. Most scholars date the work to a time from the first to the third century CE. The original language of the *Odes* was probably either Greek or Syriac, and it is generally thought to have been a Christian document that first circulated in Syria. [275]

The other theory about the place of origin for the Gospel of John is the city of Ephesus in Asia Minor. This is the view that is held by most of the Early Church fathers who have commented on the matter.[276]

John specifically states the purpose of his Gospel at 20:31, where he writes:

> But these words are written that you may believe that
> Jesus is the Christ, the Son of God, and that by believing
> you may have life in his name.

The purpose of the fourth Gospel, then, is to confirm and to secure Christians in their basic faith. John also employs 3:16 and 8:24 to communicate this purpose of the Gospel. In the former verse, John tells us:

> For God so loved the world that He gave His one and
> only Son, that whoever believes in him shall not perish
> but shall have eternal life.

This is clearly an example that the writer(s) of the Gospel of John believed in the Divine Plan Theory. In the latter passage, John relates:

I told you that you have died in your sins. If you do not
believe that I am He, you will indeed die in your sins.

Some early Christian interpreters used this verse in the Gospel
of John as a proof text for the doctrine of Original Sin. Augustine of
Hippo, for example, was one of those early Christians. The Early Church
father, Eusebius, tells us that John wrote his Gospel to supplement
the Synoptics "where they were lacking."[277] The Muratorian Canon
suggests that John's fellow disciples in Asia Minor urged him to write
down his account. The Muratorian Canon contains the earliest list of
the books of the New Testament. The manuscript consists of eighty-
five lines and is usually dated to around the year 170 CE, but it could
have been written much earlier.[278]

The specific audience for whom the Gospel of John was written
is not clear, but the Muratorian Canon suggests that it may have been
written for fellow believers in the churches of Asia Minor.[279]

There is a variety of theological themes to be found in the Gospel
of John. One of those themes is the dichotomy between Light and
Darkness. In John's Gospel, the Light is associated with God and the
Good, as well as eternal life, while dark and darkness are associated
with death, the Devil, and evil, in general.[280] This theme is reasserted
in the fourth gospel at 1:5 by the notion that "Those in the Darkness do
not understand the Light." Evildoers hate the Light in John's Gospel,
and they hate going into it.

There is a plethora of mentions of Light and Darkness in the
Gospel of John. Jesus is called the "Light of the World" at 8:12 and
9:5. The Devil is called the "Prince of this World," at 12:31, 14:30
and 16:11. At 12:46, Jesus tells the crowd that he has come "as Light
to the World, so that those who believe in him will not remain in the
Darkness."

Another theme, in addition to Jesus' "pre-existence" and the clash
between Light and Darkness in the Gospel of John, has to do with the
developing of Christology in the book, a view that is distinct from the
other Gospels. Related to this is the belief throughout the book that
Jesus Christ is the Messiah, and that he is God as well. In the very
opening verse, the Gospel claims that the *Logos* was with God and is

God. Indeed, throughout the fourth Gospel, many references are made to the divinity of Jesus.

Perhaps the most notable of these passages comes at 8:57 and 58, where Jesus declares, "Before Abraham was born, I am." Here Jesus may be making an allusion to Exodus 3:14 when the God Yahweh answers a question about His identity simply by saying, "I am Who I am." By this, He means the One, Existing Being, the Holy God. By this, then, Jesus recognizes that he is God.

Another assertion of the divinity of Jesus can be found at 10:30–33, where Jesus relates, "I and my Father are one." After making this claim, the Jews around him picked up stones because of Jesus' blasphemy, in that he claimed to be God. At the end of the Gospel, we get another indication that Jesus is God when, at 20:28, the disciple Thomas claims that "Jesus is his God."

In terms of literary style, the Gospel of John varies from the Synoptics in many ways. Scholar J. Ramsey Michaels categorizes these variations into two types. That is, the style and content of the teachings of Jesus. And secondly, the chronology and the structure of the ministry of Jesus.[281] Another peculiarity of the style of the Gospel of John is that the Fourth Gospel is known as the "Spiritual Gospel" from the Prologue all the way to the Epilogue at 21:1–25.[282]

Indeed, John's Gospel soars to its greatest spiritual heights when Jesus attempts to make known the warm love between Father and Son, as well as the relationship to be gained by being in union with them. In fact, John uses the word "love" and the verb "to love" far more often than the other three Gospels combined.[283] Usually, the words for love in John's Gospel are *agapeo* and *agape*, which are used two dozen times in John. The Fourth Gospel does not, however, employ the classical verb *philos* and *phileo*, which means "to love."

Some have argued that this Epilogue seems a bit out of place because the final lines in chapter 20 seem to bring the Gospel to a close. This has led some scholars to posit the view that the Epilogue was a later edition to the original book. This has led some to suggest that there may have been two authors of the Fourth Gospel—John the Apostle and a later editor, perhaps one of the followers of John or a student of his.[284]

One bit of evidence that supports the idea of the later editor/ contributor is that there are twenty-eight Koine Greek words in chapter 21 that are not found elsewhere in the book or in the Synoptics.[285]

Rather than simply recording Jesus' public addresses, John records many dialogues with individuals, both disciples and enemies. John gives us an intimate portrait of Jesus, including his longest recorded prayer to his Father in Heaven at 17:1–26.

Two final aspects of the Fourth Gospel are relevant for this introduction. The first has to do with the content of the Gospel, and the other has to do with the language of the Gospel of John. In regard to content, if it were not for the Gospel of John, we would not have known that Jesus' public ministry was for a period of three years. We know this because there are four Passovers in John at 2:13, 5:1, 6:4 and 13:1.

Of the sixty-two narratives that appear in the Gospel of John, thirty-two of them contain material not found in the Synoptics. Some of this material that is peculiar to John includes:

- Turning water to wine at the Wedding Feast of Cana (chapter 2)
- The requirement to be "born again" (chapter 3)
- The woman at the well (chapter 4)
- The thirty-eight-year cripple (chapter 5)
- The Bread of Life discourse (chapter 6)
- The woman taken in adultery (chapter 8)
- The man born blind (chapter 9)
- The shepherd and sheep (chapter 10)
- Lazarus raised from the dead (chapter 11)
- Washing of the disciples' feet (chapter 13)
- Jesus foretelling his betrayer (chapter 13)
- Jesus foretelling Peter's denial (chapter 13)
- Jesus as the Way to the Father (chapter 14)
- Jesus as the true vine (chapter 15)
- The work of the Spirit (chapter 16)

- Praying for peace for the Disciples (chapter 16)

- Jesus praying for his disciples (chapter 16)[286]

It is only in the Gospel of John that the works of Jesus are called "signs." Indeed, the emphasis on miraculous "signs" in the Gospel of John is unique. The use of the term "I am" is also peculiar to John's Gospel at 8:24, 28 and 58. The Gospel of John uses the Greek particles *oun* and *hina* more often than any of the Synoptics—120 times for the former, and 130 times for the latter.[287]

John's Gospel stresses the deity of the incarnate Son with his seven "I am" statements. These come at 6:35, 8:12, 10:7, 10:11, 11:25, 14:6 and 15:1.[288] In total, about 93 percent of John's Gospel does not appear in the Synoptics.[289] The Gospel of John has twenty-two direct quotations of the Old Testament, or Hebrew Bible, as well as one hundred and five allusions to the Hebrew text, far more than the other Gospels.[290]

The word *Ioudaios*, or "the Jews," occurs over seventy times in the Gospel of John, some of these are ethnic comments, some are about the inhabitants of Judaea, and some refer to the Jewish religion.[291] John does mention "the Jews" far more often than any of the other three Gospels.

It is clear that the writer of the Gospel of John has critical knowledge of Jerusalem with his references to Bethesda at 5:2, Solomon's Porch at 10:23, as well as the city and the Temple at 8:20, 18:1, 19:20, 19:41, and many other passages.[292]

In regard to the peculiar language of the Gospel of John, the text uses many more contrasts than do the other Gospels. These include light and darkness, truth and lies, the Kingdom of God and the Kingdom of the Devil, Good and evil, and many others. Nearly 35 percent of the Gospel of John is about one day in Jesus' pubic ministry. That is, the day before his Crucifixion.[293]

The Gospel of John is called the "Gospel of Believing" many times, but not in the Synoptics. The verb "to believe," or *pisteou*, occurs ninety-eight times in the fourth Gospel. There are no references to demonic possession in the Gospel of John. This word comes from the Greek verb *pistos*, or "to know." This verb is the origin of the English word epistemology, as well as many other words.

The verb "to witness," or *martureo*, is employed thirty-four times as a verb, and thirteen as a noun. These same words are only used sixteen times in Matthew, Mark, and Luke.[294]

The name for the demonic, *Beelzebub*, does not appear in the Fourth Gospel, but it can be found in Matthew, Mark and Luke.

The words "glory" and "glorify" are employed much more often in the Gospel of John. The noun "glory" is used nineteen times, while the verb "to glorify" is employed twenty-two times.[295] The expression "Came down from Heaven" is used in the Fourth Gospel over forty times.[296] The Greek term for "glory" is *doxa*, from which we get "doxology." And the word for "glorify" is *kauchema*.

The expression "Amen, Amen," or "Verily, Verily," occurs twenty-five times in the Gospel of John. It is used to refer to Christ at 1:51, about Christ's glory at 8:58, his eternality at 10:1 and 7, of Christ's uniqueness at 6:32, his mission in 13; 21, his betrayal and in his death at 12:24.[297]

The Gospel of John uses the noun "Love" (*agape*) and the verb "to Love" more than the other three Gospels combined. The word "world" is employed seventy-eight times in the fourth Gospel, to indicate that Jesus' message was intended to the widest possible audience. The word that John usually employs for "love" is *agape*, which can be found throughout the Gospel at places like 5:42, 13:35, 15:10 twice, 16:13, 17:26, and many others.

The word for "world" in John's Gospel is the term *Kosmos*, which, of course, is the origin for the English cosmos. It is employed more often in the Fourth Gospel than in the other three combined.

In the place of the word *parabole*, or "parables," the author of the Gospel of John prefers the use of *paroimia*, a word that means "proverbs." We see this difference at John 10:6, 16:25 twice, and at 16:29.

In the Gospel of John, we often find extended discourses rather than the pithy parables in the Synoptic Gospels. Examples of these "extended" discourses can be found at the story of Nicodemus in chapter 3, the Samaritan woman in the fourth chapter, the Bread of Life narrative in chapter 6, and the Farewell Discourse, that extends from chapter 13 to chapter 17.

The idea of the "Kingdom of God" is largely ignored in the Gospel of John. It is only employed five times in the Synoptic Gospels, whereas the idea is used 130 times in Matthew, Mark and Luke. In its place, John uses the expression "eternal life" in the place of the "Kingdom of God." Eternal Life is used forty-one times in the fourth Gospel, but only sixteen times in the Gospel of Matthew, Mark and Luke.

Finally, the Gospel of John contains two sets of seven—seven signs and seven "I am" statements. The first collection of seven occurs at:

1. Water to wine (2:1–11)
2. Nobleman's son healed (4:46–51)
3. Impotent man healed (5:1–9)
4. Feeding the 5,000 (6:1–14)
5. Walking on water (6:16–21)
6. Healing of the blind man (9:1–7)
7. Resurrection of Lazarus (11:1–46)[298]

The seven "I am" statements in the Gospel of John appear in the following places:

1. The Bread of Life (6:35)
2. The Light of the World (8:12)
3. The Door (10:9)
4. The Good Shepherd (10:11)
5. The Resurrection and the Life (11:25)
6. The Way, the Truth, and the Life (14:6)
7. The Vine (15:1)[299]

There are also many things that do not appear in the Gospel of John but can be found in the Synoptics. Among these items are the following:

- No genealogy.
- No baptism.
- No temptation in the wilderness

- No appointing of the Apostles.
- The two words for "Forgive" do not appear in John's Gospel (*aphiemi* and *charizomai*).
- There is no demonic possession in John.
- There is no transfiguration.
- There is no account of Christ's Ascension.
- The word "repent" does not appear in the fourth Gospel (*meta-noeo*).
- The Coming of the Son of Man is not in the Gospel of John.
- The word *parabole*, or "parables," is not in John.
- There is no sending out others to preach in the fourth Gospel.
- And many other things.[300]

Before we move to a discussion of evil and suffering in the Gospel of John, we first will make some comments on why the Gospel of John is so different from the Synoptic texts, the topic of the next section of this ninth chapter.

Why is the Gospel of John so Different from the Others?

Most contemporary Bible scholars believe that Mark was the first to write his Gospel, most likely between 55 and 65 CE. The Gospel of Mark is a relatively fast-paced portrayal of the ministry of Jesus. It was probably written for a Gentile audience, most likely for Gentile Christians, perhaps living in Rome.

New Testament scholars disagree, however, about which Gospel followed Mark. That is, Matthew or Luke. Ninety-five percent of Mark's Gospel is in Matthew and Luke, so the priority becomes a problem for scholars.

Matthew's Gospel appears to be addressed primarily to a Jewish audience. This makes sense, given the fact that many of the original converts to Christianity were Jews. Matthew's purpose, accordingly, was to prove that Jesus was the Messiah, while many of the Jewish authorities of his day rejected him.

Like Mark, the Gospel of Luke was originally intended for a Gentile audience, in large part because the author himself may have been a Gentile. Luke wrote his Gospel with the purpose of providing a historically accurate account of the life of Jesus, his death, and his resurrection, or so Luke 1:1–4 proposes.

In many ways, while Mark and Matthew sought to codify Jesus' story for a specific audience (Gentile and Jew, respectively), Luke's purposes were far more apologetic. He wanted to prove that Jesus' story was true.

The generation of people with first-hand knowledge of Jesus was now dying off, and the writers wanted to lend reliability and credibility, and staying power to the Early Church—particularly after the destruction of the Temple in 70 CE.

The major purposes and themes of the Gospel of John were different. Jesus is portrayed primarily as an authoritative miracle worker and the Son of God. The writer's purposes are theological. He is responding to popular movements at the end of the first century, including mystery religions and the movement of Gnosticism. The writer of John's Gospel was engaged in theological debates against heresies that had become rampant.

At the same time, John's Gospel most likely was written at the very end of the first century CE. It is probably the product of the Apostle John and one of his most important students, as we have suggested earlier in this chapter.

The Gospel of John is also a more thorough account of the person of Jesus, particularly in terms of his divinity. One key to showing this is that the personal pronoun "I" is only employed seventeen times in the Synoptics, while it is used 118 times in the fourth Gospel. Jesus spends far more time in the fourth Gospel explaining his nature than he does in the other three.

The purposes and themes of John's Gospel were to show Jesus as the Divine Word, the *Logos*, the pre-existent Son of God, who is one with God (10:3). This Jesus took on flesh in order to be a tabernacle among us (1:14). In other words, the author of the fourth Gospel took great pains to make it crystal clear that Jesus was indeed God in a human form.

Another way to see the major differences between the Gospel of John and the Synoptics is to examine the Koine Greek vocabulary of the four Gospels with respect to words associated with evil and suffering. The word *kakos* that is employed dozens of times in the Synoptic Gospels is only used three times in the Gospel of John at 7:7, 18:23 and 30, but the NRSV translates the word as "evil," "wrongly," and "criminal" in the three passages, nothing like the Synoptics.

The Greek word *poneros* appears many times in Matthew, Mark and Luke, but only three times in the Gospel of John at 2:13, 3:12 and 17:15, where it is rendered "evil One." The Koine Greek term *phaulos*, usually translated as "wicked," is employed six times in the New Testament, and two of those are at 3:20 and 5:29. The word *atheteo*, the verb "to despise" or "to reject," is used a dozen times in the New Testament, but only a single time at John 12:48.

Finally, another term that means "to rot," *sapros*, is used many times in the Synoptics and Paul, but this word does not appear in the Gospel of John. Thus, our conclusion should be obvious: the language about evil, suffering and destruction is very different from that of the Synoptic Gospels and the Epistles of Paul.

What is true about words related to evil in the Gospel of John is also true of terms related to "suffer" and to "suffering." *Patheos*, meaning "one who suffers," does not appear in the fourth Gospel. *Pascho*, a word that implies "suffer," is used forty-two times in the New Testament but not in John. *Pathema*, a Koine Greek word that designates the "suffering of an evil," appears sixteen times in the New Testament but is not to be found in the Gospel of John.

Similarly, the word *odunao*, a verb that means "to cause to suffer," occurs throughout the Synoptics and the Epistles of Paul, but this particular verb is not employed in the fourth Gospel of the New Testament. Thus, what is true about words related to evil in the Gospel of John is also true of terms related to suffering in the fourth Gospel. Many Koine Greek words that appear elsewhere in the New Testament cannot be found in the Gospel of John.

The Johannine vocabulary of words associated with the Demonic is also very different from the Synoptics and from the Letters of Paul. The word *daimon*, or Devil, does not appear in the fourth Gospel. Nor does the Koine Greek word *daimonion*, or "Devils," while it appears thirty-two times in the rest of the New Testament. The word *ekbello*, which means "to cast out," can be found twenty-five times in the New Testament, but not in the fourth Gospel.

The Greek adjective *daimoniodes*, which designates "demon-like," can be found throughout the New Testament, but it does not appear in the Gospel of John. The fourth Gospel does contain the word *daimonizomai* one time. It means "to be possessed." It appears thirteen times in the New Testament, but only once in John at 10:21. Indeed, the writer of the Gospel of John seems to have been disinterested in the idea.

The conclusion we can make about Greek words related to demons and possession by demons is drastically different in the Gospel of John than in the Koine vocabularies of the writers of the Gospels of Matthew, Mark and Luke, as well as the Koine Greek glossary of the Apostle of Paul.

This brings us to a discussion of the many places in the fourth Gospel, where the issues of theodicy and the problem of evil may be found as answers and responses to the issues of evil and suffering in the Gospel of John.

Evil and Suffering in the Gospel of John

The writer of the Gospel of John uses, or assents to, at least eight different answers and responses to the questions of theodicy and the problem of evil. These answers and responses are the following:

- The Influences of Demonic Forces Theory
- The Original Sin Perspective
- Retributive Justice Theory
- The Free Will Defense
- The Contrast View
- The Two *Yetzerim* Theory
- The Test View
- The Divine Plan Perspective

In this section of Chapter Nine, we will examine several examples of each of these answers/responses in the fourth Gospel, the Gospel of John, beginning with the Influences of Demonic Forces Theory. Among the passages in the Gospel of John that indicate a belief in demons are the following:

- 6:70

- 7:7

- 8:44

- 10:20

- 12:31

- 13:27

- 14:30

- 17:15

In the first of these, John tells us, "Jesus answered them, 'Did I not choose you, the twelve? Yet one of you is a devil.'" He was speaking of Judas, son of Simon Iscariot, for he thought that one of the twelve will betray him. Jesus' use of a future tense verb here may be an indication of the Divine Plan Theory, as well.

At the Gospel of John 7:7–9, the writer combines the Demonic Forces View with the Divine Plan Theory when he writes:

> The world cannot hate you, but it hates me because I testify that its works are evil. You go to the festival. I am not going to the festival because my time has not yet fully come. After he said this, he stayed in Galilee.

The use of future tense verbs and the idea of the "time to come" are evidence that Jesus knows what will occur in his life. The idea of the works of the world being evil may be a reference to the Original Sin Theory, or it may indicate the epoch of which the Devil is in charge of what goes on in the Earth.

At the Gospel of John 8:44, we find one of the most peculiar passages about the demonic in the fourth Gospel, as well as the remainder of the New Testament. This text tells us this:

> You are from your father, the Devil, and you do your
> father's desires. He was a murderer from the beginning
> and does not stand in the truth.

The Gospel of John uses the noun *Diabolos*, or "Devil," in this verse from John 8. In 8:48, 49 and 51, John also employs the word *daemon*, or "demon," three times. Most interpreters understand John 8:44 as a reference to Satan, appearing as a snake in the narrative of Genesis 3. His temptation there arouses the "desires" of Adam and Eve, leading to the first murder of one of their sons. John 8:44 also may be related to the Fallen Angels narrative when it refers to not standing "for the truth."

At 10:20, the Apostle John indicates that some of those in the first century believed in demonic possession when John writes:

> Many of them were saying, "He has a demon, and he is
> out of his mind... Others were saying these are not the
> words of a demon. Can a demon open the eyes of the
> blind?"

Clearly, John believed there were some in his time that believed Jesus was possessed by a demon. But this passage comes immediately after Jesus healing the blind man in chapter 9, so John responds to the claim of possession by arguing that one possessed of a demon could not heal a blind man.

At 12:31, the Apostle John tells us, "Now is the judgment of this world, now the ruler of this world will be driven out." Of course, the ruler of this world is Satan. This becomes clear in two other passages in the Gospel of John, where Satan is called the "ruler of this world," and then the "prince of this world." At 13:27 of John's Gospel, the Apostle speaks of Judas Iscariot being given a piece of bread, and then John says, "and Satan entered into him." This is the only time in the Gospel of John that the Apostle uses the word Satanas, or "Satan."

Finally, at 17:15, John relates, "I am not asking you to take them out of the world, but I ask you to protect them from the evil One" (*Poneros*). From these eight passages, we may conclude that the Apostle John assented to the view of the Influences from Demonic Forces in his fourth Gospel.

The writer of the fourth Gospel had several names for the Demonic, in addition to its uses of *Satanas*, or Satan, and *diablos*, or the Devil. Among these additional names to designate the Demonic are "the Prince of this World" at 12:31; the "wicked one" employed at 5:19; and "Liar," that is used along with Satan at 8:44 of the Gospel of John, and *Poneros*, or the evil One, at 17:15.

One thing that is peculiar about the Gospel of John is that there are no exorcisms to be found there. Whereas, for example, Matthew, Mark and Luke give an account of Jesus' healing of the Gerasene demoniac, where Jesus exorcises a demon, or perhaps demons out of a man and into a herd of swine, causing the animals to run down a hill and into a lake where they drown themselves. [301] There is, however, no comparable narrative to be found in the fourth Gospel.

Another curious thing about John's language regarding the demonic is that he does not use the verb *peirasmos*, or "to tempt," but it does appear in dozens of examples in the Synoptic Gospels where it is often predicated of Satan or the Devil.

Although John does not mention the Original Sin Theory directly, some scholars suggest that the narrative in chapter 3 of John's Gospel, and its insistence that one must be "born again" in the Spirit, may be connected to Original Sin. At 3:5–7, John relates:

> "Very truly I tell you no one may enter the Kingdom of God without having been born from above." Then Nicodemus said to him, "How can one be born again after having grown old? Can one enter a second time into the mother's womb and be reborn?" Then Jesus answered, "Very truly I tell you no one may enter the kingdom of God without being born of water and Spirit. Do not be astonished that I said to you, 'You must be born from above.'"

May it not be that even in the very earliest church that the sacrament of baptism was believed to eradicate the signs of Original Sin, much like the same belief in the Medieval, and more modern churches. If the answer to that question is "Yes," then we may add the Original Sin Theory to our list of the Apostle John's answers and responses to the phenomena of evil and suffering. The use of the word *hudor*, or "water," may be an indication that this view is the correct one.[302]

Another place in the history of the church where some interpreters find Original Sin in the Gospel of John is chapter 8:34 that relates:

> Very truly, I tell you, everyone who commits a sin is a
> slave to sin.[303]

Now this may be an assertion of the universality of human sin, or the claim may come with the realization that we all sin because by our very natures, we suffer from Original Sin, inherited directly from Adam and Eve.

In many places in the fourth Gospel, John employs the Retributive Justice Theory. We will point to three or four of these passages to make our point. The narrative at chapter 5 that concerns Jesus performing a healing on the Sabbath may be seen as an example of the Retributive Justice Theory, for the man was lame and then placed in a pool so he could be healed. Jesus may well be saying your sins did not have you deserve this.

At John 5:14, after Jesus had found a sinning man in the Temple and he healed him and said, "Behold, you are made whole. Go and sin no more unless a worse thing will come upon you." Clearly, it is the Retributive Justice Theory that lies behind this comment.

Finally, one curious passage that also may be about Retributive Justice comes at the Gospel of John 12:37–40. In the verses, John writes, "Those who did not believe in Jesus could not believe," because, quoting Isaiah 6:10, "God has blinded their eyes and hardened their hearts." Here John seems to suggest that these non-believers could not freely choose to follow Jesus, because their fates already have been sealed.

A similar episode can be seen at 9:1–4. In this narrative, one of his disciples asked if a blind man had sinned or if his parents had sinned to bring on the blindness, an obvious case of the Individual, or Collective, Retributive Justice Theory, either the sin of the individual, or of his family. But Jesus' response is instructive, "Neither, it was for the greater glory of God that this man was born blind." Theologically speaking, what began as an episode of the Retributive Justice Theory has now morphed into an example of the Divine Plan Perspective.

At 15:6, John gives us another example of Retributive Justice. In that verse, he says to his disciples:

> Whoever does not abide in me is thrown away like a branch and withers. And such branches are gathered up and thrown into the fire and burned.

Thus, Jesus speaks of a retribution for those who do not abide in him. So far in this section of Chapter Nine, we established that the Apostle John appears to have assented to the Influences of Demonic Forces Theory, to the Retributive Justice View, and possibly to the Original Sin Theory. In several passages there is evidence that John also utilized the Free Will Defense in his Gospel.

The best place in the Gospel of John to see an application of the Free Will Defense is in 8:31–36. We make this claim because John employs the words *eleutheroo* and *eleutheros* at verse 32 and again at verse 36. The first of these is a verb that means "to make free" or "to be released from some type of bondage." Figuratively, it implies the removal of restrictions from sin, or darkness, and thus to be delivered by God into true spiritual freedom.[304]

These two Greek terms for freedom, eleutheroo and eleutheros, are only employed in John's Gospel in these two verses in chapter 8. These same words, as we shall see in Chapter Ten to follow, can be found much more frequently in the letters of Paul, such as at Romans 8:2 and 21, as well as Galatians 5:1.

The other way that we find the use of the notion of free will in the Gospel of John is with the many uses of the noun *kardia*, or "heart," in the fourth Gospel. Many of these appear to be references to the Two *Yetzerim* Theory, such as at 12:40, 13:2, 14:1 and 27, and 16:6 and 22. In the first of these, John quotes the Prophet Isaiah and the idea of the "hardening of the heart."

In the second John passage on the heart, the one at 13:2, the text speaks of the evil of the heart of Judas, an obvious reference to the *yetzer ha ra*. The passage at 14:27 does the same thing. John 16:6 speaks of "sorrow filling the heart," and at 16:22, John informs us, "your hearts will rejoice," a reference to the *yetzer tov*, or the good inclination or imagination.

In his Gospel, the Apostle John also regularly appears to assent to the Contrast View. This can be seen at 1:5, 3:19–20, 8:12, 9:39, and 12:35–36, for several examples. In the first of these, John relates, "The light shines in the darkness, and the darkness did not overcome it."

At 3:19–20, the Apostle John relates:

> The Light has come into the world and the people loved darkness rather than the Light because their deeds were evil. For all who do evil and hate the Light and do not come to the Light, so that their deeds may not be exposed. But those who do what is true come to the Light, so that it may clearly be seen that their deeds have been done in God.

At chapter 8:12, Jesus again returns to the theme of the contrast of Light and Dark, when he says, "I am the light of the world. Whoever follows me will never walk in darkness but will have the Light of Life." At 9:39, Jesus switches the contrast from Light and Darkness, to sight and blindness. Jesus says, "I came into the world so that those who cannot see, may see, and those who do see may become blind."

The Apostle John has Jesus return to the dichotomy of Light and Darkness at 12:35–36, when Jesus reveals, "The Light is with you a little while longer, walk while you still have the Light, so that the Darkness may not overtake you. If you walk in the Darkness you will not know where you are going. While you have the Light, believe in the Light, so that you may become Children of Light."

The expression "Children of Light" is employed throughout the New Testament. In addition to John 12:36, it also can be found at Luke 16:8 and in Paul's letter to the Ephesians at 5:8 and 5:9, and First Thessalonians 5:5. The Greek of the phrase implies a belonging of all those "who are in the Light." At John 14:1 and 27, the Apostle again may be assenting to the Contrast View. These verses tell us:

> Do not let your hearts be troubled. If you believe in God, believe also in me.

And at the Gospel of John 14:27, the Apostle of the fourth Gospel relates, "Peace I leave with you, my peace I give you. I did not give to you as the world gives. Do not let your hearts be troubled and do not be afraid." Again, the use of the word *cardia*, or heart, may refer to the Jewish view that the heart was the "seat of the self," and the maker of moral decisions.

The Test View is not one that can often be found in the Gospel of John. It does, however, appear at 6:5–6, where John employs the verb to test, or *peirazo*. The same verb also is used at John 8:6:

> They said this to test him, so that they might have some charge to bring against him.

Another Koine Greek word is also employed in the New Testament to designate a "test" or a "temptation." This word is *ekpiradzo*. It is not used in the Gospel of John, but it can be seen at Matthew 4:7 and Luke 10:25, as we have shown in the previous chapter. We will see in the next chapter that Paul also employs this verb at First Corinthians 10:9 and 13, among other places.

Earlier in this chapter, we argued that the narrative about the man born blind at the beginning of chapter 9 of the Gospel of John moves from a discussion of the Retributive Justice Theory to the reason for the blindness being "for the greater glory of God," and thus the Divine Plan Theory. We also see this view in many other places in the Gospel of John in two separate ways by using future tense verbs and traditional understandings of the Divine Plan Theory.

At the Gospel of John 18:4, for example, we see a version of the latter approach. The Apostle John relates:

> Then Jesus, knowing all that was about to happen to him, came forward and He asked them, "Who are you looking for?"

Clearly, this verse indicates the omniscience of Jesus, as well as an indication of the Divine Plan Theory. At John 16:23, we see an example of the Divine Plan Theory with the use of future tense verbs. The text relates:

> On that day you will ask nothing of me. Very truly I will
> tell you, if you ask anything of the Father, He shall give
> it to you.

Other indications of the Divine Plan Theory by the use of future tense verbs in the fourth Gospel may be found at 4:21 and 5:25, as well as 11:23–26 and 12:31. At 4:21, Jesus says to the Samaritan woman, "Believe me, the hour is coming when you will worship the Father neither on this mountain nor in Jerusalem."

We find a similar remark at John 5:25:

> Very truly I tell you, the hour is coming, and is now here,
> when the dead will hear the voice of the Son of God.

Jesus mentions the "Hour" at 12:23–33, also with the employment of future tense verbs. In both verses, Jesus says, "The hour has come for the Son of Man," another indication of what is to come in the future, a plan that Jesus already knows. Just a few verses earlier at 12:31, Jesus informs us that "The ruler of this world will be driven out," again using a future tense verb.

Jesus mentions the Hour in many places in the fourth Gospel. He uses the term at the Wedding Feast at Cana at 2:4 and to the Samaritan woman at 4:21 and 23, as we have shown. At John 5:25 and 28, Jesus mentions the Hour to the Jews. At 7:6, when he is being arrested, he says, "My hour has not yet come." And the next chapter at 8:20, the text also relates that "My time has not yet fully come."

Already, we have spoken of the Hour in connection to chapter 12 of the Gospel of John, particularly 12:23 and 12:27, as well as to the reference to the Hour at 13:1. We also see the employment of the word "Hour" at John 16:2, 4, 21, 25 and 32, and most of these speak of the coming of the Hour, using future tense verbs.

The Greek word *Hora*, or "Hour," which figuratively means a time of sixty minutes, but allegorically refers to a Divine pre-set time, a period of accomplishment is also used nearly thirty times in the Gospel of Matthew, as well as five times in the Gospel of Mark.[305] The word *Hora* is not used in the Gospel of Luke.

The Greek word *Hora* is also the origin of words for "hour" in many modern languages, including Spanish, Portuguese, English, French, Italian, German, Dutch, and many other modern tongues.

We may also see the application of the Divine Plan Theory through the use of a future tense verb when Jesus, speaking of the Hour, says, "On that day, you will ask nothing of me," meaning the resurrection of the dead at the End of Time.[306]

From these evaluations of these passages, then, we may conclude that the Apostle John was a firm believer in the view that God in Heaven has a Divine Plan by which, in the end, all evil will be seen as working out for the Good. The author of the fourth Gospel expresses this view in places like 18:4, where it is clear that Jesus knows the Plan, as well as in his use of future tense verbs when he speaks of things like the "Hour."

From our tentative analyses, we have shown that the writer of the Gospel of John seems to assent to, or is a proponent of, the following answers and responses to the questions of theodicy and the problem of evil:

- The Influences of Demonic Forces Theory
- Original Sin Theory (possibly)
- The Retributive Justice Perspective
- The Free Will Defense
- The Two *Yetzerim* Theory
- The Contrast Perspective
- The Test View
- The Divine Plan Theory

In addition to these eight answers and responses to the questions of evil and suffering in the Gospel of John, there are also some indications that the Apostle John was an advocate of what we have labeled the "Practical Approach" to the issues of theodicy and the problem of evil. This is the subject matter of the final section of this ninth chapter.

The Practical Approach in the Gospel of John

Like what we have seen in Chapter Eight on the Synoptic Gospels that all seem to endorse the Practical Approach to evil and suffering, the same view also can be seen in the fourth Gospel, the Gospel of John. In several narratives of John's Gospel, the Apostle features Jesus' compassion and pity on the poor, the needy, the lame, the blind, as well as in the case of Lazarus, raising him from the dead.[307]

Among the many places to see the compassion and pity of Jesus, the Practical Approach, are the turning of water to wine at the Wedding Feast of Cana in chapter 2, the healing of the official's son in chapter 4 of John, the healing at the pool of Bethesda in chapter 5, The feeding of the five thousand in chapter 6 of John's Gospel, returning sight to the man born blind in 9:1–4 of the Gospel of John, the raising of Lazarus from the dead in John 11, and the catching of 153 fish in the fourth Gospel's chapter 21.

In each of these miracles of Jesus in the Gospel of John, Jesus assesses the needs of one who is suffering, and then makes a plan of how that suffering can be ameliorated. In the Gospel of John, each of these episodes is described as a "Sign," or *Seimion*, a neuter noun that is used seventeen times in the Gospel of John.

Another indication of the compassion of Jesus in the Gospel of John comes at 13:1. In this verse, the Apostle John relates:

> Now before the festival of the Passover, Jesus knew
> that his hour had come to depart from this world and
> to go to the Father; and having loved his own in the
> world, he loved them to the end.

In chapter 19:26–27, Jesus shows compassion to the Apostle John and to his own mother, Mary. He says about John to Mary, "Here is your son." And to John he says, "and here is your mother."

At the Gospel of John 7:37, we find another indication of the compassion of Jesus Christ, when he says, "Let anyone who is thirsty come to me, and let the one who believes in me drink." When Jesus heals the official's son at John 4:46–49, he has compassion for the official when he tells him:

Unless you see signs and wonders, you will not believe.

The word for signs in this verse is the same word we saw earlier, *seimion,* but the word for "wonders," the Koine Greek noun, *Teras,* is used sixteen times in the New Testament, and only this single time in the fourth Gospel. This word for "wonders" is used many more times in the Acts of the Apostles and in the Letters of Paul, such as at Romans 15:19 and Hebrews 2:4, as well as many other places, as we shall see in Chapter Ten.

This brings us to the major conclusions in Chapter Nine. As indicated earlier, the subject matter of Chapter Ten will be the places in the Letters of Paul and in the Acts of the Apostles, where the issues of evil and suffering may be found. We move, then, to the conclusions of this chapter.

Conclusions

We began this ninth chapter with a very general introduction to the fourth Gospel, the Gospel of John. In that introduction, we made many observations about the Apostle John's Gospel and how it is similar and different from the Synoptic texts of Matthew, Mark and Luke. Indeed, we have shown that of the sixty-two narratives that appear in the fourth Gospel, more than half of them are not in the Synoptics.

In this first section of Chapter Nine, we also made the argument that the fourth Gospel was authored by the Apostle John, Jesus' "most beloved" disciple, and that it is most likely this Gospel was written in the city of Ephesus in Asia Minor. We also indicated in that section of Chapter Nine that there may have been more than one author to the Gospel of John.

We also explored in the first section of Chapter Nine some peculiarities in regard to the content of John's Gospel, as well as the uniqueness of his vocabulary. Indeed, we have seen that the fourth Gospel contains many signature words and expressions, such as "Amen, amen." The use of the noun "love" and the verb "to love," as well as the terms "glory" and the verb "to glorify," and the noun Hora or the "Hour," among many other words and expressions peculiar to John's Gospel.[308]

We also introduced, in the first section of this chapter, the two sets of "seven" that only appear in the fourth Gospel. They are the set of seven "signs" and the set of seven "I am" statements, which may be connected, as we have said, to Yahweh's answer in Exodus 3:14 that "I am Who I am."

In another section of this ninth chapter, we made some observations about why the Gospel of John is significantly different from the Synoptic texts. The principal reason we have provided in that section of the chapter is that the Gospel of John is very different theologically from Matthew, Mark and Luke.

In the central section of Chapter Nine, we have described and then discussed the eight principal answers and responses to the issues of evil and suffering to be found in the Gospel of John. In that section, we argued that the Apostle John's views are wider and deeper than any other text in the New Testament, with the possible exception of the Epistles of Paul, as we shall see in the next chapter.

Among the answers and responses to the questions of theodicy and the problem of evil that we have seen in the fourth Gospel were the Retributive Justice Theory, the Influences of Demonic Forces Theory, the Free Will Defense, the Two *Yetzerim* Theory, possibly Original Sin Theory, the Test View, the Contrast Perspective, and Divine Plan Theory.

We also have seen in this central section of Chapter Nine on the Gospel of John, that at times, the Apostle John appears to have combined two or more of these, such as when the discussion of the man born blind in chapter 9, morphs into an example of the Divine Plan Theory when Jesus relates, "It is for the greater glory of God that the man was born blind."

In the final section of this chapter, we turned our attention to the response to evil and suffering, which was introduced in Chapter Eight and called the "practical approach." In that section, we maintained that, as we have seen in each of the Synoptic Gospels, the practical approach may regularly be detected in the Gospel of John, as well.

Indeed, in this final section of Chapter Nine, we have provided, as well as discussed, many examples in the Gospel of John, where Jesus shows compassion to the poor, the needy, the lame, the blind, and to those who otherwise may be suffering.

Among the examples of the practical approach we presented in this final section of this chapter were the seven "signs," or miracles of the Gospel, as well as when Jesus indicates that Mary is John's mother, and he her son.

In this chapter, we also made observations about some of the earliest Christian papyri, including the Egerton Gospel, as well as fragments that have been designated as P45, P46 and P47.

Finally, we have shown that the Greek vocabulary regarding words related to evil and suffering is sufficiently different than the Greek vocabularies of other writers of the New Testament, particularly from the Greek of Matthew, Mark and Luke, as well as the Apostle Paul.

In Chapter Ten, we will explore the writer of the New Testament who expressed the widest, as well as the deepest, responses and answers to the issues of evil and suffering—that is the letters, or Epistles, of Paul.

Chapter Ten:
Evil and Suffering in the Epistles of Paul

The casual reader of the Bible might be surprised to discover that the person who wrote more books of the Bible than any other person was not Moses, Solomon, or any of the original apostles. It was the apostle Paul.

—Roy Demarest, "The Epistles of Paul"

Some of the letters of Paul in the New Testament are to an individual and some are to congregations. These letters are written in a form that includes the same general elements in the same order.

—Robert Stein, "Introduction to the Letters of Paul"

Let us now consider the epistles of Paul himself. They have more than one character, that all display that spirit gifted from on high, which expatriates on the wide range of the thoughts of God, and its wonderful energy can enter at the same time into every detail.

—John Nelson Darby, "Introduction to the Epistles"

Introduction

The main purpose of this chapter is to explore the places in the Letters, or Epistles, of Paul, where he had something to say about the issues of evil and suffering. We will begin the chapter with an introduction to the idea of *Epistole*, the Koine Greek term for "Epistles." This will be followed by the second section of Chapter Ten, in which we give a general introduction to the life of Paul.

These two sections of Chapter Ten will be followed by the central section of the chapter, a discussion of the answers and responses that Paul of Tarsus makes to the questions of theodicy and the problem of evil. We begin, then, with some comments on the literary genre in the first century CE, known as the *Epistole*.

The Epistle in the First Century

Paul, in his letters, uses three different Greek terms for "letter," or "epistle." The first of these is the word *epistole* mentioned earlier. The is the most common term that designates a letter for Paul. *Epistole* is used twice in the Acts of the Apostles, at 15:30 and 23:33, and it is employed by Paul thirteen times in his various books.

The second word for "letter" in Paul's letters is a cognate of the first. This Greek word *epistello* is employed in a few places in the Letters of Paul, including at Hebrews 13:22, for example. The third Koine Greek word to designate a "letter" or a piece of writing is the term, *gramma*. This word is used by Paul at Romans 2:27 and 2:29, as well as a variety of other places. The English words, grammar and grammatical, comes from this Greek term.

In first-century Christianity, an epistle was a letter written on a scroll that most often was dictated by the author to a recorder or secretary. They were primarily a form of written communication during the time of the New Testament. There are twenty-one Epistles in the New Testament. These extend from Romans to Jude. Thirteen of these Epistles are associated with Paul.[309]

The letters attributed to Paul are the following:
- Romans
- First Corinthians
- Second Corinthians
- Galatians
- Ephesians

- Philippians
- Colossians
- First Thessalonians
- Second Thessalonians
- First Timothy
- Second Timothy
- Philemon
- Titus
- Hebrews

The Epistles of Paul are either directed to an individual or to an entire congregation or community in the Church. The letters generally follow a template that consists of the following:

- An introduction or greeting
- The body of the letter
- Exhortation and instruction
- Conclusion[310]

A secular letter in the first century began with a greeting. Two examples can be seen at Acts 15:23 and James 1:1. Jewish letters often began with the word *Shalom*, or "Peace." Early Christians had their own form of greeting. Christian letters often began with *Charis*, or "Grace," from the verb *chairo*, or "to be cheerful." The word is the origin of the English "charisma." Other early Christian letters begin with the greeting *Eirene*, or "Peace." Two examples can be found at Philemon 1:2 and Romans 1:7. The name "Irene" comes from *Eirene*.

Within the Letters of Paul are a group known as the "Prison Epistles."[311] These include Ephesians, Colossians and Philemon, one of Paul's letters to an individual. These works were written during the two years when Paul was under house arrest in Rome, as Acts of the Apostles 28:30 to 31 indicates.

What is known as the "Pastoral Letters," which include First and Second Timothy and Titus, were written by Paul to Church leaders.

These Epistles include instructions for teaching and for worship service, as well as Church orders within the earliest of the Christian churches, like those to whom Paul wrote.

Paul's letters are not always so easy to follow, either in English translation or in the original Greek. The order in which they were written, rather than the way in which they appear in the New Testament, helps us to understand why particular books were written and provides us with the correctly sequenced story of the development of the life and career of Paul of Tarsus.

Given the best and latest scholarship on the matter, the order of the writing of the Epistles of Paul looks like this, as well as the time around which they were written:

- Letter to the Galatians (around 50 CE)
- First Letter to the Thessalonians (51 or 52)
- Second Letter to the Thessalonians (52)
- First Letter to the Corinthians (56)
- Second Letter to the Corinthians (56)
- Letter to the Romans (57)
- Letter to the Ephesians (60)
- Letter to the Colossians (60)
- Letter to Philemon (61)
- Letter to the Laodocians (61, now lost)
- Letter to the Philippians (61 or 62)
- First Timothy (63)
- Letter to Titus (63 or 64)
- Second Letter to Timothy (66 or 67)[312]

Most of Paul's Epistles were dictated to what was known as an *amanuensis*—a scribe or a secretary—who attempted to record Paul's words verbatim. We find mentions of these recorders at Second Thessalonians 2:1, Second Corinthians 1:19, Philippians 1:1, Colossians 1:1 and Philemon 1:1.

Paul wrote his letters over a period of approximately twenty years between the year 47 and the year 67. The estimations of the dates of the letters have varied from scholar to scholar, but most now agree that they were written in this time period.

The subject matter in the letters of Paul can be summed up in a cluster of ten or so topics that include the following:

- Marriage.

- Divorce and remarriage.

- *Glossolalia*, or "speaking in tongues."

- The nature and extent of a Christian conscience.

- Spiritual Gifts.

- Resurrection and survival after death.

- The role of women in the Church.

- Conduct at church services and other activities.

- The proper rules of parenting.

- The place of God's law in relation to Christian salvation.

The Letters of Paul certainly contain discussions of many other topics, but the ten we have listed here cover more than 90 percent of the topics discussed in those letters. We will now make some very brief remarks about each of the fourteen Epistles of Paul.

Romans claim that Jesus Christ is the Savior of all men and women, whether Jew or Gentile. It shows the way to everlasting life through the life, death and the resurrection of Jesus, the Son of God.[313] Both First and Second Corinthians were written to the church at Corinth, and they deal with the need to recognize and eliminate sin in our lives. The congregation at Corinth is instructed to love one another and to look forward to the glorious return of the Second Coming of Christ to the Earth.[314]

In his letter to the Galatians, Paul attempts to convince Gentile Galatians that they need to be circumcised to be made right with God. Paul claims that we only can be justified and forgiven of our sins if we have faith in Jesus Christ. He says to the Galatians, "We must live in the Spirit, produce the fruits of the Spirit, and not break the law. [315]

In the Letter to the Ephesians 1:10, Paul speaks of how it is that Christ brings all people together. When we embrace Christ, Paul says, we embrace a new way of life, a way of love and a way of helping one another, both Christians and non-Christians. The Letter to the Philippians is an Epistle to the Congregation at Philippi, a city on the Mediterranean coast in Macedonia. Paul encourages the Philippians to continue their good work and dedicated service to God. Paul was very fond of the Christian community in Philippi, who were a constant source of encouragement for him.[316]

In his Letter to the Colossians, a congregation in Asia Minor, Paul warns the people against the incursion of pagan philosophical ideas that circulated around the area at the time, such as asceticism and Gnosticism. The way to God is only through Jesus Christ and the rejection of these other religious and philosophical ideas.[317]

Both of the letters to the Thessalonians, a city west of Philippi, deal with the question of when Jesus will return to the Earth. Many Christians of the day, including people in Thessalonia, believed that Christ would return imminently. In Second Thessalonians, however, Paul reveals that the end of the world must be preceded by events that have not yet occurred.[318]

The Pastoral Letters of First and Second Timothy, as well as Titus, were written to Christian ministers. Some of the topics of these letters are, *Who qualifies as an Elder? How does one become a Deacon?* And, *How are widows to be helped?*[319] Paul also instructs the Christians in these letters to avoid useless arguments, foolish disputes and contentious situations.

The very short letter to Philemon is an epistle to a member of the congregation at Colossae, also in Asia Minor. Paul tries to encourage a reconciliation between Philemon and a slave who had run away from his household to become a Christian.[320]

Finally, the Epistle to the Hebrews does not name its author, but some early Christian traditions ascribed the book to the Apostle Paul. The letter to the Hebrews mostly deals with what it calls the "New Covenant" between God and His people. The writer of Hebrews relates that the Old Covenant is being replaced with the New Covenant made possible by a new High Priest, the person of Jesus Christ.[321]

Instead of physical blessings for obedience to the letter of the law, like in the Books of Moses, the New Covenant must be understood in the Spirit of the Law, by the people of all nations, not just the Jews. Paul tells the Hebrews that all people should have the opportunity to experience everlasting life through Jesus Christ. [322]

In addition to the Epistles of Paul, the New Testament also contains eight other letters known as the "Catholic Epistles." These are Hebrews, James, First and Second Peter, First, Second, and Third John, and Jude. Historically, Paul wrote Hebrews as we have suggested earlier, James was written by the half-brother of Jesus, the Apostle Peter wrote First and Second Peter, Jude was composed by another half-brother of Jesus, and the three letters of John were written by the same man who wrote the Gospel of John and the Book of Revelation.

The Life of Paul

Information about the life of Paul of Tarsus comes from three main sources:

- His Epistles.
- Non-Biblical Sources, like archeology and Roman materials.
- The Acts of the Apostles.

The Acts of the Apostles is the fifth book of the New Testament, coming after the four Gospels. It is a valuable source for the earliest period of the Christian Church. The book was written in Koine Greek ostensibly by the same man who wrote the Gospel of Luke that ends with the Apostles at the Pentecost. Acts was most likely written in Rome between 75 and 85 CE.[323]

The Acts of the Apostles pursues the growth of the Early Church to the Gentile world under the guidance of the Holy Spirit. Acts concerns itself with the spread of Christianity gradually moving away from its Jewish roots. The three missionary journeys of Paul are given a prominent place in Acts.

In fact, without the Acts of the Apostles, a picture of the primitive church would be impossible to reconstruct. With Acts, the Epistles of

Paul are far more intelligible. It concludes rather abruptly after Paul had brought the Gospel to Rome, which was then the center of the Gentile world. With the Acts of the Apostles, the facts of the life of Paul of Tarsus would nearly be impossible, even though he is the author of almost half of the New Testament books.

The first mention of Saul/Paul in Acts comes at Acts 7:8. His role in the martyr of Stephen is detailed in the same chapter. Chapter 8 of Acts deals with his persecutions of the Church in Jerusalem. Chapter 9 gives an account of Paul's conversion to Christianity when he was knocked off his horse and blinded.

In chapters 13 and 14 of Acts, Luke gives an account of the mission of Barnabas and Paul. Acts 15 is concerned with the Council of Jerusalem, and in chapters 16 to 20, we may find an account of Paul's second missionary journey. In chapter 21, Paul makes another trip to Jerusalem. Paul appears before the Sanhedrin in chapters 22 and 23. Paul appears before Felix, Festus and Herod Agrippa in chapter 27 and 28 of Acts.

We also see Paul's attempted journey to Rome in chapters 27 and 28, as well as his stay on the island of Malta. The Acts of the Apostles ends abruptly with no description of the end of the Apostle's life, nor of his death in 67 or 68 CE.

We learn from Acts 22:3 that Paul was born "Saul" in the city of Tarsus in the southeast portion of Asia Minor. Paul tells us that he was also a Roman citizen by birth and that he was raised in a Pharisaic, Jewish home. He was educated at the feet of Gamaliel, a noted Rabbi in first-century Judaism.[324]

It is difficult to set the days of events in the life of Paul. He offers only rare events that can be dated, such as expressions like, "after three years," at Galatians 1:18 or "After some days," at Acts 15:36. This often makes definitive dates in the life of Paul difficult to determine. Central to the task of dating the events of Paul's life is the issue of how best to understand the accounts in Acts of Paul's visit to Jerusalem and compare it to the account we are given in the Epistle to the Galatians.

Whether the two events described in Galatians are related to what is sometimes called the "Famine Relief," in chapter 11 of Acts, or the Apostolic Council visit in Acts 15, is not entirely clear. This discussion is important because understanding which event is related to which in the life of Paul helps us to date the Epistles. For example, is the Letter to the Galatians before or after the Council of Jerusalem, which is believed to have taken place in 49 CE.[325]

One way to solve this problem is simply to say that Galatians 2 and Acts 15 both describe the Jerusalem Council, and Paul's account in Galatians does not mention the earlier Famine Relief visit to the city described in the eleventh chapter of the Acts of the Apostles.[326]

Another important clue in the dates of Paul's works and the place that Acts plays in that dating scheme is Paul's appearance before a man named Gallio, a Roman Proconsul in Achaia. Inscriptions that tell us the dates of Gallio's term in office, tell us that he was Proconsul from July of 51 until July of 52 CE. By using this Roman record, as well as examining the events of Acts 18:12–17, where Paul is taken by the Jews to stand trial before Gallio, we can determine with some accuracy the dates of events before and after Paul's journey to the city of Corinth.[327]

From all of this, we can date the start of Paul's second missionary journey to 47 and 48 CE. We know this because, according to Acts 18:11, Paul stayed in Corinth for a year and a half. Since we know the dates of other events before the second missionary journey, we can be sure that the Apostolic Council took place in 48 CE. This then allows us to date the Famine Relief visit to Jerusalem, during Paul's first missionary journey, mentioned in Acts 11, to approximately the years 45 to 47 CE.

Using other details from Acts, we may conclude that Paul's third missionary journey, according to Acts 18–21, must have occurred around the year 52 or 53. We know that a man named Festus replaced Felix as the governor of Judaea in 59 CE. And we know that Paul was under house arrest prior to Festus becoming governor. From this, we may conclude that Paul completed his third missionary journey and then returned to the city of Jerusalem, most likely in the year 57.

We know that after appearing before Festus, Paul invoked his right as a Roman citizen and wished to plead before Caesar in Rome. We learn from Acts 27:9 that Paul's ill-fated voyage to Rome occurred after the Day of Atonement, which would tell us that it was September or October.

Acts 28:11 tells us that after being shipwrecked, Paul spent three months on the island of Malta. We also learn subsequent details of the voyage of Paul to Rome from Acts 28:14–16. Using this chronology, we may conclude that Paul finally made it to the city in the Spring of the year 60. The Acts of the Apostles give us little details about the remainder of Paul's life. He appears to have continued his ministry for a while but was arrested a second time during the persecutions of Emperor Nero. It is likely, therefore, that Paul remained in prison in 64 and 65, and then he was killed by Nero, executed really, most likely in the year 67, simply for being Christian.[328]

The only other date in the life of Paul most likely occurred in the year 35 when Paul was around thirty years old. He was on his way to the city of Damascus, and God struck him with a thunderbolt, knocking him off his horse and causing him to go blind. Bits and pieces of Paul's conversion, around the year 35 CE, can be gathered from Acts 9:1–31, 22:1–22 and 26:–24.

A short time after his conversion, Paul regained his sight and began his first missionary journey with the Apostle Barnabas in chapters 13 and 14 of Acts. Then followed the history or chronology we outlined earlier in this chapter. This brings us to an analysis of the places in the Epistles of Paul, where the Apostle speaks of the phenomena of evil and suffering, the central section of Chapter Ten.

Evil and Suffering in the Letters of Paul and Acts of the Apostles

As indicated by the heading of this section of Chapter Ten, we shall consider views on the issues of theodicy and the problem of evil both in the Epistles of Paul, as well as comments made in the Acts of the Apostles. In these works may be found the greatest variety of answers and responses to the issues of evil and suffering in the New Testament. In fact, as we shall see, we may find all of the views introduced earlier in this study, plus a new point of view we have not yet seen.

It is in the Epistles of Paul that we find the most evidence for the belief in the Original Sin Theory, particularly in Romans, as well as First Corinthians. In Romans, this view may be seen at 2:9, 5:12–20,

6:17–21, 7:15–24 and 8:21–22. The passage that advocates the Original Sin Theory in First Corinthians comes at 15:21–23.

In the first passage from Romans 2:9, Paul relates, "There will be anguish and distress for everyone who does evil, the Jew first and also the Greek." Paul may be indicating here that some humans sin, and some do not, or he may be suggesting that all will receive distress and anguish because all suffer from Original Sin. At Romans 5:12–20, we see Paul's most clear dedication to the Original Sin Theory, particularly in verses 12 and 19.

At Romans 5:12, Paul tells us:

> Therefore, just as sin came into the world through one man and death came through sin, and so death spread to all because all have sinned.

Clearly, Paul is referring here to the original sin of Adam and Eve, and the Apostle's beliefs that through that sin, the possibility of death entered the world, and that subsequent human beings will inherit that first sin. At Romans 5:18 and 19, Paul reaffirms his beliefs, when he relates:

> Therefore, just as one man's trespass led to condemnation for all, so one man's act of righteousness leads to justification and life for all. For just by the one man's disobedience the many were made sinners, so by one man's obedience the many will be made righteous.

The two "one man," of course, refer to Adam who disobeyed so that all may sin and die, and the other "one man," Jesus Christ, whose obedience made it possible that all human beings may be saved.

The notions of being "slaves to sin," as well as "slaves to righteousness," can be seen in Romans 6:17–21, where the Apostle Paul relates, "But thanks be to God that you have once been slaves of sin, having become obedient from the heart to the form of teaching to become slaves of righteousness...For just as you once presented your members as slaves to impurity and to greater and greater iniquity, so now present your members as slaves to righteousness for sanctification."

Paul continues in the next three verses:

> When you were slaves of sin, you were free in regard
> to righteousness. So what advantage did you then get
> from which the things of which you are now ashamed?
> The end of those things is death. But now you have been
> freed from sin and enslaved to God, and the advantage
> you get is sanctification. The end is eternal life. For the
> wages of sin is death, but the free gift of God is eternal
> life in Christ Jesus, our Lord.

Perhaps the passage where the Apostle Paul says the most about the Original Sin Theory, while at the same time also advocating the Two *Yetzerim* Point of View, as well as the Moral Qualities Theory and the Divine Plan Perspective, can be found at Romans 8:18–27. In verses 18–20, Paul assents to the Divine Plan Theory by the use of the future-tense verb "about to be revealed." Verse 24 and its mention of patience suggests an example of the Moral Qualities Position. At verse 27, Paul speaks of God "searching the hearts," perhaps a reference to the *yetzer ha ra* and the *yetzer tov*.

The word *Kardia* is used by the Apostle Paul thirty-seven times to indicate the seat of the Self. These may be found in Romans, First and Second Corinthians, Galatians, Ephesians, Philippians, Colossians, First Thessalonians, First and Second Timothy, and seven times in the Letter to the Hebrews.[329]

In the remainder of chapter 8 of Romans—that is verses 31 to 38—Paul appears to return to the Divine Plan Theory with the employment of future-tense verbs such as "also will give" in verse 32 and "will be able" in verse 38. We will return to the Moral Qualities View, the Two *Yetzer* Theory, and the Divine Plan Perspective in Paul, later in this tenth chapter. It is enough now, however, to point out that the Apostle seems to combine these perspectives at the end of chapter 8 of Romans.

At First Corinthians 15:20–22, as we have indicated earlier, Paul again turns to the advocacy of the Original Sin Theory. He tells us this:

> For since death came to the world through a human
> being, for all die in Adam so all may be made alive in
> Christ.

Again, it is clear that the Apostle Paul was an advocate of the view that death entered the world as a by-product of Adam's sin, and also that it is through the death and resurrection of Jesus Christ that all may be "made alive," and then possibly gain eternal life. This brings us to many of the places that Paul seems to advocate what we have called the Retributive Justice Theory. We will give three examples to show that the Apostle Paul assented to this view.

The first of these comes at Romans 12:17 and 21, where the theory is mentioned explicitly. The Apostle tells us, "Do not repay anyone evil for evil, but take though for what is noble in the sight of all." This is followed a few verses later with the provision of, "Do not be overcome by evil, but overcome evil with good."

At Galatians 6:7–8, we see another example of the Retributive Justice Theory. The Apostle Paul tells the Galatians to:

> Render service with enthusiasm, as to the Lord and not
> to men and women, we will receive back again knowing
> that whatever good we do we will receive back again
> from the Lord, whether we are slaves or free.

In this case, the application of retribution is to be understood as good and as a by-product of doing the good. At First Corinthians 1:19, the Apostle Paul again applies the Retributive Justice Theory when he relates:

> I will destroy the wisdom of the wise, and the
> discernment of the discerning, I will thwart.

Earlier, we have spoken of Romans 2:9 to be an example of the Original Sin Theory, but it also may be seen as a version of the Retributive Justice Theory when Paul relates, "Anguish and distress will come for all who sin." From these four examples, it should be clear that Paul assented to the employment of the Retributive Justice Theory. We will now turn our attention to Paul's uses of the Influences of Demonic Forces Theory, of which there are many in his Epistles.

The Apostle Paul's assent to the Influences of Demonic Forces Theory may be seen in verses from Ephesians, Hebrews, First and Second Corinthians, as well as in the First Letter to the Thessalonians.

Among these passages of Paul are Ephesians 6:10–12; Hebrews 5:3; First Corinthians 5:5 and 7:5; Second Corinthians 2:9 and 11, 11:14 and 12:7; and First Thessalonians 2:9 and 2:18.

At Ephesians 6:10–12, Paul combines the Influences of Demonic Forces Theory, with the Moral Qualities Perspective, when the Apostle writes:

> Finally, be strong and in the strength of his power. Put on the whole armor of God, so that you may be able to withstand the wiles of the Devil.

The first half of the verse, with its language about strength and armor, may be seen as an example of the Test View or the Moral Qualities Perspective, while at the same time, the "wiles of the Devil" is an indication of the Influences of Demonic Forces Theory. At First Corinthians 5:5, Paul speaks of "being turned over to the hands of Satan," and 7:5 argues against the idea of Satan tempting one "because of a lack of self-control." A couple of verses later, at First Corinthians 2:11, Paul relates, "And we do this so that we may not be outwitted by Satan, for we are not ignorant of his designs."

Satan is mentioned again by Paul at Second Corinthians 11:14, where the Apostle relates, "And no wonder! evil Satan disguises himself as an Angel of Light," a possible reference to the Fallen Angels Narrative. At Second Corinthians 12:7, Paul provides another example of the Demonic Forces Theory, when he observes, "Even considering the exceptional character of the revelations. Therefore, to keep me from being too elated, a form was given me in the flesh, a messenger of Satan, to torment me." The word *Satanas* appears nine times in Paul, and twice in Acts.

Finally, at Second Thessalonians 2:9, the Apostle Paul speaks of "The coming of the lawless one is apparent in the working of Satan, who uses all his power, signs, and lying wonders and every kind of wicked deception for those who are perishing because they refused to love the truth and so be saved." From these many passages, it should be clear that the Apostle Paul was an advocate of the Influences of Demonic Forces Theory.

The Apostle Paul's views on the nature of the self, the two *yetzerim*, and the will are very complicated due to the fact that he understood these issues both from the perspective of a Jew, as well as from the Greco-Roman understanding of these matters. In some places, like Romans 1:21, 2:5 and 29, and 6:17, Paul uses the word *cardio*, to indicate the heart and its decision-making capacity. But he also uses a variety of words that designate "mind," "thought" and "imagination." Among these Greek terms are *prothomia*, that is rendered "plots" in Acts 20:19; *dianoia*, which means "mind" and "imagination," and is used by Paul at Hebrews 10:16 and 12:3; the word *noema* also is sometimes translated as "mind," such as at Second Corinthians 3:14, 4:4, and 11:3.

Paul frequently uses the word *nous* also to stand for "mind." This word is employed dozens of times in Romans. Some of these are at 1:28; 7:23 and 25; 8:5, 7, and 27; 11:34; and 12:2, among many other places. From all of this, we may conclude that, at times, Paul understood the self the way the ancient Jews did. That is, the heart makes one's moral decisions.

At other times, however, Paul uses the language of Greek philosophy and its emphasis on words like *nous*, from which we get the English verb "to know" and the noun "knowledge." In modern times, of course, the seat of the self is now the brain and no longer the heart as the Jews had it.

Yet, the Apostle Paul does not use the most popular word for the self among the Greek philosophers. That word is *psyche*, or "Soul." However, this word is found in many places in the Acts of the Apostles, including 2:27 and 31, 2:41 and 43, 3:23, 4:32, 7:14, and 14:2 and 22.

This brings us to a discussion of Paul's uses of the Contrast View, of which there are many examples. Some of these may be found at Ephesians 5:8, 11 and 14; First Thessalonians 5:5; Romans 6:23 and 13:12; and Second Corinthians 4:4 and 6 and 6:14. The Contrast View can also be seen at Acts 26:18. In fact, we find this view much more often in Paul and Acts than any other place in the New Testament.

At Ephesians 5:8, Paul tells them:

> For once you were in darkness, but now in the Light,
> you are light. Live as children of Light—for the fruit of
> the light is found in all that is good, and right, and true.

A few verses later, at verses 11 to 13, Paul continues the metaphor when he tells us, "Take no shameful part in the unfruitful works of darkness, but instead expose them. For it is shameful to even mention what such people do secretly; but everything exposed by becomes visible, for everything that becomes visible is light."

At Acts 26:18, Luke relates:

> To open their eyes so that they may turn from darkness
> to light and from the power of Satan to God.

At Second Corinthians 4:4 and 6, Paul again appears to consent to the Contrast View when he says, "In their case, the god of this world has blinded the minds of disbelievers, to keep them from seeing the light of the Gospels." And at verse 6, "For it is the God who said, 'Let the light shine out of darkness...'" In the same book, at 6:14, Paul gives the following advice:

> Do not be mismatched with unbelievers. For what
> partnership can there be between righteousness and
> lawlessness? Or what fellowship can there be between
> Light and Darkness?

At First Thessalonians 5:5, Paul relates, "For you are all children of light and darkness for that day to surprise you like a thief, for you are all children of light and the day. We are not of the night or the darkness." At Romans 13:2, Paul gives us another example that might be interpreted as the Contrast Theory. He tells us, "Therefore, whoever resists authority resists what God has appointed, and those who resist will incur judgment." Here Paul makes a dichotomy between those who follow God and the authorities, and those who do not and resist those authorities. At 6:23 of the same book, the Apostle Paul relates, "For the wages of sin is death, but the free gift of God is eternal life in Christ Jesus, our Lord." From these five examples, we may conclude that the Apostle Paul consented to the theory we have called the Contrast View.

In a variety of places in his Epistles, as well as in the Acts of the Apostles, Paul seems to have regularly employed what we have labeled the Test View. Some of these come at Second Corinthians 2:8, Ephesians 6:14 and 15, and Acts 20:19. The latter verse, the one in Acts, Paul tells us, "I have served the Lord with all of humanity and with tears, enduring the trials that came to me through the plots of the Jews."

At Second Corinthians 2:8, Paul again points to the Test View when he writes, "So I urge you to reaffirm your love for him. I wrote for this reason: to test you and to know if you are obedient in everything." At Ephesians 6:14 and 15, Paul advises the believer to "Stand and fasten the belt of truth around your waist, and put on the breastplate of righteousness, as shoes for your feet put on whatever will make you ready to proclaim the Gospel of peace." Here Paul uses the language of a warrior who puts on the breastplate to be tested.

At the Letter to the Galatians 4:14, Paul again speaks of believers "being put to the test, and you did not scorn me nor despise me." At Hebrews 3:8, the Apostle Paul provides the advice:

> Do not harden your hearts as in the rebellion, as on the
> day of testing in the wilderness.

At Second Corinthians 12:7, the Apostle Paul combines the Test View with the Influences of Demonic Forces Theory, when he relates, "Even considering the exceptional character of the revelations, therefore, to keep me from being too elated, a thorn was given to me in the flesh a messenger of Satan to torture me."

In many other examples, the Apostle Paul clearly refers to what we have called the Test view. Some of these passages come at Hebrews 2:8–9, 4:15 and 5:8–9, as well as several other verses in the Acts of the Apostles.[330] The same view also can be seen at First Corinthians 10:9 and 13, as well as 3:12–15.

What we have called the Moral Qualities Approach also appears to be one of the responses to evil and suffering that was utilized by the Apostle Paul. This view may be found at Romans 5:3–4 and 8:25; Hebrews 5:8; Ephesians 6:14–15; First Corinthians 4:12; and Second Timothy 2:3.

The Moral Qualities View can be seen in these Pauline words at Romans 5:3–4: "And not only that, but we boast in our sufferings, knowing that suffering produces endurance, and endurance produces character, and character produces hope, and hope does not disappoint us, because God's love has been poured into our hearts through the Holy Spirit that has been given to us."

At Romans 8:25, we see another example of the Moral Qualities View in the Apostle Paul's Epistles. Paul observes, "But if we hope for what we cannot see, we must do it with patience." At Second Corinthians 4:12, Paul tells us, "As we grow weary from the work of our own hands, when reviled, we bless, when persecuted, we endure." Patience and endurance, of course, are two of the principle attributes that suffering is believed to produce.

In Second Timothy 2:3, Paul again calls to mind the Moral Qualities Position when he writes, "Share in suffering like a good soldier of Christ Jesus." And at Hebrews 5:8, Paul relates:

> Although he was a Son, he learned obedience from
> what he suffered, and having been made perfect, he
> became the source of eternal salvation for all of those
> who obey him.

At Second Timothy 2:24, we find another example of the Moral Qualities Theory. In this verse, Paul uses the word *anexikakos*, a word that implies the "enduring of evil." Others suggest it might be rendered "bearing up under evil." This is the only use of this Greek word in the New Testament.

From these six examples, it should be clear that the Apostle Paul was a believer in the Moral Qualities Theory. This brings us to the places in the Epistles of Paul, where the Apostle appears to assent to what we have labeled the Divine Plan Theory throughout the course of this study. This same view also may be seen at the Acts of the Apostles 2:23. This verse in Acts tells us this:

> This man, handed over to you according to the definite
> plan and the foreknowledge of God, you crucified and
> killed by the hands.

The Divine Plan Theory also can be seen in the Epistles of Paul at Romans 3:8. In this verse, Paul asks, "And why not say as some people slander us that, 'We do evil so that good may come.'" At First Corinthians 2:9, the Apostle Paul again hints at what we have labeled the Divine Plan View. He tells us:

> What no eye has seen, nor ear heard, nor the human heart conceived, what God has prepared for those who love him.

At Romans 8:28 to 29, the Apostle Paul gives us his most convincing evidence that he believed in the Divine Plan Perspective, when Paul begins these verses with, "We know that all things work together for the good." Paul also seems to display the Divine Plan Theory at Ephesians 1:11, when Paul observes:

> In Christ, we also have obtained an inheritance, having been destined according to the purpose of Him who accomplishes all things according to His counsel and His will.

The Greek word for "counsel" in chapter 1 of Ephesians is *bole*, or *bolay*. Paul also uses it at Hebrews 6:17. It generally means to "give advice" or "to have a plan." Thus, the use of this verb also implies the Divine Plan Theory.

In the same book and same chapter, at verse 4, Paul observes, "Just as He chose us in Christ, before the foundations of the world to be holy and blameless before him in love." This seems to imply that Jesus, and God, had this Plan long before the creation of the World.

In addition to these many passages in Acts and the Letters of Paul where the Divine Plan Theory may be found, the same theory can also be seen in Paul's use of future-tense verbs throughout his Epistles also to imply the Divine Plan Perspective. One fine example of this phenomenon can be seen in the eighth chapter of Romans, verses 18 to 39.

The Apostle Paul employs future-tense verbs at verses 18, 21, 23, 36, and 39, all to show that God has a Divine Plan that "all things will work out for the Good." In the same section of Romans 8, Paul also endorses the Divine Plan Theory at verses 18 to 20, as well as 28 to

30. Another place where we might see Paul's belief in the Divine Plan Theory is at The Letter to the Romans 12:21, where Paul advises us, "Do not be overcome by evil, but overcome evil with Good." This, of course, is the essence of the Divine Plan Theory. Something may appear to be evil now, but in the end, it will all work out for the Good.

One final point is in order with respect to the Apostle Paul's views of the Divine Plan Theory that has to do with his Greek vocabulary. It is only in the Epistles of Paul of the books of the New Testament that the word *Prorizo*, or 'Predestination," is employed in the New Testament. This is also true of the word *Profiles*, which means, "to see" beforehand, that is only used at Galatians 3:8. At Acts 2:23 and 4:28, Luke provides two other passages where the idea of Predestination is employed, as is the case at Ephesians 1:4 to 5, where Paul again uses the term "Predestined."

Similarly, the Greek term *Prognosis*, or "forethought," can only be found in the Letters of Paul. The word *Prorao*, which may be translated as "foresaw," is only employed at Acts 2:25. And finally, the Koine Greek *Proginosko*, a word only employed by Paul in the New Testament at Romans 11:2, is generally rendered as "Foreknew" by New Testament scholars.

There are two other New Testament Greek words only employed by Paul. One of these, the term *Dysphemia*, can be found at Second Corinthians 4:13 and 6:8 but is also found in Plutarch and in other classical Greek writers. This word means "to give a bad report," or even the activity of a slanderer.[331] The other Koine Greek term, only used by Paul at the Second Epistle to Timothy at 2:24, is *Anexikakos*. The root of this word, *kakos*, we already know. It designates "evil." The rest of the word is associated with a verb that means "to endure." Thus, *Anexikakos* means something like "to bear up" with regard to evil, as in the Test View.

In addition to this peculiar vocabulary of Paul, he also at the same time regularly uses the many other terms related to evil introduced in Chapter Eight of this study. For example, Paul uses the word *poneros* twenty-two times in his Epistles, with another seven employments of the words in the Acts of the Apostles, including 17:5; 18:14; 19:12 and 15; 25:18 twice; and 28:21.

Paul does not appear to use the Hidden God Theory in his Epistles, but in one place in the letter to the Hebrews at 4:13, there is an instance of what might be called the "Reverse Hidden God Theory." In this verse, Paul relates:

> And there is no creature hidden from His sight, but all things are open and laid bare to the eyes of Him with whom we have to do.

This verse is not about the Hiddenness of God. Rather, it is just the opposite. It is about the Knowledge of God and the idea that he knows everything, including all that goes on in the "hearts" of all humans.

What we may garner so far in Chapter Ten is the author of Acts and the Epistles of Paul may be said to have endorsed the following answers and responses with respect to the issues of evil and suffering:

- Retributive Justice Theory
- The Free Will Defense
- The Two *Yetzerim* Perspective
- The Influences of Demonic Forces Theory
- The Original Sin Point of View
- The Test View
- The Contrast Perspective
- The Moral Qualities Point of View
- Divine Plan Theory
- The Practical Approach

Of all the biblical writers we have seen in this study, in the figure of the Apostle Paul, we find a deeper and broader number of answers and responses to the questions of theodicy and the problem of evil than any other writer. This brings us to the final section in which we will explore an eleventh view that so far we have not seen in this study. We shall call this final view the Identification Theory.

Paul's Identification Theory

In this final response to evil and suffering to be found in Acts and the Epistles of Paul, the Apostle suggests in several places in his letters that all believing Christians should share in the suffering with Christ, or in some way to identify with his suffering. In Ephesians 8:17, for example, Paul tells us that the sharing in the suffering of Jesus is also a sharing "in His glory." At Second Corinthians 1:5, Paul observes:

> For just as the sufferings of Christ are ours in abundance,
> so also our comfort is abundant through Christ.

The Apostle Paul makes exactly the same point at Romans 8:17, when he observes, "We suffer with him so that we might also be glorified with him." Sometimes Paul speaks of identifying with Christ's death rather than his sufferings. At Romans 6:3 to 4, for example, Paul relates:

> Do you not know that all of us who have been baptized
> in Christ Jesus also was baptized in his death. Therefore,
> we have been buried with him by baptism into death,
> so that just as Jesus was raised from the dead by the
> glory of the Father, so that we too might walk in the
> newness of life.

A couple of verses later, still in chapter 6 of Romans, Paul concludes, "For if we have been united with him in a death like this, so too might we be united with him in a resurrection like his." One of the best ways to see this "Identification Theory" in Paul is to examine the Letter to the Philippians 3:7–11. At verses 10 and 11, Paul summarizes the passage this way:

> I want to know Christ and the power of his resurrection
> and the sharing of his sufferings by becoming like him
> in death, if somehow I may attain the resurrection of
> the dead.

At Romans 8:18, Paul appears to combine the Identification Theory with the Divine Plan Point of View, when he writes, "I consider that your suffering of this present time are not worth considering when thinking of the glory to be brought to us when it will be revealed to us."

This Identification Theory is not peculiar to the Apostle Paul. It also can be seen in several places in the Acts of the Apostles, such as at 5:30, 10:39, 13:29, and at 16:22–24. The Identification Theory also may be found in several verses of First Peter. Among these passages are chapters 1:3–6 and 4:12–16.

In the following section of this chapter, we will give a summary of the answers, responses and views on evil and suffering to be found in the Acts of the Apostles, the final section of this chapter.

Evil and Suffering in Acts of the Apostles

In the New Testament's Acts, there can be found at least five of the traditional answers and responses to the issues of theodicy and the problem of evil. Those views are the following:

- The Influences of Demonic Forces Theory

- The Two *Yetzerim* Point of View (Free Will Defense)

- The Test Perspective

- The Moral Qualities View
- Divine Plan Theory

Two of the best places to find the Demonic Forces Theory in Acts are at 5:3 and 26:18. In the former, the writer of Acts combines the Demonic Influence Theory with the *Yetzerim* Point of View, when he says, "Then Peter said to Ananas, 'How is it that Satan has so filled your heart?'" At Acts 26:18, we see the combining of the Contrast View with the Demonic Influences Theory. The writer tells us:

> To open their eyes and to turn them from darkness to light, and from the power of Satan to the power of God.

Other passages in Acts that seem to be promoting the Two *Yetzerim* Theory by identifying the self with the *Kardia*, or "heart," are 5:3–4, 7:23 and 51, 8:21, 15:19, and 28:27. We will examine three of these passages to establish the point that the writer of Acts endorsed this view.

At Acts 7:23, the text relates, "When Moses was forty years old, his heart decided to visit his own people, the Israelites." At Acts 8:21, we learn, "You have no part or share in this ministry because your heart is not right before God." Acts 28:27 tells us, "For the people's heart had become calloused, and they hardly hear with their ears and they have closed their eyes."

The theory we have called the Test View can be seen in a number of places in the Acts of the Apostles, including 20:19. There we are told:

> I served the Lord with great humility and with tears and in the midst of severe testing by the plots of my Jewish opponents.

Several examples of what we have called the "Moral Qualities View" also can be detected in the Acts of the Apostles. Perhaps the most interesting of these comes at 26:18, where we find a combination of the Moral Qualities View, the Contrast Perspective, and the Retributive Justice Theory.

This text tells us this:

> To open their eyes and to turn them from darkness to light and from the power of Satan to the power of God, so that they may receive forgiveness of sins and a place among those who are sanctified by faith in me.

The Moral Qualities part, of course, are the "forgiveness" and "sanctification." The light and darkness indicate the Contrast Perspective, and the forgiveness of sins is related to the Retributive Justice Theory. It is quite common in Acts to combine answers and responses as it does in this instance.

There are a variety of passages in the Acts of the Apostles that would seem to point in the direction of the Divine Plan Theory. The best of these may be found at Acts 2:23. This text relates, "The man was handed over to you by God's deliberate plan and foreknowledge, and you, with the help of wicked men, put him to death by nailing him to the cross."

The word for "plan," often also translated as "counsel," is *boule*. It signifies a Divine purpose or an immutable plan. The same word can be found at Acts 4:28, 5:38, 13:36 and 20:27. The last of these speaks of "the whole purpose of God," another indication of the Divine Plan Theory. This word *boule* is also employed in Acts at 27:12 and 27:42.

The word for "foreknowledge" at Acts 2:23 is the Koine Greek's *Prognosis*. This word is only employed two times in the New Testament, one of which is at Acts 2:23. The other verse where the word *prognosis* is used is at First Peter 1:2.

Finally, another theory we have not seen so far in this tenth chapter is one that only appears in Acts and the Epistles of Paul. This view suggests that God does not cause evil. He merely "permits" it. So, in this view, God allows evil to exist by His permission. The two best indications of this theory can be seen at Hebrews 6:2–3 and First Corinthians 16:7. In these verses, Paul uses the words *epitrepo* and *suganome*, both of which are related to verbs that mean "to permit" or "having permission."[332]

The former passage, in the context of a discussion of baptism and the resurrection of the dead, relates, "And this we will do if God permits it." The same view may be seen at First Corinthians 16:7, where Paul tells us this:

> For I do not want to see you now and make only a passing visit. I hope to spend some time with you, if the Lord permits.

In both of these passages from Paul, he seems to indicate that God only "permits" evil. He does not cause it to happen. Nevertheless, he also indicates that any evil or other actions of humans only occur because of the permission of the Almighty God. This Permission Theory we have outlined here can only be seen in the Epistles of Paul.

This brings us to our conclusions of this tenth chapter. Then we have supplied two Appendices in which we catalog the ancient Hebrew and Greek words and expressions we have used in this study, as well as a third glossary on other foreign words and expressions.

Conclusions

We began this chapter with a section on the nature and extent of an *epistole*, or Epistle in the New Testament. In that section, we pointed out that the writers of the New Testament employed three separate terms for a "Letter." These were *Epistole, Epistello*, and *Gramma*, from which comes the words "grammar" and "grammatical." In this opening section of Chapter Ten, we also outlined the main parts of a New Testament Letter, or Epistle, including the introduction, the body of the letter, the exhortation and instruction, and the conclusion.

In this opening section of chapter ten, we presented a catalog of the fourteen letters that historically have been attributed to the Apostle Paul. Additionally, we gave a short introduction to each of these books.

In the second section, we have given a short introduction on the life of Paul of Tarsus. As we have seen, the three main sources for discerning the facts of the life of Paul are his letters, the Acts of the Apostles, and extra-canonical records from archeology and Rome. In this biographical material, we mentioned that Paul was born into a Pharisaic Jewish family and originally was given the name Saul.

We have also shown in this biographical section of Chapter Ten that after his conversion Paul took three separate missionary journeys throughout the Mediterranean Region, that he was in prison on two different occasions in his life, and that he was shipwrecked on the island of Malta.

In the central or main section of this chapter, we have introduced, cataloged, and then discussed the major places in Paul's Epistles, as well as in the Acts of the Apostles, where answers and responses to the phenomena of evil and suffering may be found. Indeed, we have suggested in this section, that Paul may be seen as a man who endorsed all of the answers and responses to the questions of theodicy and the problem of evil that we have seen throughout this study.

In fact, we have shown in chapter ten that Paul can be seen as an early Christian who assented to the use of the Retributive Justice Theory, Original Sin, the Influences of Demonic Forces Theory, and the Free Will Defense, as well as the Two *Yetzerim* Theory, the Contrast View, the Moral Qualities Answer, the Test Perspective, and to the Divine Plan theory.

We also have shown in the close of Chapter Ten that Paul appears to have endorsed what we called the "Practical Approach" to evil and suffering. Additionally, we suggested that Paul was an advocate of what we labeled the "Identification Theory." As shown, this theory involves Paul's contention that Christians should identify themselves not only with the sufferings of Jesus, but also with his death, his resurrection and his glory.

In Chapter Ten, we introduced what we have called the "Permission Theory" that can only be found in the Epistles of Paul. This is a theory we had not seen before the mention of it in this tenth chapter. We pointed out that Paul regularly used most of the Greek terms related to evil, which were introduced at the beginning of Chapter Eight, and that at times, Paul seems to have had a peculiar Greek vocabulary when it came to words related to Predestination and the idea of Foreknowledge.

We have shown in this tenth chapter that Paul held what we have called the "Reverse Hidden God Theory," in which the emphasis is not on God being absent. Rather it is on God's Knowledge.

In sum, then, Paul exhibited the greatest variety of answers and responses to the questions of theodicy and the problem of evil in all of the Biblical writers we have examined in this study. He displayed these answers and responses that can only be understood as coming from his Jewish, as well as his Roman background. In short, Paul of Tarsus knew more about the issues of evil and suffering in the Bible than any of the Judeo-Christian thinkers on these matters.

Afterword

This is not the end. It is not even the beginning of the
end, but it is, perhaps, the end of the beginning.

—Winston Churchill

I have spent my nearly fifty-year academic career on questions related to evil and suffering beginning in high school in the 1960s when I met Professor William F. Albright of Johns Hopkins University, who taught me my first bit of Classical Hebrew in his study at home in Baltimore, and continuing through college at the University of Maryland and graduate school at Yale and Oxford, and then on to a Ph.D. at Saint Mary's College of Saint Andrews University in Fife, Scotland. The central concerns of my academic studies have been questions relate to the philosophical issues of theodicy and the problem of evil.

Along the way, in my academic career, I have had many mentors. At the University of Maryland, they were Drs. John Titchener and Thomas Benson. At Yale, Professor Marvin Pope, the great Book of Job scholar. Dr. James Barr, the Regius Professor of Hebrew, was my mentor at Oxford, and at Saint Andrews my supervisors were George Hall, Bill Shaw and Peter Coxon, teacher of Biblical Hebrew. And with all of these mentors, my emphases have been on the theological responses to evil and suffering in the Judeo-Christian-Islamic tradition.

In January of 2020, a few years after I retired from teaching, a deadly virus known as COVID-19 began to emerge as a worldwide pandemic. It appears to have started in the Wuhan Province of China. By the Spring of 2020, it had infected millions of people and spread to 120 countries. As I write this, the Corona Pandemic continues, the disease having killed 87,000 people in the United States.

When I became aware of the virus in January of 2020, I thought I would continue to do what I have always done—to think and write about evil and suffering. Thus, I began planning a book on Biblical views on evil and suffering. This was an effort to do what I have always done. That is, to use my skills to show what the Bible has said about times of crisis and turmoil.

In my academic career, I have been trained as both a philosopher and a Biblical scholar. I have learned the Biblical languages, as well as other tongues such as Classical Greek and Medieval Latin of the Church so that I could read and study texts in the original languages. What better way, then, to make a contribution to the worldwide pandemic than to employ my skills in making a contribution to the current crisis?

And so this book should be seen as a summary and some reflections on what the Bible has had to say about the issues of evil and suffering when human beings are in times of calamity. I might suggest that the reader of this study have a copy of the Bible at his or her side when going through the book. This would allow the reader more easily to follow the arguments and explication to be found in the book.

I sincerely wish that this book may be helpful to some believers in the authenticity of the Biblical message. I hope the reader enjoys it and finds it helpful in this time of great worry and concern.

Stephen John Vicchio

Appendix A:
Glossary of Ancient Hebrew Words and Phrases

Abaddon	the underworld
Akedah	to bind
Alqosh	city in Galilee
Arbeh	locusts
Asah	plan or design / or understanding
Bachan	to test
Bara	to make
Berith	Covenant
Binah	knowledge
Chashab	plan or purpose
Chephets	adversity
Dibbah	evil or infamy
Esah	plan or purpose
Gaar	to rebuke
Ha	the
Hebel	vanity
Hokmah	wisdom
Iyyov	Job
Kashaph	sorcerers
Maroyth	curse
Mashal	proverb

Mashalim	proverbs
Ma'veth	death
Mechiloth	wind instrument
Mirchtam	a musical term
Makashabah	thoughts or devices
Maski	special skill in singing
Megillot	five scrolls
Messiach	Messiah
Nachash	serpent
Nadar	vow
Ne'dabah	free will offering
Neder	curse or vow
Nefesh	soul or self
Neginoth	string instrument
Optia	verb to see
Qoholeth	Ecclesiastes
Ra'	evil
Ra'ah	evil
Ra'aw	evil
Ruah	spirit
Sareph	fiery serpent
Ha Satan	the Satan
Se'irim	satyrs
Seydam	demons
Shalom	peace
Sharaq	hissings
Sheb'uah	curse
*Sheminth_*	an octave
Sheol	the underworld
Shir	a musical term
Sync	together
Tam	blameless

Tannim	sea monster
Tehillah	a psalm
Tehillim	many psalms
Tekoa	village in northern kingdom
Tsaraph	to test or to try
Va	and
Yahweh	name for God
Yacar	to chasten
Yashar	upright
Yetzerim	imagination or inclination
Yetzer ha ra	evil imagination
Yetzer tov	good imagination
Zimma	plan or purpose

Appendix B:
Glossary of Koine Greek Terms and Phrases

Adekana	wrong
Agape	love
Agapeo	to love
Amanunesis	secretary or recorder
Anexikakos	to bear with suffering
Anomia	lawlessness
Anomos	without law
Beelzebub	word for the Devil
Blasphemo	blasphemy
Blasphemia	blasphemy
Bole or *bolay*	council or plan
Charis	grace
Chairo	to be cheerful
Daimon	demon
Dokimia	to test or to try
Damimonian	devils
Daimonizomai	devils
Diablos	the Devil
Dianoia	mind
Dike	justice
Dysphemia	a bad report
Eirene	peace

Ekpiradzo	to try
Elhidna	viper
Eleeo	mercy
Eleuthero	to make free
Eletheros	to make free
Epistole	letter
Epistello	letter
Esh	asp
Glossolalia	speaking in tongues
Gramma	letter
Hina	particle
Hora	hour
Horidzo	to limit
Horidzo	to set a limit
Ioudaios	the Jews
Kakia	evil
Kata Ioannes	John says
Katalaleo	evil one
Kathaplezo	evil one
Kakokia	evil
Kakokthia	evil
Kakolegio	bad character
Kakopathia	evil and suffering
Kakopatheo	harmful
Kakos	evil
Martureo	to witness
Metriopathia	sympathy
Noema	mind
Nous	mind
Oketeiro	sympathy
Ophis	serpent
Oun	particle

Peira	test
Pierazo	to test
Phileo	love
Philos	to love
Pirasmos	a trial
Pisteou	to believe
Poneria	evil people
Ponero	evil
Pomeron	evil men
Ponapoteos	to wish evil on
Poneros	evil
Ponerau	evil one
Ponos	anguish or pain
Profiles	to see ahead
Proginosko	foreknew
Prognosis	forethought
Prorizo	predestination
Prothomia	plots
Psyche	soul
Rehe'mah	evil
Royszedon	bad
Satanas	Satan
Seimion	signs
Slagchnizomai	compassion
Sumpathes	to be sympathetic
Teras	wonders
Theos	God

Appendix C:
Other Foreign Words and Phrases

Angra Mainya	Bad god in Zoroastrianism (Persian)
Ahura Mazda	Good god in Zoroastrianism (Persian)
Atman	soul (Sanskrit)
Bedeutung	evil (German)
Brahma	ultimate reality/world soul (Sanskrit)
Creation ex nihilo	creation out of nothing (Latin)
Ex nihilo	out of nothing (Latin)
Gathas	Zoroastrian texts (Persian)
Iblis	Devil (Arabic)
Kul	be (Arabic)
Maya	illusion (Pali)
Mens rea	evil intent (Latin)
Nomos	law (modern Greek)
Quelle	source (German)
Qur'an	Muslim Holy Book (Arabic)
Rahab Chaos	monster (Ugaritic)
Reshaph	flames (Ugaritic)
Sedu	evil god (Assyrian)
Shaytan	Satan/Devil (Arabic)
Surah	chapter (Arabic)
Tat tvam asi	that you are (Sanskrit)
Zaphon	Canaanite god (Ugaritic)

Endnotes

1   G. W. Leibniz, *Theodicy* (Charleston: BiblioBazaar, 2007). Leibniz made up the word "Theodicy" and many scholars used the word after him, including Immanuel Kant.

2   Epicurus, quoted in Stephen Vicchio, *The Voice from the Whirlwind* (Westminster: Christian Classics, 1989), p. 218. In his *Dialogues Concerning Natural Religion*, David Hume quotes this same passage from Epicurus for exactly the same purposes. See Note 8. Epicurus lived from 341 to 270 BCE and was the founder of the philosophical movement established in his name. He thought the purpose of philosophy is to "make people happy."

3   Vicchio, pp. 1–2.

4   Martin Amis, *The Second Plane* (New York: Vintage Books, 2009), p. 111.

5   Louis Pojman, *Philosophy of Religion* (New York: Wadsworth, 1998), p. 163.

6   Ibid.

7   Ibid.

8   David Hume, *Dialogues Concerning Natural Religion* (New York: Hackett Books, 1998).

9   See Note 1.

10 Alvin Plantinga, *God, Freedom, and Evil* (Grand Rapids: Eerdmans, 1974). Plantinga was the foremost advocate of the Free Will Defense in the twentieth century.

11 William Rowe, "The Problem of Evil and Some Varieties of Atheism," *American Philosophical Quarterly*, vol. 16 (1979). William K. Rowe (1931–2015) was educated at the Universities of Michigan and Chicago and taught for many years at Purdue University.

12 J. L. Mackie, "Evil and Omnipotence," *Mind*, vol. 64 (1955), pp. 200–212. Mackie (1917–1981) was an Australian-born philosopher who taught in many universities in the English-speaking world.

13 Vicchio, pp. 1–2.

14   Max Weber, *Das Problem der Bedeutung* (Berlin, 1892). Weber is sometimes mentioned as the "Father of Sociology." He was born in Prussia in 1864 and died in 1920.

15   Ibid., pp. 5–6.

16   Ibid., p. 6.

17   Ibid., p. 7.

18   Ibid.

19   Ibid., p. 8.

20   Peter Berger, *The Sacred Canopy* (New York: Anchor Books, 1990). Peter L. Berger (1929–2017) was an Austrian-born theologian and sociologist of knowledge.

21   Ibid., p. 11.

22   Ibid.

23   Ibid., p. 12.

24   Ibid., p. 11.

25   Clifford Geertz, "Religion as a Cultural System," in *Culture, Custom, and Ethics* (New York: Basic Books, 1974), pp. 133–156. Geertz (1926–2006) was an American anthropologist. He advocated what was known as "Symbolic Anthropology."

26   Vicchio, pp. 5–43.

27   Ibid., p. 7–9.

28   Mithraism was a Roman religion popular during the time of Christ in the first century CE. Manicheanism was also a Roman religion, principally in the third to fifth century CE. Augustine of Hippo, for a time, was a follower of Manicheanism in his youth.

29   *Tat tvam asi* is a Sanskrit expression that is found as early as the Vedas. It signifies the relation of the individual, or *atman*, to ultimate reality, or *Brahma*.

30   Vicchio, pp. 26–27.

31   Ibid., pp. 30–34.

32   Ibid., p. 27.

33   Immanuel Kant, *Treating Persons as Ends* (London: Rowan Littlefield, 1987).

34   Vicchio, pp. 95–112.

35   Ibid., pp. 101–102.

36   The "Fallen Angels" narrative is an early Christian theory that posits that before the creation of Adam and Eve, a group of rebellious angels, led by Satan, disobeyed God and were cast down to Hell. This idea will be seen several times throughout this study.

37   This may be an Old Testament reference to the Fallen Angels narrative.

38 Vicchio, pp. 113–152 (RSV).

39 Ibid.

40 Ibid., pp. 126–129.

41 Vicchio, pp. 125–129.

42 Ibid.

43 Irenaeus, *Against Heresies* (New York: Christian Classics, 2020) and John Hick, *Evil and the God of Love* (London: Palgrave Macmillan, 1966). Irenaeus is thought to have been the progenitor of teleological answers and responses in the Christian tradition.

44 For *bosh*, see Judges 3:25 and 5:28, as well as Job 6:20 and 19:3.

45 *Bazah* may also be found quite frequently in the Psalms, such as at 15:9, 22:8, 22:24, 51:17, and 59:33, as well as many other places.

46 The word *kakos*, and its derivatives, is the most often used word in the New Testament to designate evil or bad, such as at Matthew 21:41, 24:48, 27:23, and Mark 7:21.

47 The word *rehe'mah* comes from the Semitic root RHM. The root generally is the source for words connected to compassion in Hebrew, as well as in Arabic.

48 The Greek word *blasphemia* is the source for all words in the New Testament for blasphemy. For example, at the Gospel of Matthew 12:31, 15:19, 26:65, and Mark 3:28.

49 For more on the attributes of God in Islam, as well as the uses of the word *Kul*, see, Stephen Vicchio, *Biblical Figures in the Islamic Faith* (Eugene: Wipf and Stock Publishers, 2008), pp. 1–21.

50 Billi J. Collins, *The Hittites and the World* (New York: Society of Biblical Literature, 2007), pp. 199–234.

51 Ibid., p. 199.

52 For more uses of *naqamah*, see: Psalms 18:47, 79:10, 94:1, 149:7, Jeremiah 11:20 and 20:10.

53 The word for "freely" in this passage is *chophsi*. It is used throughout the Torah in places such as Leviticus 19:20 and Exodus 21:2, 5, 26 and 27, as well as at Deuteronomy 15:12, 13 and 18.

54 Psalm 91:8 is the only place the word *Shillumah* appears in the Hebrew Bible, or Old Testament. The Semitic root from which it comes are words related to revenge and avenge. This root is CHNPH.

55 Rabbi Avi Weiss, "The Divine Plan," *Devar Torah* (January 8, 2018).

56 Stephen Vicchio, *Job in the Ancient World* (Eugene: Wipf and Stock, 2006), p. 3.

57 Ibid.

58   Vicchio, pp. 36–39.

59   Second Kings 18:13–15.

60   Vicchio, pp. 36–44.

61   Ibid., pp. 38–39.

62   Rabbi Michall Loving, "Yetzerim: The Fire Within Us," *Cleveland Jewish News* (October 18, 2001), pp. 1–3.

63   Among these themes are the application of the Mosaic Law, God's Eternal Covenant with His People, the Outlook to all Nations, and the Exile and Restoration, for example.

64   Theology of Work, https://bit.ly/3bBXfyr.

65   Isaiah 27:1. This same image of Leviathan can also be found at Job 3:8 and 40:15 to 41:26, Psalm 74:14 and 104:26.

66   Ibid.

67   *The City of God*, book 12, ch. 8.

68   Isaiah 55:11.

69   Jeremiah 17:10.

70   Augustine of Hippo saw this verse as a proof text for Original Sin.

71   Ezekiel 1:3.

72   Ezekiel 8:1–8.

73   Ezekiel 1:15–21.

74   Ezekiel 1:28.

75   Ezekiel 14:14 and 20. The "Dan'el" in these verses is not the man in the Kethuvim and his book. Archeology has shown us he is a moral worthy from Ugaritic texts. See the "Tale of Aqhat," a thirteenth-century BCE text.

76   This expression, "Have no pleasure in the death of the wicked" occurs three times in Ezekiel. These come at 18:23 and 32, and at Ezekiel 33:11.

77   The verb *bachan*, "to test," is used thirty-nine times in the Old Testament, or Hebrew Bible.

78   Augustine makes the same point about this verse.

79   Ibid.

80   See: Stephen Vicchio, *Job in the Ancient World* (Eugene: Wipf and Stock, 2007), pp. 8–25.

81   This is the order of the books in the New Revised Standard Version.

82   Sirach, or *Ecclesiasticus*, when it was written and in what language are matters of debate among scholars. Some say Hebrew, others Aramaic, or even Greek. 175 to 150 BCE is the best guess for when.

83   The 150 BCE date is related to materials from the Dead Sea Scrolls, as seen later in Chapter Four of this study.

84   Katharine Dell, *Riddles and Revelations* (Edinburgh: T & T Clark, 2019), pp. 103–114.

85   Order from the author.

86   See: https://www.oca.org/orthodoxy/the-orthodox-faith/doctrine-scripture.

87   Roman Catholic *Breviary*, ed. Gregory Bellarmine (Lancester: Christian Books Today, 2020).

88   Calendar of the Saints, https://bit.ly/2SgH2ao.

89   *Biography*, https://www.yourdictionary.com/hosea.

90   Ibid.

91   Hosea 14:2 and 3.

92   The word *yacer* is employed dozens of times in the Hebrew Bible, or Old Testament. It is usually rendered as "chasten."

93   Dell, chapters one to four.

94   The word *arbeh*, a variety of "locust," is used twenty-four times in the Hebrew Bible, or Old Testament. Five of those are in the minor prophets.

95   Gordon Bridger, *Obadiah* (Downers Grove: InterVarsity Press, 2010).

96   Bridger, pp. 10–11.

97   Amos 7:10–13.

98   Amos 5:4–5.

99   Augustine of Hippo holds this same view.

100   The word *ne'dabah* is one of the many words for "voluntary" and "freely" in the Hebrew Bible, or Old Testament. It is also employed at Psalms 54:6 and 110:3, as well as Ezekiel 46:12 and Second Chronicles 35:8, in addition to Hosea 14:4.

101   Amos 5:9–10.

102   The word *ra'* is the most common noun for "evil" in the Hebrew Bible, or Old Testament. It is used 667 times there.

103   Stephen Um, *Micah: What Does God Require of Us?* (Epsom Surrey: Good Books Limited, 2018).

104   Ibid., pp. 9–10.

105   Ibid., p. 10.

106   Ibid.

107   Micah 2:3.

108   Walter Meiser, *Nahum* (Ada: Baker Books, 1980).

109   Meiser, pp. 23–24.

110   Meiser, pp. 25–26.

111   Byron Allen, *The Book of Habakkuk* (Mearsville: Christian Faith Publishing, 2020).

112   Manual of Discipline, https://www.britannica.com/topic/Manual-of-Discipline.

113   Ibid., pp. 17–19.

114   Habakkuk 1:3–4.

115   Habakkuk 1:5–7.

116   Psalms 74:14 and 104:26.

117   Habakkuk 3:16.

118   Allen, pp. 17–19.

119   Daniel W. Baker, *Nahum, Habakkuk, and Zephaniah* (Downers Grove: IVP Academic, 2015).

120   Baker, p. 23–24.

121   Ibid.

122   Augustine of Hippo held this view, as well.

123   Jacob Dexter, *Study Haggai* (New York: Amazon Digital Services, 2019).

124   Haggai 2:13.

125   See: Daniel 6:17, Esther 2:10, and Exodus 28:11 and 39:30, for example.

126   Darius the Great (550 to 467 BCE) was born in what is now Iran. He was the third king of what were called the "King of Kings." He ruled from 522 until 467.

127   Abhashef Patel, *Darius the Great* (Independently Published, 2019). pp. 14–19.

128   Zechariah 12:1–14.

129   Zechariah 3:1–4.

130   Zechariah 9:7.

131   Kevin Youngblood, *Jonah* (Grand Rapids: Zondervan Press, 2015). Timothy Keller, *The Prodigal Prophet: Jonah* (New York: Viking, 2018).

132   Jonah 4:6–11.

133   Jonah 1:7–16.

134   Jonah 4:1–5.

135   The Hebrew word for "plant" at Jonah 4:6–11 is *kikayon*. The word only appears here.

136   Jonah 1:11.

137   This word for "wickedness" is *ra'ah*. It is used ten times in the Book of Jonah, once in chapter 1 and nine times in chapters 3 and 4.

138   The Persian word on the Book of Jonah is *'ir hayona*.

139   These dates come from Marvin Pope's *Job* (New York: Doubleday, 1973), pp. xxxii–xl.

140   Job 1:1–6 on Earth, 1:6–12 in Heaven, 1:13–22 on Earth, 2:1–8 in Heaven, 2:11–13 on Earth.

141   Job 1:1 and 42:7–8.

142 Job 1:13–22.

143 Job 2:10.

144 These exchanges begin in chapter 3 and conclude in chapter 31.

145 Job 39:1 to 41:34.

146 Job 40:15 to 41:34.

147 Job 42:1–5 in poetry. Verses 7–17 in prose.

148 See: Edward Greenstein, *Job: A New Translation* (New Haven: Yale University Press, 2019).

149 Job 42:17.

150 Job 42:10–17.

151 Job 11:7 to 9. The word *Sheol*, or the land of the dead much like Hades in Greek mythology, appears eight times in the Book of Job. These come at 7:9, 11:8, 14:13, 17:13, 17:16, 21:13, 24:19 and 26:4.

152 The word *naqiy*, or "innocent," appears forty-two times in the Hebrew Bible, or Old Testament, including six times in the Book of Job. These come at 4:7, 9:23, 17:8, 22:19, 22:30 and 27:17.

153 This is particularly clear in chapter 3 where Job curses the day he was born.

154 There are over fifty Aramaic, Syriac and Arabic words in the Book of Job. Some scholars argue there is as many as 120 of these words.

155 Job refers to his "sins in his youth" at 13:26, 20:11 and 25:7.

156 The word *kethuvim* in classical Hebrew is the name given to the third part of the Hebrew scriptures. This section is also known as the Hagiographia. The books of the Kethuvim include Psalms, Proverbs, Job, the Song of Songs, Ruth, Lamentations, Ecclesiastes, Esther and the Book of Daniel.

157 The Book of Daniel can be dated to the period between 167 and 164 BCE.

158 The word *tehellim* is the female plural of *tehellah*. The word most likely comes from the Aramaic *tillim*.

159 N. T. Wright, *The Case for the Psalms* (San Francisco: Harpers, 2013).

160 Thus, the predominant name for God changes over the course of the Psalms.

161 The only difference between Psalm 53 and Psalm 14 is the name for God.

162 The word *shigianoth* is used at the beginning of Psalm 7.

163 The word *alamoth* is used in the superscription of Psalm 46. It is also employed at First Chronicles 25:20.

164 The word *niganoth* appears in the beginning of Psalms 4, 6, 54, 55, 67 and 76, as part of the titles of those Psalms.

165 The Wisdom Books are Job, Psalms, Ecclesiastes and Proverbs.

166 James Crenshaw, "Mashal," in *Beyond Orality* (New York: Routledge, 2019) ch. 3.

167 Ibid.

168 The words *mashal* and *mashalim* occur thirty-eight times in the Hebrew Bible, or Old Testament, twelve of those in the Wisdom Books.

169 Author's research.

170 Raymond C. Ortlund, *Proverbs* (Wheaton: Crossways Publishing, 2012) pp. 14–16.

171 Ibid., p. 16.

172 The word *binah*, or "understanding," is used thirty-eight times in the Hebrew Bible, or Old Testament, including nine times in Job and eleven times in Proverbs.

173 The expressions *yirah Elohim* and *yirah Yahweh*, or the fear of God and fear of the Lord, are used forty-one times in the Hebrew Bible, or Old Testament. About half of those are in Psalms, Proverbs and the Book of Job. See Tremper Longman, *The Fear of the Lord is Wisdom* (Michigan: Baker Books, 2017).

174 Ibid., pp. 17–20.

175 The Hebrew *hokmah* and the Aramaic *chokmah* occur 149 and eight times respectively in the Hebrew Bible, or Old Testament.

176 The same word is used fourteen times in the Book of Daniel.

177 The Hebrew words for "whisper" and whispering" are *lachash*, *demanah* and *shemets*. Each of these words is used infrequently.

178 The classical Arabic expression *fa-waswasa*, or "whispers" or "evil suggestions," is used five times in *Al-Qur'an*. These come at Surah 7:20, 20:120, 50:16, 114:4 and 114:6.

179 Alfred Overstreet, "Are Men Born Sinners," https://bit.ly/3d4gkd0.

180 The classical Hebrew word *yacer,* or "to chasten," is used forty-three times in the Hebrew Bible, or Old Testament. About half of these are in the Wisdom Books.

181 Michael Fox, *A Time to Tear Down* (Grand Rapids: Eerdmans, 1999), pp. 1–26.

182 Ibid., pp. 3–5.

183 Ecclesiastes 9:11 (NRSV)

184 Ibid.

185 Fox, pp. 17–50.

186 The expression "under the sun" is used twenty-nine times in the Book of Ecclesiastes.

187 The expressions the "fear of God" and the "fear of the Lord" appear in Ecclesiastes seven times at 3:14, 5:7, 7:18, 8:12 (twice), 8:13, and 12:13.

188 The word *nadar* in classical Hebrew means a "vow" or a "promise." This word appears thirty-one times in the Hebrew Bible, or Old Testament, and three in

Ecclesiastes at 5:4 (twice), and 5:5. The word *neder*, that comes from the same NDR Semitic root, also means a "vow." This word occurs sixty times in the Hebrew Bible, or Old Testament, frequently in Job and Proverbs, but it does not occur in the Book of Ecclesiastes.

189   See: Matthew 27:38–44.

190   Thomas Aquinas discusses the bad angels in the *Summa Theologica*, Book I, question 109, articles one to four.

191   Gregory the Great, *The Moralia in Job* (Memphis: Veritatis Splendor Publications, 2012), vol. 1, p. 262.

192   Cyrus the Great (601–530 BCE) was the fourth king of the ancient Persian Empire. Darius (550–487) ruled the Persian Empire from 522 to 487 BCE until the time of his death. Ken Johnson, *The Ancient Book of Daniel* (2012), www. biblefacts.org.

193   Ibid., pp. 19–20.

194   Ibid., p. 21.

195   Ibid., pp. 23–24.

196   Daniel 9:16.

197   Daniel 2:21–22.

198   Raymond Surburg, *Introduction to the Intertestamental Period* (Saint Louis: Concordia Press, 1975), pp. 7–12.

199   Ibid., pp. 12–14.

200   *The Gospel of Thomas*, ed. David Capps (2012), www.gnosticwisdomfoundation. org.

201   Marvin W. Meyers, *The Nag Hammadi Scriptures* (San Francisco: Harper One, 2010).

202   Capps, pp. 11–15.

203   Ibid.

204   Ibid., p. 9.

205   Ibid., p. 10.

206   Ibid., p. 11.

207   Ibid., p. 8.

208   Ibid., p. 12.

209   Ibid., p. 13.

210   Ibid.

211   Ibid., p. 19.

212   *The Book of Tobit*, ed. Adolf Neubauer (Eugene: Wipf and Stock, 2015), pp. 20–23. For more on the Book of Tobit and suffering, see: Stephen Vicchio, *Job in the Ancient World* (Eugene: Wipf and Stock, 2006), pp. 119–122.

213 Ibid., p. 5.

214 *The Testament of Job*, ed. Maria Haranabakis (Edinburgh: T & T Clarks, 2014). For more on the Testament of Job and suffering, see: Vicchio, pp. 122–130.

215 Sirach 49:9. Also see: Vicchio, p. 119.

216 Sirach 49:9.

217 First Enoch 10:10–13.

218 M. Brushi, *The Damascus Document Reconsidered* (Jerusalem: Shrine of the Book, 1992), p. 19. For more on suffering in the Dead Sea Scrolls, see: Vicchio, ch. 8.

219 Ibid., p. 20.

220 Geza Vermes, *Christian Beginnings* (London: Penguin, 2013), p. 215.

221 F. Onayemi, "Sin, Punishment, and Forgiveness in Ancient Greek Religion," *Journal of Philosophy and Culture* 3, no. 1 (2006): 72–100.

222 Ibid., pp. 72–73.

223 First Enoch 17.

224 Surburg, pp. 26–39.

225 For more on Zoroastrianism, see: John Waterhouse, *Zoroastrianism* (San Diego: Book Tree, 2006) and Peter Clark, *Zoroastrianism* (Sussex: Sussex Academics, 1998).

226 Waterhouse, pp. 19–21. Clark, pp. 7–10.

227 Ibid.

228 It has been estimated that in first-century Palestine, 30 percent of the population was tri-lingual.

229 Ronald Nash, "What were the Mystery Religions?" https://bit.ly/3c25JPH.

230 Antiochus IV (215–164 BCE) ruled Palestine from 176 to 164 BCE.

231 Phillips Barry, *Antiochus IV* (Mysore: Isha Books, 2013), pp. 1–13.

232 Anthony Saldarini, *Pharisees, Scribes, and Sadducees in Palestine Society* (Grand Rapids: Eerdmans, 2001), pp. 10–27.

233 Ibid., pp. 13–14.

234 Ibid., p. 17.

235 Nash, p. 42.

236 Pompey (106 to 48 BCE) was Emperor, General and Statesman.

237 Herod Antipas (20 BCE to 32 CE) is the Herod in the New Testament at the Gospel of Luke 13:32.

238 Ibid.

239 Acts of the Apostles 26:32 to 28:16.

240 Waterhouse, pp. 20–29.

241 The *Gathas* is series of seventeen hymns organized in five groups by their meter.

242   Waterhouse, p. 22–27.

243   Waterhouse, p. 29.

244   Thomas Horn, *The Book of Judith* (Crane, MO: Defender's Publishing, 2012), p. 83.

245   Hebrew 2:9–10.

246   Waterhouse, p. 92.

247   First Maccabees 4:46 and 9:27.

248   *Phaulos* is only used these four times in the New Testament.

249   These words connected to *ponos* are the second most common in the New Testament.

250   This word *kakos* and other words connected to it are the most common expressions for "evil" employed in the New Testament.

251   Second Timothy 3:13.

252   *Beelzebub* appears in Matthew, Mark and Luke, but it is not in the Gospel of John.

253   Because of the word's buzzing sound.

254   The term "evil One" appears seventy-nine times in the New Testament.

255   The word *kakos*, and its derivatives, appear fifty times in the New Testament.

256   Book of Job 1:1–6 and 2:6–12.

257   Raymond Brown, *The Gospel of John and the Epistles of John* (Collegeville: Liturgical Press, 1988), pp. 12–15.

258   Ibid., p. 6–9.

259   Ibid., 4–6.

260   This theory is now known as the "Augustinian Hypothesis."

261   Hugo Grotius (1585–1645), Hugo Gates Jameson (1778–1855), Basil Butler (1902–1986) and John Wenham (1913–1966.)

262   Jakob Griesbach (1745–1812) was a German New Testament scholar.

263   For more on the Q source see: John Kloppenborg, *The Q Source* (Westminster: John Knox Press, 2012).

264   Ibid., 1–12.

265   Ibid.

266   Austin Farrer (1904–1968) was one of the best-known analytic philosophers in Britain in the twentieth century.

267   J. H. Roper (1872–1941), M. D. Goulder (1927–2010) and Mark Goodacre (b. 1967).

268   *Sympathies, metriopathia, oketeria* and *etheos* are all used for "compassion" and "mercy" in the New Testament.

269   Gospel of John 1:1–3, 3:12–13 and 8:58.

270 John 21:11.

271 This is the Egerton Gospel, ed. Lorne Zelyck (Leiden: Brill, 2019).

272 Ibid., pp. 10–12.

273 Ronald Cameron, *The Other Non-Canonical Gospels* (Louisville: Westminster John Knox Press, 1982), pp. 11–14.

274 Egerton Papyrus2, https://bit.ly/3djpLp0.

275 The "Odes of Solomon" is a collection of forty-two odes attributed to King Solomon. They have been dated by scholars from the first to the third century CE.

276 The ancient port city of Ephesus was located on the western coast of present-day Turkey. Ancient ruins have been preserved there.

277 Eusebius, *Ecclesiastical History*, 6.14.5–7.

278 Muratorian Canon, https://bit.ly/2Wv7zC8.

279 Ibid.

280 John 8:12, 9:5 and 20:15–18.

281 J. Ramsey Michael, *The Gospel of John* (Grand Rapids: Eerdmans, 2010), pp. 8–14.

282 Ibid., p. 10.

283 The word *agape*, or "love," and the verb *apageo* appear eight times in Matthew, five in Mark, ten in Luke, and thirty-seven times in the Gospel of John.

284 Michael, pp. 25–39.

285 Michael, pp. 26–27.

286 Author's research.

287 *Oun* and *hina* in Koine Greek mean "for" and "therefore."

288 For more on these "I am" statements, see: https://bit.ly/2yt0Pgh.

289 Author's calculations.

290 Seventy-three times in the Gospel of John.

291 The Jews only appear twelve times in the Synoptics.

292 These are items that only a first-century CE Palestinian Jew would know.

293 This day is what Christians call "Holy Thursday."

294 *Martureo*, for example, is used five times in the opening chapter of the Gospel of John, and only once in Matthew, once in Luke, and not at all in Mark.

295 Cameron, p. 19.

296 Ibid.

297 Ibid., pp. 20–22.

298 For more on the "Seven Signs" see: https://bit.ly/35LMyr1.

299 See Note 281.

300 Author's research.

301 See: Mark 5:1–17 and Luke 8:23–37.

302 The word *hudor*, or "water," is used much more often in the Gospel of John—nineteen times—than in the Synoptics, which is seven, seven and six times.

303 John 8:34.

304 *Eleuthero* is used eleven times in the New Testament. None of those are in the Gospels.

305 The word *hora*, or "hour," is employed twenty times in Matthew, twice in Mark, none in Luke, and twenty-three times in the Gospel of John.

306 John 16:23.

307 The Lazarus narrative is chapter 11 of John's Gospel. It is only found there.

308 See Note 305.

309 Madison Pierce, *Divine Discourse in the Epistles* (Cambridge: Cambridge University Press, 2020), pp. 6–10.

310 Ibid., p 5.

311 The prison epistles are Ephesians, Philippians and Colossians because Paul wrote them in the two periods when he was in prison.

312 Pierce, pp. 25–29.

313 Romans 5:8 and 9 to 11.

314 First Letter to the Corinthians 2:1–12.

315 Galatians 5:25.

316 Colossians 1:25.

317 Colossians 2:4, 8 and 18.

318 Thessalonica was an ancient city in Macedonia.

319 First Timothy 3:1–7.

320 Paul calls Philemon "a dear friend and fellow worker."

321 Hebrews 9:1–10.

322 Paul mentions "everlasting life" in Hebrews 5:9.

323 Scott Hahn, *Acts of the Apostles* (San Francisco: Ignatius Press, 2013), p. 17.

324 John Polloch, *The Life of Saint Paul* (Colorado Springs: David C. Cook Books, 2012).

325 Hahn, p. 24.

326 Ibid.

327 Ibid., pp. 25–26.

328 Polloch, p. 43.

329 See: Romans 1:21, 9:2, 10:6 and 8–10.

330 The words "test" and "try," or *peira* and *peiraamoi*, appear five and one times in Acts. These come at 5:9, 9:26, 15:10, 16:7, and 24:6 and 26:2.

331   The word *dysphemia* appears only one time in the New Testament at Second Corinthians 6:8.

332   There is a variety of other words in the New Testament to designate "permit" and "permission." Among these are the word *eao* and the term *apheime*, in addition to *epitrepo* and *sugganome*.

Acknowledgements

In the writing of this book, I must acknowledge the discussions I have had with Pete Celli; Rocco Vicchio; Jack Vicchio; my wife, Sandra Vicchio; my dear friend Marguerite Villa Santa; and Steve Kent for help with IT issues.

About the Author

Before his retirement in 2016, Stephen Vicchio taught for more than forty years at the University of Maryland, Johns Hopkins, St. Mary's Seminary in Baltimore, and other universities in Britain and the United States. He has authored over two dozen books, as well as essays and plays, mostly about the Bible, philosophy and theology. Among his books since 2000 is his interpretation of the Book of Job, *The Antichrist: A History*; *Biblical Figures in the Islamic Faith*, and books about the religions of American presidents George Washington, Thomas Jefferson and Abraham Lincoln, including *Ronald Reagan's Religious Beliefs* out now with CrossLink Publishing.

www.ingramcontent.com/pod-product-compliance
Lightning Source LLC
Chambersburg PA
CBHW031944080426
42735CB00007B/252